Technologically Mediated Human Resource Management

This book explores the enactment of technologically mediated Human Resource Management (HRM) in the gig economy from various perspectives.

The gig economy offers a new form of work which is in line with the ongoing consumer desire for convenience. Also known as the online platform, on-demand or digital platform economy, the gig economy is perhaps one of the most distinctive and extreme sides of the increasingly digitalised and fragmented nature of work. This volume examines various challenges that exist between online labor platforms and human resource management in the realm of the gig economy. The chapters in this book explore issues like institutional complexity, technological supervision of gig workers, recruitment in the gig economy, quality of work and work fairness. They further illustrate the importance of gig work being incorporated within the parameters of HRM research given the existence of many activities and practices that are typically associated with HR functions within traditional organisational forms.

This book will be a beneficial read for advanced students and researchers of Management, Economics, Business and Marketing. It was originally published as a special issue of *The International Journal of Human Resource Management.*

Anthony McDonnell is Professor of Human Resource Management, Deputy Dean and co-director of the Human Resource Research Centre at Cork University Business School, University College Cork, Ireland. His research interests include gig work, talent management and global staffing practices of MNCs.

Ronan Carbery is Senior Lecturer in Management, Director of the Executive MBA, and co-director of the Human Resource Research Centre at Cork University Business School, University College Cork, Ireland. His research interests include gig work, learning and development, and talent development.

John Burgess is Professor of Human Resource Management at Torrens University, Australia. His research interests include the HRM practices of multinational enterprises, the transition from education to employment, working time arrangements and health, the transition from military to civilian employment, and the policy implications of contingent employment.

Ultan Sherman is Lecturer in Management and a member of the Human Resource Research Centre at Cork University Business School, University College Cork, Ireland. His research interests lie broadly in the relationship between work and psychology with a particular focus on the psychological contract.

Technologically Mediated Human Resource Management

Working Relationships in the Gig Economy

Edited by
Anthony McDonnell, Ronan Carbery, John Burgess and Ultan Sherman

Routledge
Taylor & Francis Group
LONDON AND NEW YORK

First published 2023
by Routledge
4 Park Square, Milton Park, Abingdon, Oxon OX14 4RN

and by Routledge
605 Third Avenue, New York, NY 10158

Routledge is an imprint of the Taylor & Francis Group, an informa business

British Library Cataloguing in Publication Data
A catalogue record for this book is available from the British Library

ISBN13: 978-1-032-48269-9 (hbk)
ISBN13: 978-1-032-48271-2 (pbk)
ISBN13: 978-1-003-38820-3 (ebk)

DOI: 10.4324/9781003388203

Typeset in Minion Pro
by Newgen Publishing UK

Publisher's Note
The publisher accepts responsibility for any inconsistencies that may have arisen during the conversion of this book from journal articles to book chapters, namely the inclusion of journal terminology.

Contents

Citation Information

The chapters in this book were originally published in *The International Journal of Human Resource Management*, volume 32, issue 19 (2021). When citing this material, please use the original page numbering for each article, as follows:

Chapter 1

Technologically mediated human resource management in the gig economy
Anthony McDonnell, Ronan Carbery, John Burgess and Ultan Sherman
The International Journal of Human Resource Management, volume 32, issue 19 (2021), pp. 3995–4015

Chapter 2

Having their cake and eating it too? Online labor platforms and human resource management as a case of institutional complexity
Jeroen Meijerink, Anne Keegan and Tanya Bondarouk
The International Journal of Human Resource Management, volume 32, issue 19 (2021), pp. 4016–4052

Chapter 3

The effects of technological supervision on gig workers: organizational control and motivation of Uber, taxi, and limousine drivers
Peter Norlander, Nenad Jukic, Arup Varma and Svetlozar Nestorov
The International Journal of Human Resource Management, volume 32, issue 19 (2021), pp. 4053–4077

Chapter 4

Fair's fair: psychological contracts and power in platform work
Genevieve Shanahan and Mark Smith
The International Journal of Human Resource Management, volume 32, issue 19 (2021), pp. 4078–4109

Chapter 5

Job quality, fair work and gig work: the lived experience of gig workers
Katie Myhill, James Richards and Kate Sang
The International Journal of Human Resource Management, volume 32, issue 19 (2021), pp. 4110–4135

Chapter 6

Recruitment in the gig economy: attraction and selection on digital platforms
Penny Williams, Paula McDonald and Robyn Mayes
The International Journal of Human Resource Management, volume 32, issue 19 (2021), pp. 4136–4162

Notes on Contributors

Tanya Bondarouk, Human Resource Management Group, School of Behavioural, Management and Social Sciences, University of Twente, Enschede, The Netherlands.

John Burgess, Centre for Organisational Change and Agility, Torrens University, Australia.

Ronan Carbery, Human Resource Research Centre, Cork University Business School, University College Cork, Ireland.

Nenad Jukic, Quinlan School of Business, Loyola University Chicago, Chicago, IL, USA.

Anne Keegan, HRM and Employment Relations Group, College of Business, University College Dublin, Dublin, Ireland.

Robyn Mayes, QUT Business School, Queensland University of Technology, Brisbane, Australia.

Paula McDonald, QUT Business School, Queensland University of Technology, Brisbane, Australia.

Anthony McDonnell, Human Resource Research Centre, Cork University Business School, University College Cork, Ireland.

Jeroen Meijerink, Human Resource Management Group, School of Behavioural, Management and Social Sciences, University of Twente, Enschede, The Netherlands.

Katie Myhill, Edinburgh Business School, School of Social Sciences, Heriot-Watt University, Edinburgh, UK.

Svetlozar Nestorov, Quinlan School of Business, Loyola University Chicago, Chicago, IL, USA.

Peter Norlander, Quinlan School of Business, Loyola University Chicago, Chicago, IL, USA.

James Richards, Edinburgh Business School, School of Social Sciences, Heriot-Watt University, Edinburgh, UK.

Kate Sang, Edinburgh Business School, School of Social Sciences, Heriot-Watt University, Edinburgh, UK.

Genevieve Shanahan, People, Organizations and Society, Grenoble Ecole de Management, Grenoble, France.

Ultan Sherman, Human Resource Research Centre, Cork University Business School, University College Cork, Ireland.

Mark Smith, University of Stellenbosch Business School, South Africa.

Arup Varma, Quinlan School of Business, Loyola University Chicago, Chicago, IL, USA.

Penny Williams, QUT Business School, Queensland University of Technology, Brisbane, Australia.

Technologically mediated human resource management in the gig economy

Anthony McDonnell, Ronan Carbery, John Burgess and Ultan Sherman

ABSTRACT

Gig work accessed through the medium of digital platforms has become an increasingly researched and debated topic owing to several features which distinguish it from other variants of temporary work. It represents a form of working that typically falls outside the standard boundaries of the organisation and employment relationships and where technology has a most pervasive role. This paper, alongside five special issue contributions, explores the enactment of technologically mediated HRM in the gig economy. We make the case for enhanced research efforts on HRM without employment contexts. More specifically, there is a need for greater appreciation of the diversity within the digital platform classification, and what this may mean for the role and value of HRM. While gig workers tend to fall outside the HRM field's remit, we expose how this is problematic given the presence of several activities and practices that one traditionally associates with the HR function.

Introduction

The gig economy, which most commonly refers to an economic system that uses digital platforms to connect workers with consumers and clients (Harris, 2017), is increasingly omnipresent in discussions and debates around the future of work. This relatively new form of work pervades many spheres of our lives in line with trends of increasing consumer desire for convenience (Mehmood & Najmi, 2017; Pasquale, 2016). The gig economy, also known as the online platform, on-demand or digital platform economy, is in many respects the most distinctive and extreme side of the increasingly digitalised and fragmented nature of work (Kaine

& Josserand, 2019). At the heart of the gig economy is the easy and cheap exchange of considerable swathes of data and technological innovations. These features have been pivotal to the development of such new ways of working that purportedly offer flexibility for workers, businesses, and individual consumers. However, the extent to which such innovation and flexibility is positive and mutually beneficial amongst all parties is coming under greater scrutiny.

Gig work represents another type of contingent labour which bears some similarities to other temporary forms but also brings key and acute differences; notably in the use of technological solutions or digital architectures, and the hyper-flexibility involved (Duggan et al., 2020). Rather than representing one homogenous entity, the gig economy takes on several heterogeneous forms which is only beginning to gain critical evaluation (e.g. Duggan et al., 2020; Howcroft & Bergvall-Kåreborn, 2019). The spread of gig work appears to be increasing across industries and countries, and as such it is becoming more pervasive within economies. Its rise, and the associated implications of this for individuals and the social fabric of work, means that interest in it is has stretched far beyond academic researchers to now include policy makers, and the wider public. While in its infancy as a research domain, scholarly interest has exploded as evident through cross-disciplinary publication patterns in labour law, consumer studies, marketing, employment relations, sociology, strategy and so forth.

What we now see is typically commentary from two opposing and dominant perspectives in relation to the merits or shortcomings of gig work for individuals and wider society. On the positive side, we have those that speak to the flexibility and autonomy that gig work offers to individuals in respect to how much or little, and when they wish to work (Duggan et al., 2021b; Kirven, 2018). In other words, this standpoint places emphasis on the entrepreneurial opportunity afforded to individuals by gig work and the benefits that this also offers consumers. Counter to this perspective, is the argument that this type of work places too great a risk on individuals in terms of financial and social insecurities (Friedman, 2014; Wood et al., 2019). In so doing, it ultimately creates an extremely individualised and detached working life (Kaine & Josserand, 2019). The lack of widespread social protection across countries for gig workers has been a magnified concern in some countries in the context of the Covid-19 pandemic (Apouey et al., 2020).

Gig work is fundamentally comprised of hyper, short-term jobs (gigs) where those that perform it are typically classified as independent contractors rather than employees. As such the gig economy involves organisations not hiring employees but mediating an exchange between worker and customers to undertake requested tasks, with all the work allocation and associated processes managed by algorithm. The classification, or misclassification, of these workers (i.e. whether gig workers are employees or independent contractors) is, however, one that continues to attract legal challenge across several jurisdictions (Collier et al., 2017; Fabo et al., 2017; Halliday, 2021). These cases have led to conflicting outcomes with some courts finding that gig workers should in fact be classified as employees, and others dismissive of them being in a formal employment relationship. For example, in 2021, the Supreme Court of the United Kingdom, determined that Uber drivers were employees, on grounds that drivers cannot negotiate with customers on price (this being set by the platform's algorithm), while in 2020, the Fair Work Ombudsman in Australia drew the opposite conclusion, concluding that Uber drivers were self-employed given they could choose their hours of work. Ultimately, most organisations in the gig economy look to deny the existence of a formal employment relationship, which, in theory should mean full independence for workers. The reality, however, appears somewhat different with emerging evidence identifying that there are significant levels of organisational control and power exercised by these platform firms (e.g. Meijerink, Keegan et al., 2021; Norlander et al., 2021; Shanahan & Smith, 2021).

In this paper, we delineate what the gig economy is and highlight its key features and characteristics. In so doing, we consider whether the reality of gig working is more nuanced and complex than is often presented. We note the need for greater appreciation of the idiosyncrasies between different forms of gig work rather than treating this 'new' economy as a uniform entity (Duggan et al., 2020). Given the transactional nature of gig work and the lack of formal employment relationships, one may determine on first inspection that HRM holds little relevance in the context of gig work. However, we argue in this paper that this is not necessarily the case. We highlight the increasing role being played by technologically mediated HRM practices in gig work where many of the broad activities traditionally associated with HR functions are increasingly enacted and enabled by algorithms. This goes to the heart of how platform organisations exercise control and power over seemingly independent workers.

The gig economy: a review of what it is and its relevance to the world of work

The gig economy can be described as a representation of a free and global market where independent workers and customers come together on an on-demand, short-term professional working relationship basis that enables much flexibility for all parties involved with little commitment. In other words, it is a labour market that is entirely made up of short-term jobs conducted by independently contracted or freelance workers. As such the term 'gig' stems from the music industry where a job lasts for a short and defined period. These gigs or jobs tend to be mediated through digital platforms that match the requester or customer with an individual directly who undertakes this work as an independent, service provider rather than an employee. Payment then tends to be for the completion of each task by the gig worker with the intermediary platform firm normally receiving a fixed-rate percentage from each gig. However, as we elucidate later there are key distinctions in some forms of gig work that mean payment systems and work assignment are heterogeneous rather than uniform.

Evaluating the size and scale of the gig economy is difficult owing to labour statistics tending to encapsulate all self-employed people which, while likely to include many gig workers, also includes more traditional freelance or contractor roles. In addition, many individuals undertake gig work as a side-line or additional income source rather than it being their primary or sole method of income generation. As such existing labour market measurement tools appear problematic to capture the real size of the gig economy and the scope of various work-based activities in this context. We are however beginning to gain a greater appreciation through focussed survey work. For example, a 2017 RSA/ISPOS survey in the UK estimated 1.1 million people being involved which puts it on a similar scale to the National Health Service in England (Balaram et al., 2017). The European Commission (2018) found 10% of survey respondents had indicated offering services through online labour platforms on at least one occasion. Looking to the US, data from 2016 indicated that 8% of all Americans had worked through an online labour platform (Smith, 2016). Thus, while the numbers involved do not indicate the mass takeover of gig work and end of more traditional employment its scale is undoubtedly noteworthy, especially given that all predictions point to further growth.

This expansion is highlighted by Berg et al. (2018), who suggest that digital labour platforms are attracting workers across multiple sectors and countries as they provide flexibility in work schedules, the option to undertake work from any place and at any time, and the ability to choose the tasks to be performed. According to Rani et al. (2021) there has been a fivefold increase in the number of digital labour platforms in the past decade. A large proportion of these platforms are concentrated in just a few locations, including the United States of America (29%), India (8%) and the United Kingdom of Great Britain and Northern Ireland (5%). The number of platforms rose from 142 in 2010 to over 777 in 2020 with the number of taxi and food delivery platforms growing almost tenfold in this period.

Gig work is an increasingly significant influence on the rise of an on-demand societal approach (Newlands, 2021). This is evident through different forms including locally specific platform-mediated jobs which is broadly classified as gig work (Schmidt, 2017). However, others call for more specific terminology to acknowledge the distinctions within the gig economy, such as *app-work* (see Duggan et al., 2020). There is also *crowdwork* which is a form that holds no locational boundaries, but still involves digital platform mediation. This has, in turn, been broken down into different constituent types by Howcroft and Bergvall-Kåreborn (2019). First, *online requester initiated* paid work is one of the most prominent forms which includes platforms such as Fiverr and Mechanical Turk. This work sees individuals perform very simple micro-tasks to more complicated projects in an online setting. Second, *profession-based freelancers* represent a type of worker-initiated work which can be unpaid or highly speculative in nature. For example, an individual may propose the development of a new App for an Android or Apple. Third, *playbour crowdwork* is requester initiated but has similarities to the previous form in that it tends to fall into the speculative and often non-paid form. For example, a software company may seek solutions to problems they have identified, and individuals may put forward solutions which can be unpaid or it may be some sort of cash prize that is offered rather than a more formalised pay arrangement. The final type – *asset-based services* – has received some critical comment and disagreement in terms of whether it represents crowd work or not (Duggan et al., 2020, 2022). Howcroft and Bergvall-Kåreborn (2019) identify this as worker initiated localised transaction work and include organisations such as Airbnb, Uber and TaskRabbit. The critique of this is that crowdwork should only represent work that can be completed remotely which this latter category does not align to (see Duggan et al., 2020, 2022). It is also argued that the nature of organisations like Airbnb is best described as *capital platform work* given its focus on leasing assets rather than necessarily the completion of discrete forms of labour (see Duggan et al., 2021a for wider debate).

Duggan et al. (2020) further emphasise that *cloudwork* describes tasks that can be completed remotely *via* the Internet and are not bound to a specific location. They view crowdwork as where a task is not given to a specific individual but to an undefined group of people online. If the task is further subdivided into smaller units for piecemeal work, with each individual remunerated with an equally small amount of money, it is *micro-tasking crowdwork*; and where tasks cannot be subdivided but work is carried out simultaneously, by a large group of individuals, but in the end only one result is used and paid for, is *contest-based crowdwork*. Cloudwork and all types of crowdwork allow for the completion of tasks remotely, thereby lacking a discernible employer. It is argued that compared to *app-workers* in particular, these individuals are less likely to develop a transparent working relationship with the gig or platform organisation (Duggan et al., 2020) which is likely to mean a differential role for HRM depending on the form of gig work.

Table 1 presents a summary of the characteristics of these different forms of gig working arrangements through providing examples of digital platforms and differentiating the defining features from the perspective of the worker, customer/requester, supplier, platform, location of labour and payment for labour. We also provide examples of technologically mediated HRM practices which will be expanded on further in the next section.

Human resource management in gig work

It is evident that there are significant challenges to our knowledge and understanding of people management in the context of gig work and the role HRM plays. Table 1 intimates that referring to gig work as a monolithic concept is problematic, most notably in a research context where such an approach may create confusion about what and who exactly is being studied, leading to inconclusive results (Gerwe & Silva, 2020). Gig work can therefore, we argue, be regarded as a new archetype for HRM, which allows for the expression and understanding of a new range of atypical working conditions, the nature of which may vary across different types of roles within the overall gig economy.

The short-term temporal nature of gig work means individuals complete tasks or provide labour for a defined time with no long-lasting connection to their 'employing' organisation (Todolí-Signes, 2017). The role of HRM may appear limited given that most gig-workers are viewed as independent contractors rather than employees. Notwithstanding the widespread legal ambiguity surrounding the employment classification of gig workers, the assumption that independent workers are not relevant to or within the remit of HRM practice and theory is questionable (see Cross & Swart, 2021). While digital platforms deny the existence of a traditional employment relationship, they nevertheless impose various measures of control on workers to ensure proper work assignment and performance management (Duggan et al., 2020). As a result, workers regularly compare themselves to employees (Petriglieri et al., 2019). Workers are often guided and controlled by technologically mediated HR practices, or algorithmic management.

Table 1. Characteristics of gig working arrangements.

Type of gig work	Example of platform	Worker	Customer/Requester	Supplier	Platform	Location	Payment	Examples of technologically-mediated HR practices
App-work	Uber, Deliveroo, Lyft, UberEats, Taskrabbit, Helpling	Independent contractor who works flexibly on a piece-rate basis.	End-user of the service; generates demand on platforms by initially requesting services *via* apps.	Exists in certain app-work arrangements as an additional partner of the online platform/ app e.g. restaurants in the case of food delivery	Platforms assign tasks to workers *via* apps based on demand, setting minimum quality standards of service and in the selection and management of those who perform the work	Tasks performed locally in person	Workers paid by platform. Platform specifies the payment level for the task.	Compensation e.g. Uber's surge price algorithm that adjusts workers' pay on the basis of labour supply and demand dynamics. Work allocation e.g. Deliveroo's algorithm dispatches orders to riders without human involvement.
Capital platform work	Airbnb, etsy	Workers use a digital platform to sell goods peer-to-peer or to lease assets	Customers are connected with a form of capital owned by an individual	N/A	Platform intermediates an e-commerce arrangement	Local (e.g. in the case of accommodation) or remote (e.g. in the case of the sale of goods)	Workers set compensation rates and are paid *via* platform	Compensation e.g. Airbnbs 'Smart Pricing' feature dynamically adjusts the cost of a night's stay based on current demand and allows hosts to set a minimum price
Cloud work	Upwork, Freelancer,	Work done by a specific individual online	Organisation or individual requests a task or project to be completed *via* a platform	N/A	Digital labour platforms provide services that are not bound to a specific location	Tasks completed remotely online	Platforms extract value from the service transaction e.g. by taking a commission, or charging workers a fee	Selection e.g. an algorithm grants or denies workers access to the Upwork platform
Crowdwork	Crowdflower, Fiverr, Workana, Appen	Work carried out by undefined group of people	Organisation or individual requests a task or project to be completed *via* a platform	N/A	Platforms connect workers with customers to sell their services by performing tasks	Tasks completed remotely online	Certain crowdwork platforms set minimum compensation for certain tasks, while others let the compensation be set by their requester. Requesters can pay workers directly plus a fee to the platform	Work allocation e.g. CrowdFlower distributes tasks to workers based on data collected information about workers' abilities and qualifications. Quality of the completed work is measured and recorded, and used in allocation of future tasks.

(continued)

Table 1. (Continued).

Type of gig work	Example of platform	Worker	Customer/Requester	Supplier	Platform	Location	Payment	Examples of technologically-mediated HR practices
Micro-tasking crowdwork	Amazon Mechanical Turk, Prolific, Clickworker	Tasks are subdivided into smaller units for piecemeal work.	Organisation or individual requests a task or project to be completed *via* a platform	N/A	Platform distributes repetitive tasks across a large and unspecified group of workers. Workers self-assign to the tasks.	Tasks completed remotely online	Each individual remunerated with an equally small amount of money	Talent management e.g. Amazon Mechanical Turk identifies talent through a 'Master Worker' qualification; a designation awarded to individuals that consistently exceed expectations. Workers cannot apply for the designation and it is determined by a proprietary algorithm.
Contest-based crowdwork	TopCoder, 99designs, Jovoto	Work is carried out simultaneously, by a large group of individuals	Organisation or individual requests a task or project to be completed *via* a platform	N/A	Customer selects and pays for only one result	Tasks completed remotely online	No guarantee of payment; customer pays for only one result	Performance management e.g. at the end of each contest on TopCoder, their algorithm rates each contestant, based on past performance and ranking compared to other contestants

Duggan et al. (2020) define algorithmic management as 'a system of control where self-learning algorithms are given the responsibility for making and executing decisions affecting labour, thereby limiting human involvement and oversight of the labour process' (p. 119). Kellogg et al. (2020) argue that algorithmic management goes beyond traditional forms of organisational control in several ways. It is generally used to direct workers through restricting and recommending behaviour, to evaluate workers through recording and rating behaviour, and to discipline workers through threatening replacement or promising reward (Kellogg et al., 2020). Consequently, algorithmic management is 'more comprehensive, instantaneous, interactive and opaque' than traditional means of control (Kellogg et al., 2020, p. 396). Meijerink, Boons et al. (2021) suggest the adoption of the term 'algorithmic HRM' to describe the 'use of software algorithms that operate on the basis of digital data to augment HR-related decisions and/or to automate HRM activities' (p. 2547).

We argue that the way in which technologically mediated HRM practices bind both digital platforms and workers to a working agreement, and the means through which they manage workers and bypass many of the regular responsibilities of employment has significant implications for HRM. Indeed, Duggan et al. (2020) note the potential redundancy of the traditional HR function in gig working because designers and developers of algorithms produce the technologically mediated HR practices that, in part, mimic traditional HR activities. Permeable organisational boundaries and increasingly fragmented forms of work combined with concerns that HR is a single actor unable to keep pace in such a complex environment network or ecosystem of stakeholders (Harney & Collings, 2021), means that there is a need to move away from the dominant 'organisational' or 'employee' conceptual lens when considering HRM in gig work. Cross and Swart (2021) similarly espouse the need to adopt a much broader focus to studying HR and individuals within an ecosystem in order to generate a more nuanced discussion and analysis of how different types of workers deploy their labour, knowledge, skills and abilities.

HR processes in the gig economy, including recruitment and selection, work allocation, performance management, reward management and employee termination, can be opaque, and not readily communicated to workers. In instances where algorithmic management is used, a lack of transparency about platform decision-making can limit workers' agency and autonomy. In terms of pay, platforms are generally not obligated to comply with local minimum wage legislation, and consequently workers are often in danger of earning below their local minimum wages, especially when time spent searching for work and overtime are considered (Halliday, 2021).

The performance of gig workers is generally controlled through algorithms which are purportedly unbiased and efficient in work allocation. The theoretical underpinning of performance management as a HR process generally focuses on performance identification and pay for performance. From the performance identification viewpoint, algorithms use harder platform control to capture the exact log of working hours, number of working assignments accepted or cancelled, punctuality, etc. (Shapiro, 2018). Newlands (2021) highlights how the allocation of work by algorithms lacks awareness of certain spatial conditions that workers encounter, which are generally beyond their control (e.g. weather or traffic conditions). This can negatively impact performance metrics and associated rewards, since the surveillance mechanisms fail to capture and account for these conditions, many of which may directly impact the worker's health and safety. From the pay for performance viewpoint, algorithms are designed around 'choice architecture' that uses certain gamic elements and institutionalised nudges as a method of exercising 'soft control' on the worker's motivation and behaviour that impacts their decisions and ultimately their performance outcomes (Rosenblat & Stark, 2016). More often, these outcomes fail to favour the worker or are not in alignment with their expectations, as the worker ends up receiving pre-determined incentives for achieving the targets that were curated by these digital platforms in the first place. In addition, workers choice appears to be severely compromised due in no small part to asymmetries of information whereby the platform organisation owns the knowledge and controls what is released (Cheng & Foley, 2019; Veen et al., 2020).

Heiland (2021) argues that control mechanisms deployed by algorithms on behalf of platforms are not solely technologically driven. In the case of food delivery, while platforms try to limit worker power through technological control, some loopholes remain, allowing workers some capacity to act autonomously. Therefore, additional forms of control are used in the form of working time regimes. Through working time regimes, platforms must fill unattractive and unprofitable shifts with workers, and thus limit the temporal flexibility of workers. Working time regimes do not only coordinate the labour process but control it by means of restricting both the worker's effort and mobility power. Working time regimes exist as a form of temporal (and thus organisational) control and are not just merely an efficient allocative instrument of labour, as workers tend to compete for shifts through their performance, which combines the issues of flexibility and control of platform labour.

The above practices demonstrate that, from a HRM perspective, the gig economy creates a new dynamic where technologies do not just mediate economic and social relations, but also help to co-constitute them

(Wood & Lehdonvirta, 2019). Digital platforms deploy technologically mediated HR practices at scale, allowing them to manage large, invisible workforces. Meijerink and Keegan (2019) suggest that the increasing prevalence of gig work redefines the role of HRM away from upholding employment relationships towards the governance of exchanges on platforms that serve to allow the co-creation of value for all parties involved. However, the long-term viability of the role of HRM in the gig economy has been questioned, particularly within the strategic context of motivating workers, ensuring high-quality performance, and providing social support (Jabagi et al., 2019). While Crawford (2021) suggests that algorithmic management is 'simply the latest (technology) in the long historical development of factories timepieces, and surveillance architectures' (p. 85), HRM activities now tend to be outsourced to system designers and coders that develop and deploy technologically mediated practices. This removes many of the costs of HRM and passes employment risks to the individual (Snyder, 2016), further eradicating the more interpersonal and empathetic aspects of people management (Angrave et al., 2016).

Special issue papers

The first paper by Meijerink, Keegan et al. (2021) unpacks the HRM activities that are used by online labour platforms under the theoretical lens of institutional complexity. As such, the paper rails against conceptions that HRM is of no relevance within the gig economy. Specifically, the paper reports on how these platforms create tensions between the competing market logic and corporation logic. The market logic is evident by how platform organisations see themselves as merely creating an online marketplace to enable independent contractors and customers to transact. The offer of considerable or full autonomy to gig workers is viewed as indicative of HRM activities that support this institutional logic. Counter to this is the competing corporation logic which accentuates the legitimisation of coordinating and controlling workers to support organisational profitability and success. HRM activities that fall under this logic, and which creates the tension include the utilisation of performance evaluations and algorithmic driven and managed compensation. Through an innovative qualitative methodology that incorporates ethnographic accounts of life as a gig worker this paper unpacks the interrelationships among several HRM activities that gig workers are subject to, the tensions from competing institutional logics at play, and the response strategies of these organisations.

The second paper by Norlander et al. (2021) focuses on perceptions of control and motivation held by three types of workers involved in transportation services namely, Uber, taxi and limousine drivers. Drawing from both a between-subjects survey and within-subjects field experiment leads the authors to identify how workers experience technological supervision. Noteworthy is that this study evaluates perceptions of motivation and control under algorithmic management conditions and more traditional human centred management, while holding the tasks being performed constant. The results show Uber drivers to report greater levels of organisational control than taxi drivers but not more intrinsic motivation, enjoyment or needs satisfaction. There were some divergent results between the two studies undertaken here but overall platforms are linked to moderately increased perceptions of control and work enjoyment amongst Uber drivers. The use of additional controls does not however appear to decrease motivation. The authors importantly report the existence of selection effects in understanding the differences between the gig workers and taxi and limousine drivers.

Our third paper in this special issue sees Shanahan and Smith (2021) draw on semi-structured interviews and participant observation methods, and Lukes' (2005) three key facets of power (i.e. decision-making; non-decision-making, and ideological power) to illustrate how food delivery platforms to promote the idea of gig work being fair. Moreover, the paper examines what the authors view as coping approaches to psychological contract violations by gig workers which both reinforce and resist the power possessed by platform firms. The findings offer some fascinating insights into how several ideological, explicit, and implicit mechanisms of power influence gig worker perceptions regarding their work. The role of principled dissent (Krause & Moore, 2018) as a coping approach is particularly prominent in that it enables individuals to continue with the exchange, thus holding the (limited) autonomy available but without supporting the platform firm view that the terms provided are fair.

The fourth contribution by Myhill et al. (2021) concentrates on the underpinning nature and quality of gig work; an area that has received scant attention to date in the literature. The authors seek to apply an approach that focuses on objective aspects that encompass a quality job but also incorporate the subjective, lived experiences of gig workers. The limitations surrounding existing models of job quality are highlighted through the research, in particular the limitations that surround objective styled characteristics. The lived experience of gig workers emerges as more complex and nuanced than existing commentary. For example, while there is critical discourse around the negative side to the tight, technological control that is endemic in gig work, workers appeared to be less concerned on much of this, instead perceiving themselves as holding greater control over when to work. Also, there was appreciation for the opportunities that existed to generate additional income despite the substantial job insecurity that is evident. Of note is that the key findings illustrate gig worker experiences vary depending on the platform and whether they undertake this work as their core income versus it being a supplementary source. This gives further credence for the need for wider empirical research into contrasting variants of gig work to be able to better contextualise and appreciate the different forms that encompass this new economy.

Our final paper by Williams et al. (2021) centres on exploring how different platform organisations attract and select independent gig workers. The data consists of an analysis of multiple websites and terms and conditions documents of online platform organisations in Australia. They reveal evidence of traditional recruitment practice alongside new algorithmic enabled aspects. The research indicates a layer of invisibility around some selection practices used which the authors argue raises concerns over the equitability of access to work on these online labour platforms. The title of the Meijerink, Keegan et al. paper (2021), in this issue, which refers to platform organisations as *having their cake and eating it too* also has resonance here in that they, 'simultaneously abdicate responsibility for selection decisions to clients, while maintaining control over attraction of workers and key selection processes, such as algorithmic shortlisting or "matching"' (Williams et al., 2021, p. 22).

Where to next? A look to future research avenues

The five papers published in this Special Issue illuminate a future research agenda on which to build upon and critique. For example, Williams et al. (2021) provides a model, developed through documentary and website analysis, that could serve as a starting point to further research and understanding on gig worker attraction, selection and turnover. Meijerink, Keegan et al. (2021) offer a useful framework that can serve to further unpack the inter-relationships among HRM activities for gig workers and the competing logics and response strategies underpinning the inherent complexity involved in this form of work. Given the urgency of change permeating work arrangements in the gig economy over the last decade, it is challenging for scholars to imagine what the future holds for this dynamic form of labour. Indeed, there is a danger that the speed with which existing technologies develop, and new technologies emerge may render a lot of the assumptions made about technologically mediated HRM and employment relationships in this space obsolete by the time they get through the publication cycle. However, if 'human work' is to remain a feature of gig working either within or beyond the boundaries of the gig economy, there are significant theoretical and practical implications for HRM (Cross & Swart, 2021). We argue that inter-disciplinary research perspectives which broadly encompasses the topic – *work in the gig economy* – has never been more important and necessary to provide critical perspectives that can be used to positively influence practice and inform policy decisions.

As evident from the papers included in this Special Issue, one of the most pressing issues requiring greater attention from HRM scholars is the need to better understand the role of the algorithm in the different variants of gig working. Algorithms at work, by design, are self-learning and dynamic and exist in ever-shifting employment contexts (Kellogg et al., 2020). This, of course, presents an obstacle to those seeking to explore how they function. Yet, given that algorithmic management has replaced several of the more traditional HRM activities such as selection and rewards, particularly in many app-work and crowdwork variants, there is a clear need to deepen our knowledge on the implications of algorithms for people management. There are many unanswered questions in this domain requiring a sharper focus from researchers. First, should there be a role for the HR function within the platform organisation in the design and development of the algorithm? Might algorithms function more effectively when it comes to people management issues if HR specialists have had an input in their construction (rather than this being the preserve of, for example, software developers)? If this is the case, in what ways can algorithms be adapted so that HR has more of a say in how gig-workers should be managed?

There is an increasing body of research arguing that algorithms are transitioning from employment 'tool' to employment 'partner' (Bankins & Formosa, 2020; Duggan et al., 2021a; Sherman & Morley, 2020), assuming the responsibilities once held by supervisors or line managers. Indeed, if algorithms are to be seen as the manager by proxy in the context of employment relationships, the implications for HR are significant. For instance, can gig workers have an employment relationship with an algorithm whereby they create a mutual exchange agreement? In this special issue, Shanahan and Smith (2021) consider the implications of how violated agreements influence perceptions of fairness in this type of arrangement. However, the idea of an algorithm being viewed by workers as the 'employer' requires further scholarly attention. If there is, for example, the potential for a more co-determined working relationship, how can HR assist workers in their interactions with the algorithm? Answering such questions, may help to bring the disparate literatures of HRM and algorithmic management closer together.

Several papers in this issue either directly or indirectly consider aspects of control and motivation in online platform work. For example, Norlander et al. (2021) found some causal effects of platforms in their second experimental study, that stood in contrast to their first study, raising the issue of possible selection effects at play. The issue of selection effects is worthy of further recognition, such as whether they are related to those that opt into gig work or if it is through attrition. This is something that has not gained much, if any, consideration prior to the publication of this paper by Norlander et al. (2021). Overall, greater research on how the types of technological control and monitoring that is made possible through these platforms impact on gig workers are required.

While untangling the complexities of algorithms at work is critical to gain deeper insights into the technologization of HRM, a growing number of researchers are focussing their attention on gig workers' experiences of being managed by an algorithm (see for example in this special issue, Myhill et al., 2021). We argue that foregrounding the lived experiences of the 'human' in the grip of an algorithmic mediated employment relationship should remain a central tenet of future exploration in the HRM field, a particular feature of papers in this Special Issue. Of course, it can be argued that the lack of clarity surrounding the precarious employment status of some gig-workers across the globe means that having a duty of care over these workers is not a universal concern for the gig organisation. Yet, a growing argument within HR scholarship contends that HRM should have responsibility for the independent workers with whom they work in a wider network (Connelly et al., 2021; Cross & Swart, 2021). There is a need, therefore, for broadening the parameters on where HRM is relevant. This view also fits with calls for a greater focus on wider societal matters as exemplified in the UN Sustainable Development Goals where, for example, HR could, and we argue should, promote moral policies and practices that are sustainable for humans and the environment. Accordingly, the employment status of gig workers may be somewhat immaterial in the context of considering the responsibilities of the HR function in terms of managing this cohort of workers. The potential implications of this line of enquiry for research is significant as it raises several important questions. In what way is the management of gig workers different to employees in more standard employment arrangements? If the nature of the working relationship grows and moves beyond its transactional and short-term focus what are the implications for the HR function in terms of reward, development, retention, etc.? Does 'best practice' within these processes neatly extend to a gig-work context or is novel thinking required in these areas to ensure these workers are managed effectively? Again, answering questions like these are crucial in comprehending how HR is to remain a valuable and necessary party in the ecosystem (Meijerink, Keegan et al., 2021).

There is also a need to consider the wider transmissibility of gig economy HR processes and practices into the more traditional employment model (Huws et al., 2018). If algorithmic management can capture and duplicate many of the traditional HR functions it raises the question as to how much of the gig economy experience can be replicated elsewhere? Can organisations outside the gig economy substantially increase their use of HR software systems that in turn sees the need for less HR professionals? The forced move for millions of workers into home working arrangements arising from the Covid-19 has seen increasing calls for greater flexibility in where and when people work once this global health crisis has abated (Wheatley et al., 2021). This leads us to question whether there could be a greater role for algorithmic style management within 'standard' employment to remotely manage staff.

As explained, gig work typically involves multiple parties (Duggan et al., 2020) and the successful functioning of the work system is dependent on each party contributing effectively. Yet, there exists concern about the implications of the gig economy for the future of work but also about the long-term sustainability of gig work as a viable form of labour (Wood et al., 2019). There is also a need to consider whether the potential implications of gig work are equal across the world. For example, gig work may provide opportunities to improve job quality, voice, and the generation of jobs in a developing economy context like Africa where over 80% of employment is informal (Heeks, 2017). Through greater platform regulation and certification, decent work conditions could be transplanted into the informal economy (Heeks et al., 2020). There is emerging evidence of several international platforms progressively introducing better work conditions into contracts (Fairwork, 2019), and thus there does exist some potential for embedding decent work conditions through digital platforms.

To effectively address the challenges presented by gig work it seems likely that HR will be required to play a pivotal role in ensuring employment opportunities in this space remain worthwhile, durable and meaningful for workers. Indeed, the idea of developing a 'career' within gig-work has received only minor attention from researchers to date (see for example, Duggan et al., 2021b). What are the responsibilities of the HR function in digital platforms regarding the career development of gig workers? How can the HR function help gig workers with the transition into and out of this form of labour? Relatedly, how do employers value work experience in the gig economy when assessing a prospective candidate for a new role? How can the HR function in digital platforms help to develop career competencies for workers unlikely to stay within the industry on a long-term basis? These, and other questions, require much consideration by researchers trying to assess how HRM can contribute to the long-term sustainability of this form of labour.

Finally, we wish to briefly touch upon methodological matters. The innovative nature of gig work brings with it the potential for more creative methodologies being applied to best address many of the future research questions set out here. In this issue we see several innovative approaches adopted (e.g. Meijerink, Keegan et al., 2021; Norlander et al., 2021) which we welcome and encourage more of. Moreover, there is much scope to strengthen the data sources used in gig economy research; many papers in the gig economy and work context tend to rely on very small samples of participants. Greater diversity of perspectives from the different actors involved in this type of work is required to really advance understanding and knowledge. The perspectives of clients and the digital platforms themselves would be especially welcome inputs into future research, though we are appreciative of the access challenges. While challenging to undertake, longitudinal research designs will be especially welcome in that they may assist in charting the evolution of gig work overtime. Given the dynamism of the legal and regulatory environment of gig work, along with the ways in which algorithms are deployed this is likely to be a highly evolving research domain, making it ripe for a more long-term focussed research designs.

Conclusion

The papers in this special issue provide empirical insight on how technologically mediated HRM is enacted in the gig economy. A variety of HRM activities deployed by digital platform organisations that gig workers are subject to including attraction, recruitment and selection, job quality, motivation and control provide an insight into how technology mediates the management of labour in gig work. Considering work and working conditions are hugely individualised across digital platform organisations, the implications for HRM along with policy and union responses will vary and will need to be tailored accordingly. More pertinently, the role and value of organisational HR functions and traditionally internal HR activities such as selection, training and development etc. may be eroded in the context of gig work. These issues notwithstanding, as long as organisations operating in the gig economy remain reliant on humans to complete the gigs, it is hard to argue against an important role for HRM in this new form of labour.

Disclosure statement

No potential conflict of interest was reported by the author(s).

ORCID

Anthony McDonnell http://orcid.org/0000-0002-9127-2452
Ronan Carbery http://orcid.org/0000-0001-8836-2038
John Burgess http://orcid.org/0000-0002-9875-3275
Ultan Sherman http://orcid.org/0000-0002-2639-746X

References

Angrave, D., Charlwood, A., Kirkpatrick, I., Lawrence, M., & Stuart, M. (2016). HR and analytics: Why HR is set to fail the big data challenge. *Human Resource Management Journal*, *26*(1), 1–11. https://doi.org/10.1111/1748-8583.12090

Apouey, B., Roulet, A., Solal, I., & Stabile, M. (2020). Gig workers during the COVID-19 crisis in France: Financial precarity and mental well-being. *Journal of Urban Health*, *97*(6), 776–795. https://doi.org/10.1007/s11524-020-00480-4

Balaram, B., Warden, J., & Wallace-Stephens, F. (2017). *Good Gigs. A fairer future for the UK's gig economy*. Report Downloaded from https://www.thersa.org/globalassets/pdfs/reports/rsa_good-gigs-fairer-gig-economy-report.pdf

Bankins, S., & Formosa, P. (2020). When AI meets PC: Exploring the implications of workplace social robots and a human-robot psychological contract. *European Journal of Work and Organizational Psychology*, *29*(2), 215–229. https://doi.org/10.1080/1359432X.2019.1620328

Berg, J., Furrer, M., Harmon, E., Rani, U., & Silberman, M. S. (2018). *Digital labour platforms and the future of work: Towards decent work in the online world*. International Labour Office.

Cheng, M., & Foley, C. (2019). Algorithmic management: The case of Airbnb. *International Journal of Hospitality Management*, *83*, 33–36. https://doi.org/10.1016/j.ijhm.2019.04.009

Collier, R. B., Dubal, V. B., & Carter, C. (2017). *Labour platforms and gig work: The failure to regulate* [Institute for Research on Labour and Employment: Working Paper, 106–17].

Connelly, C. E., Fieseler, C., Černe, M., Giessner, S. R., & Wong, S. I. (2021). Working in the digitized economy: HRM theory & practice. *Human Resource Management Review*, *31*(1), 100762. https://doi.org/10.1016/j.hrmr.2020.100762

Crawford, K. (2021). *The Atlas of AI. Power, politics, and the planetary costs of artificial intelligence*. Yale University Press.

Cross, D., & Swart, J. (2021). The (ir) relevance of human resource management in independent work: Challenging assumptions. *Human Resource Management Journal*. https://doi.org/10.1111/1748-8583.12389

Duggan, J., McDonnell, A., Sherman, U., & Carbery, R. (2022). *Work in the gig economy: A research overview*. Routledge

Duggan, J., Sherman, U., Carbery, R., & McDonnell, A. (2020). Algorithmic management and app-work in the gig economy: A research agenda for employment relations and HRM. *Human Resource Management Journal*, *30*(1), 114–132. https://doi.org/10.1111/1748-8583.12258

Duggan, J., Sherman, U., Carbery, R., & McDonnell, A. (2021a). Multi-party working relationships in gig work: Towards a new perspective. In J. Meijerink, G. Jansen, & V. Daskalova (Eds.), *Unravelling the gig work paradox*. Edward Elgar

Duggan, J., Sherman, U., Carbery, R., & McDonnell, A. (2021b). Boundaryless careers and algorithmic constraints in the gig economy. *The International Journal of Human Resource Management*, 1–31. https://doi.org/10.1080/09585192.2021.1953565

European Commission. (2018). *New report shows that digital employment platforms are gaining a foothold in Europe's labour markets*, European Commission [website]. Retrieved May 5, 2021, from https://ec.europa.eu/social/main.jsp?langId=en&catId=89&newsId=9146

Fabo, B., Karanovic, J., & Dukova, K. (2017). In search of an adequate European policy to the platform economy. *Transfer: European Review of Labour and Research, 23*(2), 163–175. https://doi.org/10.1177/1024258916688861

Fairwork. (2019). *The five pillars of fairwork: Labour standards in the platform economy.* Oxford, UK: Fairwork Foundation. http://fair.work/wp-content/uploads/sites/97/2019/10/Fairwork-Y1-Report.pdf

Friedman, G. (2014). Workers without employers: Shadow corporations and the rise of the gig economy. *Review of Keynesian Economics, 2*(2), 171–188. https://doi.org/10.4337/roke.2014.02.03

Gerwe, O., & Silva, R. (2020). Clarifying the sharing economy: Conceptualization, typology, antecedents, and effects. *Academy of Management Perspectives, 34*(1), 65–96. https://doi.org/10.5465/amp.2017.0010

Halliday, D. (2021). On the (mis)classification of paid labor: When should gig workers have employee status? *Politics, Philosophy & Economics, 20*(3), 229–250. https://doi.org/10.1177/1470594X211015467

Harney, B., & Collings, D. G. (2021). Navigating the shifting landscapes of HRM. *Human Resource Management Review, 31*(4), 100824. https://doi.org/10.1016/j.hrmr.2021.100824

Harris, B. (2017). Uber, lyft, and regulating the sharing economy. *Seattle University Law Review, 41*(1), 269–285.

Heeks, R. (2017). *Decent work and the digital gig economy: A developing country perspective on employment impacts and standards in online outsourcing, crowdwork, etc.* [GDI Development Informatics Working Papers; No. 70]. Global Development Institute, University of Manchester. http://hummedia.manchester.ac.uk/institutes/gdi/publications/workingpapers/di/di_wp71.pdf

Heeks, R., Graham, M., Mungai, P., Van Belle, J.-P., & Woodcock, J. (2020). *Systematic evaluation of platform work against decent work standards: Development of a new framework and application in the global south.* Manchester Centre for Digital Development Working Paper 85. http://www.gdi.manchester.ac.uk/research/publications/di/

Heiland, H. (2021). Neither timeless, nor placeless: Control of food delivery gig work via place-based working time regimes. *Human Relations*, 001872672110252. https://doi.org/10.1177%2F00187267211025283. https://doi.org/10.1177/00187267211025283

Howcroft, D., & Bergvall-Kåreborn, B. (2019). A typology of crowdwork platforms. *Work, Employment and Society, 33*(1), 21–38. https://doi.org/10.1177/0950017018760136

Huws, U., Spencer, N., & Syrdal, D. (2018). Online, on call: The spread of digitally organised just-in- time working and its implications for standard employment models. *New Technology, Work and Employment, 33*(2), 113–132. https://doi.org/10.1111/ntwe.12111

Jabagi, N., Croteau, A. M., Audebrand, L. K., & Marsan, J. (2019). Gig workers' motivation: Thinking beyond carrots and sticks. *Journal of Managerial Psychology, 34*(4), 192–213. https://doi.org/10.1108/JMP-06-2018-0255

Kaine, S., & Josserand, E. (2019). The organisation and experience of work in the gig economy. *Journal of Industrial Relations, 61*(4), 479–501. https://doi.org/10.1177/0022185619865480

Kellogg, K. C., Valentine, M. A., & Christin, A. (2020). Algorithms at work: The new contested terrain of control. *Academy of Management Annals, 14*(1), 366–410. https://doi.org/10.5465/annals.2018.0174

Kirven, A. (2018). Whose gig is it anyway? Technological change, workplace control and supervision, and workers' rights in the gig economy. *University of Colorado Law Review*, *89*(1), 249–292.

Krause, A. J., & Moore, S. Y. (2018). Working in imbalance: How employees revise their psychological contracts in a post-breach environment. *Employee Responsibilities and Rights Journal*, *30*(4), 253–278. https://doi.org/10.1007/s10672-018-9321-0

Lukes, S. (2005). *Power: A radical view*. 2nd ed. Palgrave Macmillan.

Mehmood, S. M., & Najmi, A. (2017). Understanding the impact of service convenience on customer satisfaction in home delivery: Evidence from Pakistan. *International Journal of Electronic Customer Relationship Management*, *11*(1), 23–43. https://doi.org/10.1504/IJECRM.2017.086752

Meijerink, J., Boons, M., Keegan, A., & Marler, J. (2021). Algorithmic human resource management: Synthesizing developments and cross-disciplinary insights on digital HRM. *The International Journal of Human Resource Management*, *32*(12), 2545–2562. https://doi.org/10.1080/09585192.2021.1925326

Meijerink, J., & Keegan, A. (2019). Conceptualizing human resource management in the gig economy: Toward a platform ecosystem perspective. *Journal of Managerial Psychology*, *34*(4), 214–232. https://doi.org/10.1108/JMP-07-2018-0277

Meijerink, J., Keegan, A., & Bondarouk, T. (2021). Having their cake and eating it too? Online labor platforms and human resource management as a case of institutional complexity. *The International Journal of Human Resource Management*, *32*(19), 1–37. https://doi.org/10.1080/09585192.2020.1867616

Myhill, K., Richards, J., & Sang, K. (2021). Job quality, fair work and gig work: The lived experiences of gig workers. *The International Journal of Human Resource Management*, *32*(19), 1–26. https://doi.org/10.1080/09585192.2020.1867612

Newlands, G. (2021). Algorithmic surveillance in the gig economy: The organisation of work through Lefebvrian conceived space. *Organization Studies*, *42*(5), 719–737. https://doi.org/10.1177/0170840620937900

Norlander, P., Jukic, N., Varma, A., & Nestorov, S. (2021). The effects of technological supervision on gig workers: Organizational control and motivation of Uber, taxi, and limousine drivers. *The International Journal of Human Resource Management*, *32*(19), 1–25. https://doi.org/10.1080/09585192.2020.1867614

Pasquale, F. (2016). Two narratives of platform capitalism. *Yale Law & Policy Review*, *35*, 309–319.

Petriglieri, G., Ashford, S. J., & Wrzesniewski, A. (2019). Agony and ecstasy in the gig economy: Cultivating holding environments for precarious and personalised work identities. *Administrative Science Quarterly*, *64*(1), 124–170. https://doi.org/10.1177/0001839218759646

Rani, U., Kumar Dhir, R., Furrer, M., Gőbel, N., Moraiti, A., & Cooney, S. (2021). *World employment and social outlook: The role of digital labour platforms in transforming the world of work*. International Labour Organization.

Rosenblat, A., & Stark, L. (2016). Algorithmic labour and information asymmetries: A case study of Uber's drivers. *International Journal of Communication*, *10*(27), 3758–3784.

Schmidt, F. A. (2017). *Digital labour markets in the platform economy: Mapping the political challenges of crowd work and gig work*. Friedrich-Ebert-Stiftung.

Shanahan, G., & Smith, M. (2021). Fair's fair: Psychological contracts and power in platform work. *The International Journal of Human Resource Management*, *32*(19), 1–32. https://doi.org/10.1080/09585192.2020.1867615

Shapiro, A. (2018). Between autonomy and control: Strategies of arbitrage in the on-demand economy. *New Media & Society*, *20*(8), 2954–2971. https://doi.org/10.1177/1461444817738236

Sherman, U. P., & Morley, M. J. (2020). What do we measure and how do we elicit it? The case for the use of repertory grid technique in multi-party psychological contract research. *European Journal of Work and Organizational Psychology*, *29*(2), 230–242. https://doi.org/10.1080/1359432X.2019.1668844

Smith, A. (2016). *Labor platforms: Technology-enabled 'gig work'*. Pew Research Center, Retrieved May 5, from https://www.pewresearch.org/internet/2016/11/17/laborplatforms-technology-enabled-gig-work/

Snyder, B. (2016). *The disrupted workplace: Time and the moral order of flexible capitalism*. Oxford University Press.

Todolí-Signes, A. (2017). The gig economy: Employee, self-employed or the need for a special employment regulation? *Transfer: European Review of Labour and Research*, *23*(2), 193–205. https://doi.org/10.1177/1024258917701381

Veen, A., Barratt, T., & Goods, C. (2020). Platform-Capital's 'App-etite' for control: A labour process analysis of food-delivery work in Australia. *Work, Employment and Society*, *34*(3), 388–406. https://doi.org/10.1177/0950017019836911

Wheatley, D., Hardill, I., & Buglass, S. (2021). *Handbook of research on remote work and worker well-being in the post-COVID-19 era* (pp. xix–xxxiii). IGI Global.

Williams, P., McDonald, P., & Mayes, R. (2021). Recruitment in the gig economy: Attraction and selection on digital platforms. *The International Journal of Human Resource Management*, *32*(19), 1–27. https://doi.org/10.1080/09585192.2020.1867613

Wood, A. J., Graham, M., Lehdonvirta, V., & Hjorth, I. (2019). Good gig, bad gig: Autonomy and algorithmic control in the global gig economy. *Work, Employment & Society*, *33*(1), 56–75.

Wood, A. J., & Lehdonvirta, V. (2019). *Platform labour and structured antagonism: Understanding the origins of protest in the gig economy*. Paper presented at the Oxford Internet Institute Platform Economy Seminar Series. March 5.

OPEN ACCESS

Having their cake and eating it too? Online labor platforms and human resource management as a case of institutional complexity

Jeroen Meijerink, Anne Keegan and Tanya Bondarouk

ABSTRACT

Previous studies have shown that online labor platforms want to have their cake and eat it too by implementing human resource management (HRM) activities to control gig workers who ought to be autonomous in their work. Our empirical study shows that using HRM activities to control gig workers creates institutional complexity and explores the strategies adopted by platform firms to address this complexity. Based on case studies of two meal-delivery platforms in the Netherlands (Uber Eats and Deliveroo), we identify freelance-related HRM activities that create tensions between the market and corporation logics. We show that online labor platforms rely on response strategies that integrate/balance, rather than rule out competing logics, including creating novel forms of HRM outsourcing, HRM devolution, and covert HRM implementation to control gig workers while simultaneously upholding their freelance status. Furthermore, we show that these response strategies are enabled by information technologies and the marketplaces that online labor platforms create, allowing for more experimental and dynamic approaches to HRM than so far theorized. The main implication of these findings is that the HRM activities for gig workers are simultaneously the source of, and the solution to, the institutional complexity associated with HRM for controlling freelance gig workers.

Introduction

In this study, we explore how online labor platforms such as Uber and Deliveroo respond to the institutional complexity associated with their use of human resource management (HRM) activities for controlling self-employed 'gig' workers that ought to be autonomous in their work (Meijerink & Keegan, 2019). Institutional complexity occurs when organizations face tensions that arise from competing institutional logics, that is, ideal-type, taken-for-granted social prescriptions of what constitute legitimate goals and activities (Greenwood et al., 2011; Thornton & Ocasio, 1999). Through their use of HRM activities, we expect that online labor platforms create tensions between two competing institutional logics: (1) the *market logic* that legitimizes profit-making through free, unregulated competition among self-employed workers, and (2) the *corporation logic* that legitimizes market share and revenue growth through coordination and control of employees by an employer (Frenken et al., 2018).

On the one hand, online labor platforms emphasize the market logic as they are for-profit labor market intermediaries that create online marketplaces where self-employed 'gig' workers and requesters (i.e. organizations or consumers) transact (Kuhn & Maleki, 2017; Meijerink & Keegan, 2019). Accordingly, gig workers are framed as independent entrepreneurs that compete, for example on price or service offerings, which may be evidenced by HRM activities such as autonomy offered to gig workers (Aloisi, 2016; Kuhn & Maleki, 2017). On the other hand, online labor platforms also use HRM activities such as performance-rating schemes (Rosenblat et al., 2017), algorithm-based compensation (Duggan et al., 2020), and narrowly defined jobs (Kuhn & Maleki, 2017) which afford control over gig worker performance and institute the corporation logic. Control-enhancing HRM activities emanating from the corporation logic contradict autonomy-enhancing HRM activities that reinforce the market logic, creating institutional complexity, and generating tensions. Institutional complexity can cause conflicts with relevant stakeholders, loss of legitimacy, and ultimately organizational failure (Battilana & Dorado, 2010; Greenwood et al., 2011). In a gig context, such tensions and conflicts are evident in the various court cases against online labor platforms around the globe, which center on the issue whether gig workers should be classified as autonomous freelancers (i.e. market logic) or employees that are controlled by an employer (i.e. corporation logic) (Frenken et al., 2018; Meijerink & Keegan, 2019).

To address such challenges and ensure organizational survival, online labor platforms – like other organizations – can adopt response strategies that alleviate tensions between competing logics. Although extant research discusses response strategies to institutional complexity (Greenwood et al., 2011; Lewis et al., 2019; Pache & Santos, 2010), these strategies may not translate well to online labor platforms as they involve favoring one logic over others. As corporations that organize markets, online labor platforms are unlikely to opt for a single logic since they see working with freelancers as desirable (a market logic) while simultaneously wanting to control these freelancers (a corporation logic) (Frenken et al., 2018). Our study therefore explores the institutional complexity of HRM for controlling freelance gig workers, and the response strategies adopted by online labor platforms for integrating competing institutional logics.

This study makes three contributions to the literature. First, we disentangle the institutional complexity associated with HRM for freelance gig workers by examining which HRM activities reinforce the market logic and which reinforce the competing logic of the corporation. Although researchers have frequently studied how institutions impact HRM activities (Lewis et al., 2019), our study reveals that HRM activities of online labor platforms are a source of institutional complexity and therefore, best conceptualized as hybrid systems. Second, while institutional complexity in the gig economy has been theorized (Frenken et al., 2018), less is known about how stakeholders experience it. The adoption of response strategies to institutional complexity depends on how it is perceived (Pache & Santos, 2010). As such, we contribute by showing how gig economy actors experience institutional complexity associated with HRM for freelancers. Finally, we illustrate the response strategies adopted by online labor platforms for balancing the tensions associated with HRM practices for freelancers. We add to institutional theory by showing how the technologies and online marketplaces, created by online labor platforms, afford novel response strategies for addressing institutional complexity in cases where organizations cannot favor one institutional logic over another.

This paper is structured as follows. We start by discussing the business model of online labor platforms and how this can be understood from an institutional complexity perspective. This is followed by outlining how HRM for freelancers may create institutional complexity and the response strategies for addressing this complexity. After presenting our methodology and the results from the case studies of two online labor platforms, we conclude by discussing the implications of our work for institutional theory and HRM research into online labor platforms.

Literature review and theoretical background

Online labor platforms' business model and the gig economy: Freelancing or employment?

Online labor platforms are for-profit labor market intermediaries that use technology to create online, multi-sided marketplaces that together make up the so-called gig economy. Although there is no consensus on a definition of the gig economy, the term is generally used to describe an economic system that consists of online labor platform firms that connect requesters (i.e. organizations or consumers) with on-demand gig workers in industries such as transportation (e.g. Uber), cleaning (e.g. Helpling) and food delivery (e.g. Deliveroo) (Duggan et al., 2020; Meijerink & Keegan, 2019). Although paid for their services, gig workers do not have an employment relationship with an organization (Aloisi, 2016; Daskalova, 2018). Rather, they are classified as independent freelancers by platform firms who facilitate their access to requesters. As such, rather than being employers to gig workers, online labor platforms claim that they are brokers providing intermediation services between self-employed gig workers and consumers/organizations that wish to outsource fixed-term activities that gig workers are willing to perform (Kuhn & Maleki, 2017; Stanford, 2017; Veen et al., 2020).

The business model of online labor platforms is based on charging fees for their intermediation services (Kuhn & Maleki, 2017; Stanford, 2017). In practice, this involves gig workers and/or requesters paying the platform for each successful match made. For instance, the ride-hailing platform Uber operates an online platform where passengers – by means of a smartphone application – can hail a taxi that is driven by a freelance driver. Uber algorithmically matchmakes between the two by dispatching a passenger's requests to one of its freelance "partners". After the freelance taxi driver accepts the passengers' requests and drops him/her off at the final destination, Uber charges passengers the fare for the taxi ride, which Uber transfers to the taxi driver after deducting a commission fee that ranges between 20% and 30% (Rosenblat & Stark, 2016). To increase the number of transactions and thus their revenue, platform firms like Uber must grow the number of gig workers and requesters willing to transact. Online platform firms seek to create so-called network externalities that occur when increased numbers of platform users improve the value of the intermediation service (Lin & Lu, 2011) by scaling up both sides of the online market place: more active requesters means that gig workers can more easily acquire gigs (and thus income); more gig workers allows requesters to more easily and efficiently outsource their activities. Network externalities improve the revenues for the platform firm by increasing workers' and requesters' willingness to pay for intermediation services (Lin & Lu, 2011; Tanriverdi & Lee, 2008).

The creation of network effects however comes at a cost. Particularly in their early stages, online labor platforms expend significant effort to scale up both sides of their online marketplaces. They do so by offering discounts on intermediation services to the freelance workers and requesters (Frenken et al., 2018; Kessler, 2015; Rosenblat et al., 2017). The financial resources that enable this mainly come from venture capital offered by early investors (Lieman, 2018). The venture capital-based discounts may however prove unsustainable over time if rival platforms also seek to create network externalities. In such cases, the online platform with the largest financial resources is likely to drive competitors out, which creates a monopsony/monopoly allowing the remaining platform to reduce subsidies and increase commission fees to grow revenue (Daskalova, 2018; Meijerink & Keegan, 2019).

Online labor platform firms allegedly benefit from not formally employing gig workers in ensuring their future profit. Some argue that online labor platforms work with freelancers to avoid having to apply labor laws, thereby avoiding the associated costs (taxes, social security, paid holidays, etc.) (Aloisi, 2016; Daskalova, 2018; Rosenblat & Stark, 2016). Working with self-employed workers also enables platform firms to exit a market at a low cost (by not having to terminate employment contracts of their workers) if they cannot outcompete rival platforms. Although working with freelancers may lower costs to a platform, it also presents challenges as sustaining network externalities requires online labor platforms to control gig workers as if they were employees in an employment relationship. These actions go against the freelance model, flouting the self-employed status of gig workers propagated by platform firms (Veen et al., 2020; Wood et al., 2019). It is precisely this tension between platforms controlling gig workers on the one hand, and having to offer them autonomy to uphold their freelance status on the other, that has sparked numerous court cases on the legal status of gig workers (Meijerink & Keegan, 2019). To understand this tension and the consequences this has for online labor platforms, we draw on the concept of institutional complexity.

Institutional complexity in the form of competing institutional logics

Institutional complexity occurs when organizations face incompatible prescriptions from different institutional logics (Greenwood et al., 2011; Lewis et al., 2019; Pache & Santos, 2010; Thornton & Ocasio, 1999). Institutional logics amount to "socially constructed, historical patterns of material practices, assumptions, values, beliefs, and rules by which individuals produce and reproduce their material subsistence, organize time and space, and provide meaning to their social reality" (Thornton & Ocasio, 1999: 804). As such, institutional logics are ideal-type representations of an organization's institutional field in terms of taken-for-granted social prescriptions as to what is seen as legitimate (Battilana & Dorado, 2010).

Thornton (2004) outlines six ideal-type institutional logics that may conflict: the state logic, market logic, family logic, religious logic, corporation logic, and professional logic. Each of these institutional logics describe what is seen to be a legitimate goal and legitimized actions to realize this goal, such as profit through free/unregulated competition (i.e. market logic), reputation through expertise development (i.e. professional logic), and market share/revenue growth through organizational control and coordination (i.e. corporation logic). These different logics may contradict one another to produce institutional complexity that manifests itself as tensions between, or incompatible prescriptions from, different institutional logics (Greenwood et al., 2011). For example, this will occur when a bank (and its shareholders) propose a pay raise or bonus for its CEO to remain competitive on the international labor market (i.e. market logic) since this is incompatible with the state logic which holds that banks serve a greater, community good.

In line with the work of Frenken et al. (2018), we posit that online labor platforms experience conflicting logics, and thus institutional complexity, as they apply HRM practices for self-employed gig workers to implement their business model. As discussed below, this complexity is rooted in incompatible prescriptions from the market and the corporation logics associated with the use of HRM activities by online labor platforms.

Online labor platforms use of HRM practices to institute the 'market logic'

Gig workers are rooted in the market logic. Actors that draw on the market logic view profit and shareholder value as legitimate goals that are achieved through free and unregulated competition without control by a single corporation or the state (Goodrick & Reay, 2011; Thornton, 2004). At least two of the actors in the gig economy are likely to propagate the market logic. First, there are the early investors that provide online labor platforms with the venture capital to create network externalities in the hope this will result in profits. Second, platform firms propagate the market logic and, specifically, the free and unregulated competition among self-employed gig workers (Frenken et al., 2018). By framing gig workers as freelancers that generate profit through free and unregulated competition based on price or service offering, online labor platforms can increase profit to the platform firm by reducing (or avoiding) costs such as taxes, social security payments and worker benefits (Aloisi, 2016; Daskalova, 2018).

Online labor platforms may implement several HRM activities to enable free and unregulated competition among freelance gig workers. First, they offer gig workers the autonomy to make decisions on where to work, which requesters to serve, which services to offer, and what prices to charge (Kuhn & Maleki, 2017; Shapiro, 2018; Wood et al., 2019). This reinforces the market logic as it offers gig workers the freedom to compete on the basis of price and/or service offering as well as to work for requesters that are willing to pay a premium price. Moreover, to ensure free competition without control by the platform firm, gig workers should be free to join and to leave the online marketplace. Although online labor platforms do implement HRM practices related to gig worker recruitment and selection (Meijerink & Keegan, 2019), they may be inclined to set very few selection/admission criteria for gig workers to support the market logic of free and unregulated competition.

HRM practices of online labor platforms for instituting the 'corporation logic'

Online labor platforms simultaneously institute the competing logic of the corporation. Actors that draw on the corporation logic view market share and revenue growth as legitimate goals that are achieved through encoding work into the routines of the organization and subjecting workers to administrative control through HRM activities (Frenken et al., 2018; Goodrick & Reay, 2011; Thornton, 2004; Van Mierlo et al., 2018). The corporation logic is embedded in online platforms in two ways. First, platforms control and coordinate their online marketplaces to create network externalities that help to attract and retain gig workers and requesters, which ultimately will grow the market share of that online labor. Second, platform firms aim to become the largest online market place in their respective industry, creating a monopsony or monopoly situation that enables them to charge higher prices and increase revenue (Frenken et al., 2018).

To institute the corporation logic of market share and revenue growth, online labor platforms need to attract, retrain, and control gig workers as if they were employees subject to organizational routines, hierarchy, and control. As discussed by Meijerink and Keegan (2019), online labor platforms can utilize a range of HRM activities to attract, retain and control gig workers. For instance, platforms like Uber, Deliveroo, and Fiverr engage in HRM practices that are similar to those seen in recruitment: "employer" branding and the creation of "employee" value propositions to attract people to work with them (Kuhn & Maleki, 2017; Veen et al., 2020). Moreover, platforms implement HRM practices related to motivation through employing compensation schemes such as piece-based reward schemes to incentivize gig workers to work long hours (Chen et al., 2015; Lieman, 2018). Other HRM activities include surge pricing, paid worker referral schemes, and higher compensation for gig workers in new areas where the online platform starts up (Chen et al., 2015; Lee et al., 2015; Lieman, 2018). Online labor platforms also implement performance appraisals (e.g. five star ratings) that build a gig worker's online reputation that cannot be taken to another platform and therefore creates lock-in effects that serve to retain workers (Rosenblat et al., 2017; Wood et al., 2019). Furthermore, platforms may provide training – alongside appraisal practices – to ensure gig workers offer high-quality services so that they meet requesters' expectations and retain them on the platform (Rosenblat et al., 2017).

Institutional complexity of HRM for freelancers

The use of HRM activities for freelance gig workers, which simultaneous institutes the market and corporation logics, likely creates institutional complexity in the form of tensions that stakeholders draw on to challenge the legitimacy of online labor platforms (Frenken et al., 2018). That is, the use of HRM activities such as compensation, appraisal, and job design reinforces the corporation logic by serving to control self-employed gig workers. This goes against the use of HRM activities like providing autonomy which aligns well with the market logic's principles of self-employment and free, unregulated competition. Institutional complexity caused by HRM for freelance gig workers comes the fore when HRM activities such as offering autonomy reinforce the market logic while other HRM activities for committing, controlling and limiting worker discretion through compensation, incentives, appraisal and discipline simultaneously challenge the market logic and instead institute the corporation logic where workers are treated like employees and not self-employed agents (Aloisi, 2016; Daskalova, 2018; Rosenblat & Stark, 2016).

Online labor platforms represent a novel organizational type that reconfigures institutional logics (Frenken et al., 2018). This makes them highly salient to societal stakeholders and vulnerable to judgements that their actions are not legitimate due to combining contradictory logics. For instance, journalists and other social commentators have reported on the incompatibility of the market and corporation logics manifest in the platforms' usage of HRM activities. They argue that online labor platforms, by means of HRM activities that align with the corporation logic, exercise control over nominally self-employed gig workers and, therefore, should be classified as employers and cease instituting an inappropriate market logic of unregulated competition among gig workers (Frenken et al., 2018).

Strategies for responding to the institutional complexity of HRM for freelancers

To avoid being seen as illegitimate, online labor platforms need to respond to the institutional complexity associated with their use of HRM activities for self-employed gig workers. Research shows that although it creates challenges, institutional complexity can be addressed, and in some cases resolved, by organizations through various response strategies (Smets et al., 2015). Organizations may do this is by determining which logic can be most easily ignored (D'Aunno et al., 1991), which logic can best be adhered to in order to achieve the greatest reward (Greve & Man Zhang, 2017), or which can be undermined/delegitimized by a competing logic (Raaijmakers et al., 2015).

Online labor platforms may use such strategies to manage workers through HRM practices without employing them. At the same time, such response strategies may not necessarily resolve institutional complexity as they involve making 'either/or' choices through approaches like acquiescence (i.e. habitual adoption of one logic), avoidance (of an 'undesirable' logic), or defiance (i.e. delegitimizing a selected logic) (Greenwood et al., 2011; Lewis et al., 2019; Pache & Santos, 2010). Online labor platforms may not be willing to adopt response strategies that require choosing/favoring a single logic given the inherently complex nature of their business model that relies on combining contradictory market and corporation logics in HRM activities. To create revenue and profit, platforms cannot favor the market logic over the corporation logic, or vice versa.

According to Greenwood et al. (2011), institutional theorists have shed little light on response strategies to institutional complexity that involve marrying two competing logics. Moreover, a recent literature review by Lewis et al. (2019) reveals that little is known about the means through which HRM addresses the competing prescriptions of different institutional logics. This is particularly relevant for online labor platforms which traditionally are not viewed as having HRM responsibilities (Kuhn & Maleki, 2017; Meijerink & Keegan, 2019). The new intermediation-based business model online labor platforms does not comply with existing norms and regulations (Aloisi, 2016; Frenken et al., 2018; Kessler, 2015). At the same time, research has shown that institutional complexity may serve as a push toward new organizational developments (Lewis et al., 2019). By working through this complexity, organizations may find new operating models, work practices, or business strategies. In fact, the online marketplaces that online labor platforms create, and the powerful information technologies they develop, may provide new possibilities for addressing institutional complexity that have not been conceptualized or empirically uncovered by previous studies. To contribute to a better understanding of these issues, we empirically explore the institutional complexity associated with HRM for self-employed gig workers (Meijerink & Keegan, 2019), and the response strategies that online labor platforms adopt to cope with this institutional complexity.

Methodology

We conducted in-depth case studies of the Dutch operations of two major online labor platforms, Uber Eats and Deliveroo. We chose these platforms for the following reasons. First, Deliveroo and Uber Eats fit our definition of online labor platforms as they match freelance gig workers to requesters that wish to outsource meal delivery activities. Second, these platforms likely create institutional complexity by combining market and corporation logics. They align with a market logic by classifying the workers on the platform as self-employed, but also use HRM activities to coordinate the efforts of multiple parties including requestors, individual consumers and restaurants (Meijerink & Keegan, 2019; Veen et al., 2020). Finally, the 'independent/self-employed' status of the gig workers and the 'intermediary' role of Deliveroo and Uber Eats is highly contested by Dutch labor unions and the media as well as in several court cases. Our choice of cases allowed us to explore the institutional complexity these platforms face, and if and how they respond to this complexity.

Data collection

The empirical study was carried out between January 2018 and March 2019, and relied on 37 semi-structured interviews with various stakeholders, approximately 16 h of gathering ethnographic accounts of real-life gig worker activities and a court hearing, and document analysis (see Table 1 for an overview of the data collection techniques).

Data collected through interviews

To collect data from all the relevant actors involved, and for purposes of triangulation, the first author and three master-level students conducted interviews with the management of Deliveroo and Uber Eats, gig workers, requesters, and labor union representatives.

The interviews with the platform firms' management (11 interviewees in total including with managing directors, requester support managers, gig worker support managers, IT specialists, and gig worker engagement managers) served to gain insights into the HRM responsibilities of the online labor platforms, gig workers, and requesters, the functioning of

Table 1. Empirical research methods.

	Sample (N)	*Total duration*
Deliveroo		
Interviews with Deliveroo managers	8	7h 45 min
Interviews with gig workers	10	9h 00 min
Interviews with requesters	3	2h 30 min
Interviews with labor union representatives	3	4h 15 min
Ethnographic accounts (i.e. 'gigs' performed)	5	2h 45 min
Uber Eats		
Interviews with Uber Eats managers	3	4h 00 min
Interviews with gig workers	2	1h 15 min
Interviews with requesters	3	2h 30 min
Interviews with labor union representatives	5	5h 45 min
Ethnographic accounts (i.e. 'gigs' performed)	20	14h 30 min

the online applications that match labor supply and demand, and the promotion of institutional logics. Moreover, these interviews with the Deliveroo/Uber Eats management provided information on the HRM activities that gig workers are subject to, and the responses adopted to mitigate the institutional complexity associated with HRM activities for freelancers.

Since HRM practices may not be implemented as intended (Bos-Nehles & Meijerink, 2018; Nishii & Wright, 2008; Van Mierlo et al., 2018), we also interviewed 12 gig workers (i.e. meal deliverers) and 6 requesters (i.e. owner-managers of restaurants) to obtain information on their experiences with the use of HRM practices. To avoid depending fully on Uber Eats and Deliveroo to recruit interviewees, we contacted gig workers and requesters directly. Lacking a sampling frame for gig workers, we searched on social media for gig workers, approached gig workers we came across in the street, attended gatherings of gig workers, and engaged in snowball sampling. As a result of these efforts, 70% of the interviewees were sampled independently of the management of Uber Eats and Deliveroo. The gig workers we interviewed were students, freelancers looking for side-gigs, or those "in-between" jobs. These represent the types of gig workers reported to be active on online meal-delivery platforms (Kässi & Lehdonvirta, 2018; Katz & Krueger, 2019). The owner-managers of the restaurants were identified and contacted through the Web/mobile applications of the two platforms, and interviewed to reveal their involvement in the HR management of gig workers.

Finally, eight representatives of the three largest labor unions in the Netherlands were interviewed on the legal activities they undertook to influence the HRM activities of Deliveroo and Uber Eats. This was helpful in obtaining data on institutional complexity and which logics are propagated by societal stakeholders.

All the interviews were tape-recorded and transcribed. The transcripts were sent to the interviewees for verification to ensure the reliability of our data. In a number of cases, interviewees proposed corrections which resulted in minor changes to the transcripts to better reflect their interpretation of the issues.

Data collected through ethnographic accounts

Alongside these interviews, the first author also signed up as a gig worker and performed 5 'gigs' (i.e. meal deliveries) for Deliveroo and 20 gigs for Uber Eats. Besides providing an understanding of the functioning of the meal delivery process, these ethnographic accounts also served to gather data on the HRM practices of both platforms. This supplemented the information gathered from the interviews and enabled first-hand experience to fill in gaps resulting from interviewee recollections and reports. The ethnographic accounts involved signing up as a gig worker, taking part in the 'onboarding process', making use of the mobile application and performing meal deliveries. Screenshots of the mobile application were made to capture data on HRM practices such as recruitment and selection, incentives and workforce planning, job design, and performance appraisal.

The first author also attended a court hearing on the legal status of Deliveroo gig workers that took place during the period of empirical research. Besides providing data on Deliveroo's HRM practices and how this creates the institutional complexity, this also helped to recruit gig workers (those that attended the court hearing) for an interview. Field notes on HRM activities, institutional logics, and responses to institutional complexity were taken during the court hearing.

Data collected through document analysis

Finally, we analyzed documents which we found online or received from Deliveroo and Uber Eats. These documents – which included emails, text messages, webpages, newspaper articles, press releases, worker contracts with Deliveroo/Uber Eats, and rulings in the Deliveroo court cases – provided additional data on HRM activities such as recruitment and selection, workforce, job design, and training.

Ultimately, using multiple data sources helps substantiate the data and safeguards the trustworthiness of the findings (Sandberg, 2005). Furthermore, interviewing different actors allows for data triangulation, by enabling cross-checking of data among multiple stakeholders (Denzin, 1987), and the development of richer insights into issues that reflect the institutional complexity of HRM for freelance gig workers. Having conducted 37 interviews, performed 25 meal delivery 'gigs', read hundreds of pages of text, and attended a court hearing, data saturation was achieved.

Data analysis

Data analysis was conducted in three phases. First, a deductive approach was taken. We used directed content analysis to code the transcripts based on a set of preliminary descriptive codes derived from the literature on HRM activities, institutional logics/complexity, and responses by the online labor platforms for addressing institutional complexity (Hsieh & Shannon, 2005). During the second phase, we analyzed the data using additional inductively generated codes and sub-codes to identify themes. As an example, the HRM activity code 'recruitment and selection' was further sub-coded to cover the different recruitment and selection techniques used for gig workers. To strengthen the trustworthiness of our findings, we debriefed the management and workers of both platforms and carried out member checks by presenting and discussing the research results and gaining feedback on insiders' perceptions of the adequacy of our categories and terms used to describe the findings (Morse et al., 2002; Sandberg, 2005). During the final phase, we carried out a cross-case analysis by listing and comparing the Deliveroo and Uber Eats cases to identify core similarities and differences (Miles et al., 2018). These similarities and differences are presented in Table 2 and discussed below.

Results

Case descriptions: The context of institutional complexity for uber eats and deliveroo

Uber Eats and Deliveroo operate in the takeaway meal industry and match freelance 'gig' workers (i.e. meal deliverers), restaurants, and individual consumers. Both platforms are strongly rooted in the market logic of profit and shareholder value. For instance, Deliveroo has managed to attract approximately $1.5 billion from venture capitalists around the globe, hoping Deliveroo will enter a monopsony/monopoly position enabling it to secure high levels of future profitability. Despite making an $8.5 billion loss, Uber went for an initial public offering (IPO) on Wallstreet in 2019, raising $8.1 billion from institutional investors banking on Uber making profits in the near future. The embeddedness of Uber Eats and Deliveroo in the market logic is further evidenced by their creation of an online marketplace where self-employed gig workers, restaurants, and consumers transact freely. Deliveroo and Uber Eats neither 'own' these restaurants, nor employ the meal deliverers they work with.

Table 2. Summary of the empirical results and comparison between uber eats and deliveroo.

	Deliveroo	Uber Eats
Background and history	• Move from employment to freelance model • Stand-alone organization • Workers offering a service to Deliveroo	• Freelance model since Dutch operations started • Part of wider Uber Technologies Inc. • Workers receiving a service from Uber Eats
HRM practices for instituting the market logic	Autonomy • Workplace autonomy • Worktime autonomy • Job resource autonomy (e.g. gear, bike, phone) • Job demand autonomy (e.g. which activities, how to perform activity) Selection • Limited selection criteria	Autonomy • Workplace autonomy • Worktime autonomy • Job resource autonomy (e.g. gear, bike, phone); • Job demand autonomy (e.g. which activities, how to perform activity) Selection • Limited selection criteria
HRM practices for instituting the corporation logic	Recruitment and selection • Social media • Use of branded gear • Referral schemes • Screening of identification form (e.g. passport) Training and instructions • Job-related training prior to joining platform • Instructions from requesters *via* app • Training for personal development Workforce management and compensation • Fixed pay per order, determined by platform • Incentives: 'Do X, Get Y' bonuses • Algorithmic restriction of delivery area • Shift system Performance appraisal • Appraisal of workers • Appraisal of restaurants	Recruitment and selection • Social media • Use of branded gear • Referral schemes • Screening of identification form (e.g. passport) • Online test Training and instructions • Job-related training prior to joining platform • Instructions from requesters *via* app Workforce management and compensation • Variable pay per order, determined by platform • Incentives: hourly guarantees • Algorithmic restriction of delivery area Performance appraisal • Appraisal of workers • Appraisal of restaurants
Experienced institutional complexity	• Gig workers favor market logic • Deliveroo managers report need to balance logics • Legitimacy of Deliveroo challenged by labor union representatives • Multiple court cases challenging status of Deliveroo riders	• Gig workers favor market logic • Uber Eats' managers report need to balance logics
Response strategies to institutional complexity	• Rejection of corporation logic • Covert HRM implementation: tips and tricks, providing gear for free etc. • HRM devolution of appraisal and instructions to requesters • HRM outsourcing to third parties	• Rejection of corporation logic • Covert implementation: tips and tricks, providing rent-free gear, etc. • HRM devolution of appraisal, instructions, and compensation to requesters

Instead, restaurants and meal deliverers are seen to be independent actors (or, so called 'partners' to the platform) that freely engage in transactions with consumers. These transactions are enabled by Deliveroo's and Uber Eats' online platform that users access through a mobile (or web) application. The application presents a list of restaurants, and their menus, from which consumers can make choices. Once a meal is ordered through this so-called consumer app, the online platform algorithmically dispatches the order to the restaurant and to a potential meal deliverer who can accept or reject the order through the restaurant app or delivery app respectively. Once a transaction is completed, Uber Eats and Deliveroo collect the payment from the consumer, pay a portion of this to the restaurant and freelance meal deliverer, and keep the remainder as a service fee charged for each successful match made.

In the Netherlands, the main competitors of Uber Eats and Deliveroo are Takeaway.com (in Dutch: Thuisbezorgd.nl) and Foodora. The four meal delivery platforms are strongly rooted in the corporation logic and engage in competition for market share. The rivalry between these four meal delivery platforms was evident during the interviews with Deliveroo and Uber Eats representatives who were hesitant to disclose detailed information about the strategies used to grow the size of their respective online marketplaces:

> *Interviewer: "When starting a meal-delivery platform, how do you ensure that a sufficient number restaurants and meal deliverers join the platform and are available to serve consumers?" Interviewee: "I would say that is part of the Uber secret versus our competitors. So, everyone has a different strategy in terms of launching cities. I don't want to share this information." (…) Interviewer: "What is the balance between organic growth and targeted growth of Uber's online marketplace?" Interviewee: "I think we are getting into another portion of the secret sauce here." (Manager Uber Eats)*

> *"Obviously, the working of our algorithms for efficiently dispatching orders is a trade secret. This is a core competence of our company for outcompeting rivals." (Manager Deliveroo)*

In terms of instituting the corporation logic of market share growth, the creation of network externalities for outcompeting rival platforms turned out to become very salient as one of the rival platforms – Foodora – decided to cease its operations in the Netherlands in August 2018, due at least in to failure to create sufficient market share to ensure profitability.

Uber Eats and Deliveroo differ in terms of three organizational aspects that have implications for the institutional complexity experienced. First, whereas Uber Eats has worked with freelance deliverers since starting operations in the Netherlands, Deliveroo initially employed the people delivering meals. When it started its Dutch operations in 2015, Deliveroo offered its meal deliverers an employment contract, assigned them 'shifts', and paid them hourly wages. In the summer of 2017, Deliveroo started to gradually replace employee-deliverers with freelance deliverers who are paid per order and are free to decide if and when, for whom, and nominally how they will perform their work. This implies a shift by Deliveroo from the corporation logic (i.e. employment relationship) to the market logic (i.e. freelance status).

Second, Deliveroo is a stand-alone organization that operates in the food delivery industry, whereas Uber Eats is part of the wider Uber Technologies Inc. organization. Besides Uber Eats, Uber Technologies Inc. also operates Uber Rides that matchmakes between taxi drivers and passangers. While the legitimacy of Uber Eats is only discussed in a very limited way, and not subject to widespread public debate, the legitimacy of Uber Rides is frequently challenged. In fact, the Dutch operations of Uber Rides (i.e. UberPop) was initially seen as illegitimate and therefore temporarily banned.

Finally, the contracts that Deliveroo and Uber Eats have with the freelance deliverers differ. In instituting the market logic, Deliveroo established a freelance contract for its meal deliverers stating they are providers of services to Deliveroo:

> *"You are a supplier in business on your own account who wishes to arrange the provision of delivery services to Deliveroo. Parties merely wish to enter into an agreement on the basis of a supplier agreement (…) You are completely independent in carrying out the agreed work. You carry out the agreed work at your own discretion and without the supervision of Deliveroo." (Freelance contract of Deliveroo, version May 1st, 2018)*

Uber Eats has terms and conditions that gig workers need to accept before joining the platform. Rather than viewing gig workers as freelancers that offer services *to* the online labor platform, Uber Eats' terms and conditions portray gig workers as users that receive services *from* the online platform: Uber Eats frames itself as an actor in the market for intermediation services (aligning with the market logic) and treats meal deliverers as "independent" consumers of its "technology services", while rejecting the corporation logic by denying that it controls any of its meal deliverers:

> *"[Uber Eats] offers services in terms of generating leads to the providers of transportation services [i.e. gig workers]. (…) You wish to enter into this agreement to access and use Uber's services. (…) You confirm and agree that [Uber Eats] is a supplier of a technology service that does not provide [meal] delivery services. (…) [Uber Eats] is not supposed to direct, manage, or have control over you or your performance under this agreement. (…) You retain the sole right to determine when, where, and for how long you will use the Provider App and the Uber services." (Uber Eats' terms and conditions, version September 5th, 2016)*

HRM practices of online labor platforms for instituting the 'market logic'

The gig workers of Uber Eats and Deliveroo are subject to a range of HRM practices that are used to institute a market logic and imply that gig workers are freelancers who can engage in free, unregulated competition.

Selection

To ensure their online marketplaces are freely accessible to everyone who meets minimal standards set mainly by state laws, Uber Eats and Deliveroo apply a very limited set of selection criteria for allowing access to their platforms. According to the management of both platforms, meal deliverers can join the platform when they (1) are entitled to work in the Netherlands, (2) speak Dutch or English, and (3) are at least 18 years of age. Employees of Uber Eats and Deliveroo (e.g. operation associates) screen potential workers according to these criteria. Prospective meal deliverers go to a platform's office where they have to identify themselves using a valid form of identification. Through this light-touch selection process, the platforms reinforce a market logic where gig workers are more or less free to join (and leave) when they wish.

Job design and autonomy

Gig workers are autonomous in many respects. Deliverers on both platforms have the autonomy to decide when to login to the delivery app and be available to perform work. In addition, meal deliverers are free to decide in which location (i.e. city) they wish to work. They can select the working times and locations which are most lucrative to them in terms of making a profit, which fits the market logic of free and unregulated competition. Gig workers have the autonomy to decline orders that are assigned to them by the dispatching algorithm. Some meal deliverers told us that they use this autonomy in particular circumstances such as when they feel the restaurant and consumer are too remote. This aligns with the market logic, as travelling to a remote restaurant and consumer reduces the profit a gig worker can make as return commutes are not financially compensated.

Uber Eats and Deliveroo grant gig workers the autonomy to enact their job demands/responsibilities as they wish, and to use whatever job resources they prefer. Both platform firms try to avoid giving instructions on 'how' gig workers should perform their job. Meal deliverers receive no instructions from Deliveroo or Uber Eats on which type of transport to use (e.g. bike, scooter, car) or which route to take. The representatives of Deliveroo in effect reinforce the market logic by avoiding instructions which would imply that they have an employment relationship with their meal deliverers:

> *"Legally, this is a very grey area because, as a platform, we are not allowed to give instructions to freelancers, because they are independent, so they are allowed to decide for themselves how they interpret the assignments, so we cannot say you should do your job in such a way. So, in terms of instructions, nothing is allowed." (Manager Deliveroo)*

Online labor platforms' HRM practices for instituting the 'corporation logic'

Although the platforms reinforce the market logic as outlined in the previous section, Deliveroo and Uber Eats simultaneously reinforce the corporation logic of growth through control and coordination which are required due to the interdependence of meal deliverers, restaurants, and consumers. Deliveroo and Uber Eats face difficulties to balance supply and demand for labor to avoid dissatisfaction on the side of the meal deliverers (too little demand for their services and thus low incomes) and/or requesters (too little supply of workers causing meal deliveries to be delayed):

> *"One of the biggest challenges for us is the continuous quest for balance. There are either too many meal deliverers which is bad because then they earn too little, or we receive too many orders which cannot be processed quickly. The balance is never perfect." (Manager Deliveroo)*

Meal deliverers and restaurants are expected to offer high-quality services to attract and retain (new) platform users for growing the market share of the platform (i.e. a legitimate goal under the corporation logic). To realize this, Deliveroo and Uber institute the corporation logic of growth and control/coordination through HRM practices for gig workers as outlined below:

Recruitment and selection

Uber Eats and Deliveroo invest significantly in recruitment. They recruit through Facebook, Google, and Instagram to reach one of their main target populations (i.e. students). They also provide the current workforce with clothing and gear (such as thermal bags for transporting meals) that display their logos in an effort to create brand awareness among potential workers and consumers. Finally, both platforms implement referral schemes offering up to 200 euro per hire.

An online application process is used where workers receive instruction videos, sign a contract, upload a copy of their passport and bank account, and can order their delivery gear (e.g. a thermal food transportation bag). In line with the corporation logic of control, Uber Eats requires potential meal deliverers to complete a brief test during the selection process. Our ethnographic study revealed that this test could be failed and retaken indefinitely until 75% of the test questions are answered correctly. Rather than *rejecting* potential workers, this 'test' is meant to be instructive in nature and should ensure that meal deliverers "understand the app" and "know about the ratings that will be used". This way of 'selecting' reinforces the corporation logic in two ways. First, it ensures workers are 'trained' to meet customer needs and second, it ensures a steady and swift supply of workers, which is needed to grow the market share of the platform firm:

> *"The registration process is done online, and that should be arranged so that if you log in tomorrow, then basically you could work tomorrow." (Manager Uber Eats)*

Training and instructions

Besides some video instructions on safety issues and the working of the delivery app, meal deliverers receive very little training. In comparison, when Deliveroo employed its meal deliverers, it offered training (e.g. on-the-job training for new hires) This was soon abandoned when Deliveroo started working with freelance meal deliverers. Nevertheless, Deliveroo does offer training services consistent with the corporation logic of growth and worker commitment, including workshops on issues which are not directly work-related (such as cooking classes, presentations skills, and bike clinics):

> *"Most meal deliverers are young and want to develop themselves. We organize workshops on how to set up your own business or improve your presentation skills. Also, we offer bike clinics and cooking classes to create a community." (Manager Deliveroo)*

Workforce management and compensation

To ensure a steady supply of meal deliverers, both platforms implement highly dynamic compensation practices. In line with the corporation logic, compensation rates are fully determined by the platform firm, leaving meal deliverers with no autonomy to compete on the basis of price. In the case of Deliveroo, meal deliverers were paid a set amount per delivery (€5 at the time of writing), while Uber Eats pays a base rate per delivery to which a so-called distance fee is added (€3.70 and €0.80 per kilometer driven respectively). Platforms change their compensation scheme at times when demand outstrips supply (such as during evening meal times). Deliveroo increases its fee up to €7 per delivery to attract more deliverers and grow the platform. Uber Eats' approach to safeguard supply when demand peaks is to offer so-called 'hourly guarantees' which are "a set level of gross fares" that meal deliverers earn. This is aligned with a corporation logic, resembling an hourly wage that might be offered to employees. To induce longer working hours and thus control gig worker behavior, the platforms offer workers additional incentives (so-called 'Do X, Get Y' bonuses) if they deliver a minimum number of orders:

> *"We work with a bonus system. For instance, if a worker delivers five orders, they will receive a 10 euro bonus. We prefer this system above increasing the fee per order as we see that meal deliverers log out after 3 or 4 orders, because they feel they have earned enough. By offering a bonus after 10 deliveries are completed, we encourage them to reach these performance levels." (Manager Deliveroo).*

Besides balancing demand and supply through varying compensation, Deliveroo also requires its workers to work in agreed blocks (that each last an hour). To avoid an oversupply of workers during off-peak hours, Deliveroo restricts the number of workers who can receive orders through the delivery app. Workers will only receive orders when they sign up for shifts and are free not to sign up for shifts:

> *"At Deliveroo you book your shifts, you don't have to book any if you can't fit them in. You can even not work for three months and then just come back." (Meal deliverer Deliveroo)*

Each Monday at 3 pm, the booking system in the delivery app opens, such that shifts for the coming week can be booked. Depending on a worker's past performance, and as an incentive to those who deliver regularly and achieve high performance scores, some meal deliverers are entitled to sign up earlier for shifts. Deliveroo's need for a reliable supply of workers, especially during peak hours, is evident from the criteria used to define performance: (1) percentage of booked shifts a worker actually attended, (2) percentage of late cancellations (i.e. signing off from a booked shift less than 24 h before the shift starts), and (3) number of high-peak participation shifts performed (i.e. on Friday, Saturday and/or Sunday from 17:00 to 20:00). The shift system therefore aligns with corporation logic by controlling worker performance and access to the platform.

Finally, where demand for meals outstrips the supply of meal deliverers (often in periods of bad weather), representatives of Uber Eats and Deliveroo explained that they may algorithmically restrict the number of restaurants that consumers can choose. In effect, consumers can only order from nearby restaurants such that meal deliverers' travel times are curtailed and the number of meals they can deliver in increased:

> *"When very few meal deliverers are available, but many customers are ordering meals, the algorithm restricts the number of restaurants that consumers can choose from. On busy days I only receive orders from consumers who are close to me, while during off-peak periods the area I service is much bigger." (Restaurant owner)*

Performance appraisal

Besides performance criteria related to availability, meal deliverers are also evaluated by consumers and restaurants using an online "Thumbs Up/Down" rating scheme. Dissatisfied consumers and restaurants can indicate what performance dimensions require improvement. Deliveroo and Uber Eats reported to keep track of the rate of orders declined by workers to control restaurants, rather than workers:

> *"There are no consequences for workers who decline orders. They are free to do as they please. It is our responsibility to ensure they have no good reasons to decline orders. (…) We use data on order acceptance to evaluate how well the process functions. If riders decline orders coming from a certain restaurant, this might be an indication of how the restaurant is performing." (Manager Deliveroo).*

Aligned with the corporation logic, platform firms control the efforts of the restaurants, by allowing meal deliverers and consumers to evaluate meal quality using a "Thumbs Up/Down" rating scheme. Meal deliverers can flag problems related to restaurants which start preparing meals too late or those treating gig workers inappropriately. Consistently poor consumer or gig worker ratings have consequences. Restaurants are put lower down the list presented to consumers in the consumer app (with fewer orders and thus less income as a consequence). Another key performance indicator is the speed at which restaurants accept orders and prepare their meals. Again, aligned with the corporation logic, the listing of restaurants in the consumer app is used to incentivize/sanction restaurants:

> *"The speed at which restaurants prepare their meals has implications for how high they are placed in the ranking. (…) This is important for restaurants to know: you go down in the ranking if you do not perform well."(Manager Deliveroo)*

> *"We have to work as fast as possible. You climb in the rating if (…) you accept within 6 seconds. It's all about seconds. It is quite hysterical, because the faster and better you work, the higher you end up in the ranking. (Restaurant owner)*

Finally, the restaurant owners shared with us that multi-homing (working with multiple platforms) is discouraged by Deliveroo and Uber Eats through increased commission fees, which reinforces the corporation logic of growth and market protection.

Institutional complexity of HRM for freelancers

Although the HRM activities described early reinforce competing institutional logics for the freelance meal deliverers, the majority of the meal deliverers we interviewed seem to experience little institutional complexity, articulating few tensions between competing institutional logics. Their almost full alignment with the market logic of autonomy may explain this fact. Some meal deliverers switched from the rivalry platform Takeaway.com, that employs its meal deliverers (for reinforcing the corporation logic), to Uber Eats and/or Deliveroo because they align with the market logic:

> *"With Uber Eats and Deliveroo I can work whenever I want. (...) That option is better for me [than Takeaway] so that I can study and also manage my expenses." (Meal deliverer Deliveroo and Uber Eats)*

> *"The major reason for switching from Takeaway to Deliveroo is the flexibility. At Takeaway, I had to work at least two weeks a month. This was not very flexible for me. Also, Takeaway imposed many rules like which clothes I should wear, and I had to ride at least 25 km/hour on average. I like it that Deliveroo does not have these rules." (Meal deliverer Deliveroo)*

At the same time, some meal deliverers criticized the legitimacy of Deliveroo's business model by referring to the institutional complexity associated with HRM activities for freelancers. Specifically, they felt the control exercised by Deliveroo's shift system, and the performance criteria used to give priority access to shifts, contradicted the autonomy/flexibility propagated by Deliveroo. As such, the shift system creates tensions between the corporation (i.e. control over working hours by the platform) and market logic (i.e. autonomy of workers to determine working hours themselves):

> *"There are some snags to working with Deliveroo. They promise you can work whenever you want, because technically speaking, you are a freelancer. However, Deliveroo works with a shift system. I understand why they do this but this restricts the freedom I should have as a freelancer." (Meal deliverer Deliveroo)*

While workers did not really challenge the legitimacy of online labor platforms, others including labor unions, journalists, and politicians do pose questions regarding their legitimacy because of the tensions and institutional complexity associated with the use of HRM practices for freelance gig workers. Specifically, they criticize online platforms for creating false self-employment, for controlling freelancers through compensation rates set by the platform firms (i.e. corporation logic) and for controlling workers in ways that flout the autonomy and flexibility they claim to offer gig workers (i.e. market logic):

> *"In our view, the meal deliverers of Deliveroo are falsely self-employed. (…) They are freelancers, but they are not free to set their own prices." (Labor union representative).*

During interviews with the managements of Uber Eats and Deliveroo, tensions arising from aligning HRM practices with both market and corporation logics also became evident. Platform firms' attempts to institute the corporation logic in terms of growing their online marketplace and their market share through training gig workers, appraising their performance, and using dynamic compensation schemes, clash with other HRM activities that align with the market logic, such as worker autonomy to make decisions and engage in free, unregulated competition. Platform firm managers reported an ongoing quest to navigate tensions between HRM activities for managing gig workers in terms of the emphasis on controlling/committing freelancers (i.e. corporation logic) versus offering them autonomy (i.e. market logic):

> *"The government may fine us for false self-employment of freelancers. That is a shame. We want to offer them freedom and flexibility, but this limits the support and training we can offer to meal deliverers. That is a challenge. (…) It is difficult that we cannot provide the support we would like to offer. (Manager Deliveroo).*

> *"Look, these are freelance meal deliverers. We will not instruct them how to do their work. Back in the days, when we employed the meal deliverers, we did provide them with training and instructions. (…) We would like to do more for them – training and supporting the meal deliverers. We decided not to do this, as this is, legally speaking, very challenging. We want to avoid meal deliverers being reclassified as employees." (Manager Deliveroo).*

The level of institutional complexity at Uber Eats is less than at Deliveroo. One of the reasons for this is that Uber Rides (the associated taxi service) faces significant institutional pressures, and this seems to shelter Uber Eats from institutional complexity-based critiques. For instance, Uber Rides was heavily criticized in the Dutch media for how it treats its taxi drivers and how it failed to take responsibility after several Uber drivers were involved in traffic accidents in which cyclists were killed. Indeed, during the interviews, the labor union representatives repeatedly criticized Uber Rides, while remaining silent on Uber Eats at the expense of Deliveroo:

> *"It is painful to see how jobs are being replaced by freelance work. Taxi jobs are taken by Uber, meal delivery jobs by Deliveroo." (Labor union representative)*

Politicians, labor unions, and the media more frequently questioned the legitimacy of Deliveroo, because it creates institutional complexity by marrying the corporation and market logics, which is more readily observable because they changed from employing deliverers (corporation logic) toward working with freelancers (market logic). As noted by a labor union representative, this change was the catalyst for undertaking legal action against Deliveroo:

> *"Last year we undertook actions against Deliveroo, because Deliveroo indicated it wanted to replace their employees with freelancers. Together with another labor union, we are considering how to make sure these people can be decently employed and have a labor contract." (Labor union representative)*

> *"We took actions against Deliveroo to ensure that these workers are being employed again. We try the best we can, but cannot go against all platforms. If we want to initiate court cases, we have to initiate multiple cases. You cannot summon Deliveroo and Uber to court at the same time." (Labor union representative)*

The same switch by Deliveroo was reported and criticized in the Dutch media, something which was also felt by the representatives of Deliveroo who equated marrying the market logic with the corporation logic (and the tensions this creates) with walking a tightrope:

> *"During the crisis period, when we switched from employees to freelancers, both the employees and the media gave us the feeling that suddenly we no longer cared for our meal deliverers. That was not the intention: we want to care for them, but the law does not offer that many opportunities. (...) It is a very fine line." (Manager Deliveroo)*

> *"I try to support the meal deliverers. This is where public opinion is against us. We are always so negatively received, with people claiming that we try to control meal deliverers as if they are employees. No, we try to support them and offer a good service. Where Deliveroo is concerned, people always assume the worst." (Manager Deliveroo)*

The institutional complexity experienced by Deliveroo was also salient in two court cases taken against Deliveroo. In both cases, the plaintiffs (a meal deliverer formerly employed by Deliveroo and the labor union FNV) drew on the tensions between the corporation and market logics to build a court case that centered on reclassifying freelance gig workers as employees. Here, the saliency of institutional complexity came to the fore, as a key legal condition (under Dutch law) for the presence of an employment relationship is control over workers by a corporation (i.e. corporation logic). The complexity is further evidenced by the fact that one court case led to the conclusion that meal deliverers are indeed freelancers while, in the other case, meal deliverers were seen as having an employment relationship with Deliveroo. In the latter court case, the judge ruled that Deliveroo controls its meal deliverers and, therefore, they ought to have an employment relationship with Deliveroo. According to the judge, the organizational control over the freelancers is evidenced by Deliveroo's use of HRM activities, highlighting the institutional complexity associated with HRM for freelancers:

> *"[The use of the roster system by Deliveroo] offers Deliveroo the ability to adjust the availability of deliverers in the direction desired by Deliveroo. (...) Deliverers who perform well according to the Deliveroo standards are given "priority access" to reserve a time slot and are therefore more likely to be offered orders at desired times. [This] justifies the conclusion that (...) there is no complete freedom for a deliverer who wishes to generate a (sufficient) income. (...) In combination with the bonus system, a deliverer is therefore encouraged to work as much as possible and perform well (...) and this significantly limits the freedom to reject orders. (...) When working, there is undoubtedly a relationship of authority and control. (...). As a result of technological possibilities, there is a great deal of freedom when it comes to availability for work, but this still fits within the nature of the employment contract, even if work is done at times to be chosen by the employee. (...) The judges consider the dependence [of workers] on Deliveroo to be more weighty than the independence of the deliverers. (Court ruling)*

Response strategies to the institutional complexity of HRM for freelancers

Uber Eats and Deliveroo implement a range of response strategies to address the institutional complexity associated with HRM for freelancers. Both implemented defiance and avoidance strategies by rejecting the corporation logic in favor of the market logic. These response strategies could be best described as 'steering the discourse' where meal deliverers are portrayed as consumers, riders, or hobbyists that seek maximum flexibility and autonomy (i.e. market logic), while rejecting the argument that they wish to be full-time employees or workers (i.e. corporation logic), and 'framing' the platform as a neutral intermediary (rather than as an employer). In propagating the market logic over the corporation logic, Deliveroo holds that meal deliverers value the freedom and flexibility associated with the freelance status:

> *"Riders work less than 10 hours a week, making this type of work a hobby-like activity. The majority of the deliverers do this as a side job. Riders will leave the platform if they are not granted maximum flexibility. Moreover, if there are too few riders, Deliveroo will offer higher compensation. These are mere market forces/dynamics. The plaintiff (i.e. the freelance meal deliverer in the court case) does not represent the large number of riders that value the flexibility offered by Deliveroo. At the same time, the plaintiff makes maximum use of the flexibility possibilities: he reserved 403 sessions and cancelled 259 of them, of which 201 at the very last moment. Freelancers are allowed to do this. Under an employment contract, the plaintiff would have received two warnings and been fired." (Deliveroo's lawyer, summarized in notes taken during court hearing)*

During one of the court hearings, Deliveroo framed itself as an "optimizer of supply and demand in the food delivery market". Similarly, Uber Eats' representatives framed the organization as an intermediary that takes care of transferring payments from the restaurants to flexible, autonomous freelancers. Accordingly, meal deliverers are referred to as 'delivery partners' (or 'riders' in the case of Deliveroo) that work 'with' Uber Eats and 'for' the restaurants:

> *"The delivery partners are paid by the restaurant. On behalf of the restaurant, Uber Eats collects from the consumer the payment for the meal and its delivery. Uber then transfers this to the restaurant partner after deducting a marketplace fee that Uber Eats charges. Delivery partners receive the turnover they make minus a 10% marketplace fee." (Manager Uber Eats)*

Besides response strategies related to framing and discourse, platform firms also implement response strategies to institutional complexity associated with specific HRM activities.

Recruitment

The use of Uber Eats' and Deliveroo's gear (i.e. thermal bag and coat with the platform firms' logo) by meal deliverers is an important recruitment method for the platform firms to recruit new deliverers for reinforcing the corporation logic of growth. In line with the market logic, the freelance deliverers are free to decide not to use this gear:

> *"Since Deliveroo started working with freelancers, it was clearly communicated that deliverers do not have to use the thermal bag offered by Deliveroo. When I was employed by Deliveroo, they really made an issue out of the bag and coat: I was obliged to put on the Deliveroo coat, because – as I was told – consumers and potential workers should see you work for Deliveroo." (Meal deliverer Deliveroo)*

While Uber Eats and Deliveroo would like those delivering on their behalf to wear branded gear, they cannot force freelance meal deliverers to do so. This incompatibility of the corporation logic (i.e. growth through recruitment by means of branded gear) and market logic (i.e. autonomy of freelancers not to use branded gear) is remedied by each platform in a different way.

Deliveroo shadows its alignment with the corporation logic, and instead motivates meal deliverers to utilize its gear, by "selling" the gear at a 100% discount through a third party vendor:

> *Interviewee: "Deliverers are expected to buy the gear in an online web shop." Interviewer: "How much does the gear cost?" Interviewee: "Nothing, the bag and coat are for free." (Meal deliverer Deliveroo)*

> *"The gear is not offered for free but sold at a 100% discount. The gear and discount is not offered through our website, but sold via Shopify, which is an external web shop. For us, this is a workaround, because directly selling gear to our riders is not possible." (Manager Deliveroo)*

Uber Eats resolves the tension by renting out its gear to meal deliverers. Although they do not charge a fee to deliverers, they do ask for a

€50 deposit. Meal deliverers are expected to compensate for the 'free' gear by offering a marketing service to Uber Eats. This marketing service is formalized in a contract that helps the Uber Eats' platform grow as a result of delivery workers promoting their business by using branded gear (i.e. corporation logic) while the renting scheme means gig workers are not forced to buy gear and are nominally allowed to maintain their independence and autonomy (i.e. market logic):

> *"You agree to render advertising services for Uber by using these Devices [i.e. insulated delivery bag and/or clothing and wearing gear such as a rain jacket and other accessories] while providing on-demand food delivery services to end consumers via the UberEATS platform (the 'Advertising Services'). You hereby confirm and agree that use of the Devices is not intended to create any employer-employee relationship with Uber. (…) Uber hereby grants you a limited, non-exclusive and non-transferable license during the Term to use and publicly display the Uber Marks on Devices provided by Uber on a royalty-free basis" (Terms and Conditions of Advertising Services of Uber Eats, accessed on December 6th, 2019)*

Training

We came across four response strategies to institutional complexity associated with training and instructing freelance deliverers. First, both platforms 'steer the discourse' to avoid implying a corporation logic of control. On this point, platform representatives note that offering training and instructions is complicated due to the self-employed status of meal deliverers. Instead, they eschew the language of training and instead 'share' what they call 'best practices', 'tips-and-tricks', or 'information' on how to satisfy restaurant and consumer needs:

> *"We provide meal deliverers with tips-and-tricks on what restaurants value. We have to be cautious however not to offer instructions and use imperative language. That is not allowed, because we work with freelancers who are free to decide how they want to execute their work." (Manager Deliveroo)*

Second, Uber Eats and Deliveroo devolve the instruction of workers to the restaurants through a feature in the restaurant and delivery app. This reinforces the corporation logic of control without the platform firm having to dismiss the market logic (i.e. working with independent freelancers who cannot be instructed). For instance, while collecting ethnographic accounts as a meal deliverer, instructions were received through the delivery app from the restaurant to wait outside the restaurant and to pack the meal in a specified manner. Meal deliverers experienced the same:

> *Interviewer: "Does anyone instruct you on how to do your work? If yes, who?"*
> *Interviewee: "Yes, this is clearly explained in the app. You receive an instruction coming from the restaurant or consumer on what you have to do, where to wait, how to transport the food, whether you should ring the bell or not, etc. Both the*

restaurants and the consumers communicate a lot of demands via the app." (Meal deliverer Deliveroo)

Third, Deliveroo and Uber Eats train and give instructions during the on-boarding process of new meal deliverers, but crucially *before* entering into a contract with them. In this way, platform firms can instruct gig workers and thus control their behavior (i.e. adopt the corporation logic) before the platform is compelled to align with the market logic:

"The only possible way [for Deliveroo to instruct meal deliverers] is during the registration process, when we show safety and instruction videos. That is still allowed. But after that, we really cannot give instructions anymore" (Manager Deliveroo)

Finally, in line with the corporation logic of growth, Deliveroo organizes personal development workshops to commit meal deliverers to its platform. However, to uphold the independence and freelance status of these gig workers (i.e. market logic), these training workshops are outsourced to third parties:

"All activities related to learning and development are taken care of by an external party. We cannot organize these training activities ourselves." (Manager Deliveroo)

Compensation

Compensating gig workers is also associated with institutional complexity. While freelancers should be able to set their own pay rates, and ideally compete on the basis of these pay rates (i.e. market logic), the level of compensation offered is fully determined and controlled by Uber Eats and Deliveroo (i.e. corporation logic). To address this situation, Uber Eats institutes an escrow payment service where, officially, the restaurant is paying for the service provided by a meal deliverer, with Uber Eats being responsible for transferring the money from the restaurant to the meal deliverer. In this way, the pay rate for gig workers is controlled and determined by the platform firm (corporation logic), but the actual payment comes from the restaurants (market logic):

Interviewer: "What type of compensation and rewards does Uber Eats offer to meal deliverers?" Interviewee: "Just to be clear, the deliverer is paid by the restaurant. Our partners [i.e. meal deliverers] receive their revenue – after a deduction of the 25% service fee that Uber charges them for making use of our platform – through our app." (Manager Uber Eats)

Performance appraisal

In line with the corporation logic of growth, it is important that meal deliverers meet the expectations and needs of platform consumers and restaurants. Rather than controlling meal deliverers directly themselves, which would go against the market logic of free and unregulated competition, Uber Eats and Deliveroo devolve responsibility for performance appraisal to restaurants and consumers by means of rating schemes in the online app.

Discussion

In this paper, we draw on institutional theory (Greenwood et al., 2011; Lewis et al., 2019) to argue that HRM for freelancers inherently involves institutional complexity and explore the response strategies adopted by online labor platforms to address this complexity. By drawing on empirical evidence from two food-delivery platforms in the Netherlands, we show that gig workers are subjected to HRM practices, and that this creates tensions between the competing 'corporation' and 'market' logics. Moreover, we show that labor platforms rely on a range of response strategies to overcome the institutional complexity represented by these competing logics. Our results have important implications for both institutional theory and research on HRM in the gig economy as discussed below.

Implications for theory and practice

Our results on competing institutional logics in the context of online labor platforms build on previous knowledge of institutional complexity and provide new theoretical insights. First, while existing studies have shown that institutional logics impact on the use of HRM activities (Lewis et al., 2019), our study shows that the adoption of HRM activities also creates tensions between institutional logics. While HRM activities such as offering autonomy and selection reinforce a market logic, HRM activities such as recruitment, training, workforce management, compensation, and appraisal align with the opposing corporation logic. Our results support the assertion by Lewis et al. (2019) that institutional logics and HRM activities are reciprocally interrelated (see Figure 1 that summarizes our empirical results). While one institutional logic (e.g. corporation logic) motivates organizational decision-makers to adopt certain HRM activities, another and competing logic (the market logic) may delegitimize the use of these HRM activities, motivating organizational decision-makers to adopt HRM activities that create an alternative institutional logic. This has implications for our understanding of the HRM activities used by online labor platforms which traditionally are not viewed as having HRM responsibilities (Kuhn &

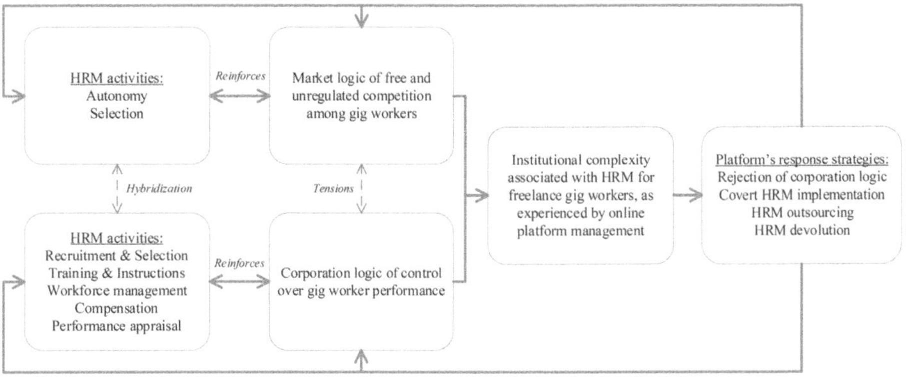

Figure 1. Interrelations among HRM activities for freelancers, competing logics, and response strategies to institutional complexity.

Maleki, 2017; Meijerink & Keegan, 2019). Given that the majority of online labor platforms deny an employment relationship, one may argue that HRM activities are absent, and therefore HR theory irrelevant, in a gig context. Our results challenge this viewpoint. While some HRM activities used by platforms imply the existence of an employment relationship (i.e. those that reinforce the corporation logic), others do not (i.e. those that reinforce the market logic). These findings do not align well with well-established HR concepts such as internal alignment, strategic fit, and HRM system strength, all of which stress that the success of HRM activities depends on how well they converge towards realizing and signaling one consistent goal (Bowen & Ostroff, 2004). On the contrary, our results imply that the success of HRM activities used by online labor platforms depends on what we call the 'hybridity' of HRM, i.e. how well HRM activities strike a balance between competing institutional logics. Striking this balance requires ongoing experimentation and multiple iterations, which may explain why HRM activities for freelancers frequently change depending on the institutional logic currently favored by an online labor platform (e.g. Deliveroo's changing approach to training practices before and after shifting to a freelance model). Our findings suggest that HRM activities used by online labor platforms are simultaneously the source of and (through the adoption of response strategies and alterations of HRM processes) solution to the institutional complexity associated with HRM for freelancers (see Figure 1). Our results suggest and hopefully motivate future research to adopt a longitudinal perspective for further exploring the dynamism (Van Mierlo et al., 2018) and recursive interrelations among HRM activities, competing institutional logics, and response strategies to institutional complexity in the gig economy (Lewis et al., 2019).

Second, although previous studies have conceptually explored the institutional complexity created by online labor platforms (Frenken et al., 2018), we empirically show which gig economy actors experience tensions between the market and corporation logics. Notwithstanding some exceptions, gig workers in our study appear to experience little institutional complexity and to favor the market logic. It is plausible that workers who favor the corporation logic view online labor platforms as illegitimate and do not to join them. In comparison, the management of online labor platforms experience institutional complexity associated with HRM for freelancers. This occurs because the platform's business model requires them to simultaneously institute the corporation logic (e.g. working with freelancers to cut labor costs) and corporation logic (e.g. controlling freelancers to ensure platform growth) (Aloisi, 2016; Meijerink & Keegan, 2019; Wood et al., 2019) even though these are in tension. While institutional HRM researchers have shown that the management of workers involves institutional complexity (Lewis et al., 2019), our results show that the management of requesters is equally associated with institutional complexity. In line with the market logic, independent businesses such as restaurants ought to have the autonomy to compete on the basis of service offerings. This is contradicted by HRM practices such as appraisal (e.g. sanctions by the platform for restaurants that perform poorly) and workforce management (e.g. algorithmic restriction of the number of consumers that restaurants can serve) that align with the corporation logic of control. These results not only imply that future research needs to differentiate between the use of HRM for gig workers and for requesters (Meijerink & Keegan, 2019), but also specify whether they study institutional complexity related to the management of gig workers or of requesters.

Third, building on existing research, we have shown how Deliveroo and Uber Eats seek to resolve institutional complexity through response strategies that others (D'Aunno et al., 1991; Greve & Man Zhang, 2017; Raaijmakers et al., 2015) have previously described, such as ignoring an institutional logic (e.g. not providing training and instructions to gig workers), adhering to the logic that achieves the greatest reward (e.g. framing gig workers as freelancers, or delegitimizing a competing logic (e.g. "meal deliverers value their freedom as a freelancer which could not be offered if hiring them as employees"). While existing studies "assume or imply that organizations enact single (...) responses" to institutional complexity (Greenwood et al., 2011: 351), our results show that online labor platforms implement these strategies in tandem. Online labor platforms implement a variety of HRM activities that each add to institutional complexity due to the incompatibilities between the market and corporation logics, and which require a portfolio of response strategies. This suggests that the number of strategies required may be linked to the number of incompatible institutional logics present as well as the degree to which they contradict each other. This is evidenced by our results showing that Deliveroo experienced greater levels of institutional complexity than Uber Eats, resulting in the adoption of a variety of response strategies by Deliveroo (see Table 2).

Fourth, our results show that the gig economy context requires new response strategies to address the institutional complexity resulting from online labor platforms being compelled to balance competing logics in order to control freelance gig workers (Kuhn & Maleki, 2017; Meijerink & Keegan, 2019; Wood et al., 2019). To achieve this, they implement novel HRM activities that are enabled by the technologies and online marketplaces they establish. These novel practices include the devolution of HRM activities to requesters (e.g. consumers engaging in performance appraisal and restaurants giving instructions *via* the app) and outsourcing of HRM to third parties (e.g. providers of e-learning modules). This is striking as previous research has shown that HRM activities are primarily outsourced or devolved to reduce costs and/or improve HRM service quality (Lepak et al., 2005; Maatman & Meijerink, 2017), and also that such services usually command financial recompense for those to whom such tasks are outsourced. Although such findings may also hold for online labor platforms, our results imply that, in the gig economy, HRM outsourcing also serves as a response strategy to address institutional complexity. Alongside outsourcing HRM, online platforms engage in another novel strategy to address institutional complexity. We call this strategy ‘covert HRM activity implementation’, that is, work practices which control freelancers but do not imply or create an employment relationship. These include offering tips-and-tricks for ‘training purposes’ or ‘selling’ gear at a 100% discount to simultaneously implement the market and corporation logics. Others have shown that institutional complexity is not necessarily undesirable as competing logics provide leeway for organizations to choose a desired logic (Lewis et al., 2019). Their business model makes it challenging for online labor platforms to adopt such ‘either/or’ response strategies to institutional complexity. This does not imply however, that institutional complexity is always undesirable and needs to be eliminated. Instead, our result suggest that tensions between competing logics also motivate the use of novel business practices that blended and balance competing logics, favoring one logic over others, such that institutional complexity can be a driver of and opportunity for organizational change and innovation.

Finally, online labor platforms may divert public attention away from one platform to another to shape its structural position in an institutional field (Greenwood et al., 2011). This occurs with Uber, where Uber Eats' operations are camouflaged by Uber Rides, which has gained significant attention from institutional players in the Netherlands. Deliveroo cannot adopt such a 'distraction' strategy as it operates a single platform, yet was in a 'central' field position as it gained attention as a consequence of switching from hiring employees (corporation logic) to freelancers (market/professional logic). This implies that a platform's field position not only shapes its strategic responses as found in previous studies (Greenwood et al., 2011; Pache & Santos, 2010), but also that strategic responses shape the manifestation of institutional complexity through shaping a platform's field position.

Limitations and directions for future research

As with any study, this one has its limitations. First, we examined a three-sided platform (consisting of gig workers, restaurants, and consumers). This inherently makes the coordination of these actors challenging, which increases the need for HRM activities that lead to additional institutional complexity. In other situations, where only gig workers and consumers interact (e.g. Uber Rides), there may well be less need for coordination, meaning that fewer or other HRM activities may be adopted. Future research on this issue is recommended to determine whether our results are generalizable to two-sided platforms.

Second, the results of this study may not be generalizable to other types of gig work. For instance, gig work can also take place virtually (e.g. Amazon Mechanical Turk), can be more creative/less structured (e.g. idea generation platforms), or require gig workers to collaborate (Duggan et al., 2020; Kuhn & Maleki, 2017; Meijerink & Keegan, 2019). Each of these types of gig work present different coordination challenges that need to be addressed with HRM activities and differ in terms of the core and extra role behaviors required for platforms to succeed and provide competitive differentiation. As such, we strongly encourage future studies to explore the role of HRM in online labor platforms that source other types of gig work than that studied here.

Third, the institutional lens adopted in this study may not help to explain all of the tensions that online labor platforms create. For example, researchers have argued that platform use of algorithms for HR purposes may restrain as well as improve workers' autonomy (Veen et al., 2020; Wood et al., 2019). Although anticipating the link between autonomy and the market logic, institutional theory says little about how so-called algorithmic management enables or limits gig worker's autonomy. Moreover, different legal jurisdictions may place more or less emphasis on autonomy as a legal condition for determining the existence of an employment relationships (i.e. corporation logic). Given differences in how (competing) institutional logics may be 'formalized' in (labor) laws, online labor platforms' experiences of tensions between institutional logics are likely to differ across countries. Therefore, to more fully understand the complexity associated with the use of HRM practices for freelance gig workers by online labor platforms, interdisciplinary research is needed that combines insights from e.g. institutional theory, HRM, labor law and information systems research.

Finally, it is quite possible that we did not obtain full details of the utilized HRM activities. For instance, competitive pressures meant that Deliveroo and Uber Eats withheld some information on the precise functioning of their algorithms and mobile applications. As a result, we were unable to uncover all details with regard to HRM activities such as workforce management and compensation. Future research on the details of algorithmic HR management for freelance gig workers is likely to be of immense practical and theoretical value in better understanding this nascent phenomenon.

Conclusions

Notwithstanding its limitations, we believe that our study has provided important insights into the use of HRM for freelancers in the gig economy and how online labor platforms address the institutional complexity that this creates through novel responses strategies. We showed that gig workers are subject to HRM activities that are needed to control their actions, which is seen as necessary to grow the platform. This aligns with the corporation logic that online platforms institute, but contradicts the market logic that online labor platforms simultaneously propagate through their reliance on freelancers that ought to be autonomous in their work and free to join (and leave) online market places that online labor platforms create. The institutional complexity that this creates can to an extent be alleviated by means of technology and the marketplaces that online labor platforms establish, and by having HRM practices implemented through third parties, including their own clients, and through covert HRM activities.

Acknowledgements

The authors thank Prof Anthony McDonnell, Prof John Burgess, Dr Ronan Carbery, Dr Ultan Sherman and the three anonymous reviewers for their valuable feedback.

Furthermore, the authors acknowledge with gratitude the help of Alina Gervald, Irene Hagens, Stefan Becking, Kimberley Morris, Vincent Schapers, and all of the people that took part in this study.

Disclosure statement

No potential conflict of interest was reported by the authors.

ORCID

Jeroen Meijerink http://orcid.org/0000-0002-0210-073X
Tanya Bondarouk http://orcid.org/0000-0002-8455-1859

References

Aloisi, A. (2016). Commoditized workers: Case study research on labor law issues arising from a set of on-demand/gig economy platforms. *Comparative Labor Law & Policy Journal, 37*(3), 653–690.

Battilana, J., & Dorado, S. (2010). Building sustainable hybrid organizations: The case of commercial microfinance organizations. *Academy of Management Journal, 53*(6), 1419–1440. https://doi.org/10.5465/amj.2010.57318391

Bos-Nehles, A. C., & Meijerink, J. G. (2018). HRM implementation by multiple HRM actors: A social exchange perspective. *International Journal of Human Resource Management, 22*, 3068–3092.

Bowen, D. E., & Ostroff, C. (2004). Understanding HRM–firm performance linkages: The role of the "strength" of the HRM system. *Academy of Management Review, 29*(2), 203–221.

Chen, L., Mislove, A., & Wilson, C. (2015). Peeking beneath the hood of uber. *Paper Presented at the Proceedings of the 2015 Internet Measurement Conference.*

Daskalova, V. (2018). Regulating the new self-employed in the uber economy: What role for EU competition law. *German Law Journal, 19*(3), 461–508. https://doi.org/10.1017/S207183220002277X

D'Aunno, T., Sutton, R. I., & Price, R. H. (1991). Isomorphism and external support in conflicting institutional environments: A study of drug abuse treatment units. *Academy of Management Journal, 34*(3), 636–661.

Denzin, N. K. (1987). *Sociological methods: A source book*. Routledge.

Duggan, J., Sherman, U., Carbery, R., & McDonnell, A. (2020). Algorithmic management & app-work in the gig economy: A research agenda for employment relations & HRM. *Human Resource Management Journal, 30*(1), 114–132. https://doi.org/10.1111/1748-8583.12258

Frenken, K., Vaskelainen, T., Fünfschilling, L., & Piscicelli, L. (2018). An institutional logics perspective on the gig economy.

Goodrick, E., & Reay, T. (2011). Constellations of institutional logics: Changes in the professional work of pharmacists. *Work and Occupations, 38*(3), 372–416. https://doi.org/10.1177/0730888411406824

Greenwood, R., Raynard, M., Kodeih, F., Micelotta, E. R., & Lounsbury, M. (2011). Institutional complexity and organizational responses. *Academy of Management Annals*, *5*(1), 317–371. https://doi.org/10.5465/19416520.2011.590299

Greve, H. R., & Man Zhang, C. (2017). Institutional logics and power sources: Merger and acquisition decisions. *Academy of Management Journal*, *60*(2), 671–694. https://doi.org/10.5465/amj.2015.0698

Hsieh, H.-F., & Shannon, S. E. (2005). Three approaches to qualitative content analysis. *Qualitative Health Research*, *15*(9), 1277–1288. https://doi.org/10.1177/1049732305276687

Kässi, O., & Lehdonvirta, V. (2018). Online labour index: Measuring the online gig economy for policy and research. *Technological Forecasting and Social Change*, *137*, 241–248. https://doi.org/10.1016/j.techfore.2018.07.056

Katz, L. F., & Krueger, A. B. (2019). The rise and nature of alternative work arrangements in the United States, 1995–2015. *ILR Review*, *72*(2), 382–416. https://doi.org/10.1177/0019793918820008

Kessler, S. (2015). The gig economy won't last because it's being sued to death. *Fast Company*, *17*, 2015.

Kuhn, K. M., & Maleki, A. (2017). Micro-entrepreneurs, dependent contractors, and instaserfs: Understanding online labor platform workforces. *Academy of Management Perspectives*, *31*(3), 183–200. https://doi.org/10.5465/amp.2015.0111

Lee, M. K., Kusbit, D., Metsky, E., & Dabbish, L. (2015). *Working with machines: The impact of algorithmic and data-driven management on human workers* [Paper presentation]. Paper Presented at the Proceedings of the 33rd Annual ACM Conference on Human Factors in Computing Systems, New York.

Lepak, D. P., Bartol, K. M., & Erhardt, N. L. (2005). A contingency framework for the delivery of HR practices. *Human Resource Management Review*, *15*(2), 139–159. https://doi.org/10.1016/j.hrmr.2005.06.001

Lewis, A. C., Cardy, R. L., & Huang, L. S. (2019). Institutional theory and HRM: A new look. *Human Resource Management Review*, *29*(3), 316–335. https://doi.org/10.1016/j.hrmr.2018.07.006

Lieman, R. (2018). *Uber Voor Alles*. Business Contact.

Lin, K.-Y., & Lu, H.-P. (2011). Why people use social networking sites: An empirical study integrating network externalities and motivation theory. *Computers in Human Behavior*, *27*(3), 1152–1161. https://doi.org/10.1016/j.chb.2010.12.009

Maatman, M., & Meijerink, J. (2017). Why sharing is synergy: The role of decentralized control mechanisms and centralized HR capabilities in creating HR shared service value. *Personnel Review*, *46*(7), 1297–1317. https://doi.org/10.1108/PR-09-2016-0245

Meijerink, J. G., & Keegan, A. (2019). Conceptualizing human resource management in the gig economy: Toward a platform ecosystem perspective. *Journal of Managerial Psychology*, *34*(4), 214–232. https://doi.org/10.1108/JMP-07-2018-0277

Miles, M. B., Huberman, A. M., & Saldana, J. (2018). *Qualitative data analysis: A methods sourcebooks*. SAGE Publications.

Morse, J. M., Barrett, M., Mayan, M., Olson, K., & Spiers, J. (2002). Verification strategies for establishing reliability and validity in qualitative research. *International Journal of Qualitative Methods*, *1*(2), 13–22. https://doi.org/10.1177/160940690200100202

Nishii, L. H., & Wright, P. M. (2008). Variability within organizations: Implications for strategic human resource management. In D. B. Smith (Ed.), *The people make the place: Dynamic linkages between individuals and organizations* (pp. 225–248). Lawrence Erlbaum Associates.

Pache, A.-C., & Santos, F. (2010). When worlds collide: The internal dynamics of organizational responses to conflicting institutional demands. *Academy of Management Review, 35*(3), 455–476.

Raaijmakers, A. G., Vermeulen, P. A., Meeus, M. T., & Zietsma, C. (2015). I need time! Exploring pathways to compliance under institutional complexity. *Academy of Management Journal, 58*(1), 85–110. https://doi.org/10.5465/amj.2011.0276

Rosenblat, A., Levy, K. E., Barocas, S., & Hwang, T. (2017). Discriminating tastes: Uber's customer ratings as vehicles for workplace discrimination. *Policy & Internet, 9*(3), 256–279. https://doi.org/10.1002/poi3.153

Rosenblat, A., & Stark, L. (2016). Algorithmic labor and information asymmetries: A case study of Uber's drivers. *International Journal of Communication, 10*(27), 3758–3784.

Sandberg, J. (2005). How do we justify knowledge produced within interpretive approaches? *Organizational Research Methods, 8*(1), 41–68. https://doi.org/10.1177/1094428104272000

Shapiro, A. (2018). Between autonomy and control: Strategies of arbitrage in the "on-demand" economy. *New Media & Society, 20*(8), 2954–2971. https://doi.org/10.1177/1461444817738236

Smets, M., Jarzabkowski, P., Burke, G. T., & Spee, P. (2015). Reinsurance trading in Lloyd's of London: Balancing conflicting-yet-complementary logics in practice. *Academy of Management Journal, 58*(3), 932–970. https://doi.org/10.5465/amj.2012.0638

Stanford, J. (2017). The resurgence of gig work: Historical and theoretical perspectives. *The Economic and Labour Relations Review, 28*(3), 382–401. https://doi.org/10.1177/1035304617724303

Tanriverdi, H., & Lee, C.-H. (2008). Within-industry diversification and firm performance in the presence of network externalities: Evidence from the software industry. *Academy of Management Journal, 51*(2), 381–397. https://doi.org/10.5465/amj.2008.31767300

Thornton, P. H. (2004). *Markets from culture: Institutional logics and organizational decisions in higher education publishing.* Stanford University Press.

Thornton, P. H., & Ocasio, W. (1999). Institutional logics and the historical contingency of power in organizations: Executive succession in the higher education publishing industry, 1958–1990. *American Journal of Sociology, 105*(3), 801–843. https://doi.org/10.1086/210361

Van Mierlo, J., Bondarouk, T., & Sanders, K. (2018). The dynamic nature of HRM implementation: A structuration perspective. *The International Journal of Human Resource Management, 29*(22), 3026–3045. https://doi.org/10.1080/09585192.2018.1443957

Veen, A., Barratt, T., & Goods, C. (2020). Platform-capital's 'app-etite'for control: A labour process analysis of food-delivery work in Australia. *Work, Employment and Society, 134*(3), 388–406.

Wood, A. J., Graham, M., Lehdonvirta, V., & Hjorth, I. (2019). Good gig, bad gig: Autonomy and algorithmic control in the global gig economy. *Work, Employment & Society : A Journal of the British Sociological Association, 33*(1), 56–75. https://doi.org/10.1177/0950017018785616

The effects of technological supervision on gig workers: organizational control and motivation of Uber, taxi, and limousine drivers

Peter Norlander, Nenad Jukic, Arup Varma and Svetlozar Nestorov

ABSTRACT

Does supervision from technological platforms alter gig workers' motivation and perceptions of control? We address this question with two field studies set in the passenger livery (pick up and drop off) industry. A between-subjects field survey ($n = 50$) finds that UberX drivers perceive significantly greater organizational control compared to taxi drivers, but do not report significantly different levels of intrinsic motivation, needs satisfaction, or enjoyment of work. In a follow-up within-subjects field experiment ($n = 79$), we identify the causal impact of technological supervision on drivers' perceptions of control and motivation. Black car limousine drivers who sometimes work on the UberBlack platform are randomly assigned to respond to questions about their perceptions while driving either for Uber or their limousine company. Limousine drivers in the Uber condition report greater market control and enjoyment of the work. We draw several conclusions: 1) large differences between gig workers and incumbent workers are selection effects, and 2) Uber's platform modestly increases perceptions of market control and task enjoyment with 3) no impact on motivation or needs satisfaction. This article contributes to the literature on the classification of gig workers, the gamification of work, and studies of technology, management, and organizations. We call for greater theoretical attention to how workers experience technological supervision and discuss how platforms change the future of employment relationships and human resource management.

Introduction

The growth of software platforms that manage remote "gig workers" through apps challenges existing understandings of employment

---

Supplemental data for this article is available online at https://doi.org/10.1080/09585192.2020.1867614.

relationships and human resource management (Duggan et al., 2020). While gig workers often see themselves as acting autonomously (Möhlmann & Zalmanson, 2017), platform technologies closely monitor, reward, and punish workers' behaviors, which workers can experience as controlling (Marquis et al., 2018). The control and power that apps exert over workers raise a central concern of employment relations: that gig workers are misclassified as independent contractors, and should be treated as employees (Collier et al., 2017; Harris, 2017). Technological supervision also undermines existing assumptions of Human Resource Management (HRM) about the centrality of human supervisors and HR departments: while apps can perhaps be designed to support workers' well-being and intrinsic motivations, apps may replace traditional supervision and HRM in many types of employment relationship (Jabagi et al., 2019).

While gig work is part of a broader move away from traditionally secure full-time jobs (Cappelli & Keller, 2013), gig workers may experience a higher degree of employer control than traditional independent contractors (Collier et al., 2017). In response to the contested classification of gig workers as independent contractors (Kalleberg, 2009; Kirven, 2018; Weil, 2014), California's Assembly Bill 5 (AB5) in 2019 deemed many gig workers employees based on the degree of employer control. Gig companies Lyft, Uber, DoorDash, Instacart and Postmates continue to contest the claim that their platforms exert control over workers, and on the website of their campaign to overturn AB5 (http://yeson22.com/), these companies argue that workers have "complete flexibility over when, where, and how they work."

Control also raises questions about motivation: in the job characteristics model, increased control and supervision of work product decreases intrinsic motivation and work satisfaction (Richard &

Oldham, 1976). However, the emerging literature on algorithmic control suggests that platforms can enhance worker motivation and enjoyment. Because the supervision of gig workers is conducted through software, algorithmic management is often limited to providing incentives and incorporating elements of "gamification" that keep workers returning to the platform through motivational techniques (Deterding, 2015; Mollick & Rothbard, 2014; Mollick & Werbach, 2015). It is possible that gig work on platforms can be designed to intrinsically motivate workers (Jabagi et al., 2019).

Scholars have called for further investigation of the effects of these technologies. In particular, there is a call for more empirical evidence on the surveillance of workers on technological platforms (Zuboff, 2015), the mechanisms through which gig companies motivate and control workers (Kuhn & Maleki, 2017), and "how platforms seek to extract and control labor effort in the production processes or workers' experiences of this work" (Veen et al., 2019; p. 2). Duggan et al. (2020) call for empirical research on power and control in these atypical employment relationships in the gig economy. We contribute to this growing literature by empirically assessing motivation and control while holding task constant.

In the passenger livery (pick-up and drop-off) industry, licensed taxi and limousine drivers perform the same tasks as gig workers for app-based Transportation Network Provider (TNP) companies such as Uber and Lyft. While on the job, gig workers for TNPs are supervised by software algorithms, and have few human interactions with the city or the platform company. TNP drivers exemplify working under conditions of algorithmic management and a potentially transformed employment relationship system. For the incumbent owner-operator and independent contractor licensed drivers, this new competition has degraded wages and working conditions while supervision and regulation continues to be based on traditional face-to-face management and relationships.

We contrast motivation and control under the newer system of platform management and a traditional, human-centered management system. While theories offer different predictions regarding platform effects, and many have speculated on how platforms affect gig workers, the effects on worker motivation and experiences of control remain an empirical question. We research two questions: first, do platforms extend greater perceived control than traditional management systems? Second, do platforms increase workers' intrinsic motivation, satisfaction of needs, and enjoyment of the work?

We present the results of two studies with drivers in the livery industry in Chicago. We find that UberX drivers report greater control compared to taxi drivers in a between-subjects field survey, and insignificant differences in needs satisfaction, intrinsic motivation, and enjoyment of work. In a follow-up study, we report causal effects of platform management in a field experiment with full-time, licensed, chauffeur limousine (black car) drivers who find rides concurrently on a platform, UberBlack, an Uber service used to pick up additional passenger rides, and through a limousine company. Limousine drivers answer questions about their work motivation and perceptions of control while blinded to experimental manipulation of whether the survey is about their experience driving for UberBlack or their limousine company. We find that limousine drivers report greater market (output-based) control, and greater enjoyment of the work while driving for UberBlack compared to limousine companies, even when the limousine drivers own their own company.

We draw several conclusions that contribute to this growing literature: 1) large observable differences between gig workers and incumbent workers are selection effects, 2) although effect sizes are modest, platforms do increase worker perceptions of control and enhance enjoyment of the work, and 3) additional controls used by platforms do not decrease motivation. We discuss the implications for theory, employment relationships, and HRM.

Theorizing motivation and control in the gig context

For many gig workers, the allure of "being your own boss" and opportunities to connect with others are reasons to enjoy work on platforms like Uber, and yet the apps do indirectly control how drivers do their jobs (Rosenblat & Hwang, 2016). While on-demand companies promote their autonomy-enhancing potential to workers, they use "soft" forms of technological control that limit choices (Shapiro, 2018). The potential for data-driven and algorithmic management to transform work goes far beyond gig economy workers and may perpetuate historical systems of coercive micro-management and output-based rewards (Mayer-Schönberger & Cukier, 2013; McGaughey, 2018). Platforms could lead to alienation and "digital Taylorism," increasing the power of employers (Leighton, 2016), and extending control over workers' time (Lehdonvirta, 2018).

Research on alternative work arrangements and organizational behavior (OB) can assist in understanding motivation and control in this context (Spreitzer et al., 2017). Organizational control is a counterpart to individual motivation: whereas control relates to organizational attempts to direct workers, motivation refers to how workers act through their own agency (Deci et al., 1999). In prior literature, control and intrinsic motivation are often positioned as opposites: a worker with intrinsic motivation does not require control, and a controlled worker is less intrinsically motivated, and potentially alienated, from the work. While several papers examine and contrast control and autonomy in the gig work context (see, e.g. Möhlmann & Zalmanson, 2017; Shapiro, 2018; Wood et al., 2019), we contribute to this emerging literature by using measures arising from the OB literature, and empirically assessing differences in the field using survey and experimental methods, and a comparison group. In the following sections, we present OB theories of motivation and control that we use in our studies.

Intrinsic motivation

Self-determination theory proposes humans have intrinsic needs for autonomy, competence, and relatedness (Gagné & Deci, 2005). Gig work may enhance these intrinsic motivators by providing workers new freedom (autonomy), opportunities to gain work experience and be productive (competence), as well as opportunities to meet others (relatedness). Job characteristics of gig work can fulfill these needs, leading to increased intrinsic motivation (Jabagi et al., 2019). Gig work on platforms also exemplifies gamification by introducing design elements into work to relieve boredom and increase satisfaction (Mollick & Werbach, 2015). The success of gamification may rely on the design of immediate contextual feedback and rewards, which, as we develop below, can be rendered through control mechanisms such as norms, bureaucratic rules or market-like incentives.

Organizational controls

Control is "any process whereby managers direct attention, motivate, and encourage organizational members to act in ways desirable to achieving the organization's objectives" (Cardinal et al., 2010, p. 56). In organizational control theory, there are three fundamental systems: market, bureaucracy, and clan (Sitkin et al., 2010). Market control systems are focused on outputs, such as profit, productivity, and customer satisfaction. Bureaucratic control systems emphasize specifying, monitoring, and enforcing rules, emphasizing behavioral "process rules" and "behavioral norms." Clan control systems consider how human resource and material elements are "qualified, chosen, and prepared" (ibid, p. 59).

As introduced earlier, the degree of control over workers is central to the debate over the gig worker employment relationship. While the legal standard for determining the degree of employer control does not rely on worker perceptions, and is meant to be a clear and objective test, organizational control theory includes concepts that are similar to behavioral control items on the legal test, reflects workers' experience of control, and is widely used in the OB and HRM literatures.

Contrasting controls between taxis, limos, and Uber

Economists, regulators, technology and legal scholars have disagreed about the extent and variety of controls used in the livery industry. Economists have described Uber and Lyft as providing arms-length, hire-on-demand, market-matching software that enables gig workers to freely find "gigs" picking up and dropping off passengers (Azevedo & Weyl, 2016). Many technology and legal scholars contest this narrative, emphasizing that platforms like Uber have a supervisory role involving control over workers, and have great power given the information asymmetries involved (Rosenblat & Stark, 2016). The following description of the systems of control in the context of livery service connects theories of organizational control with the facts on the ground. While the debate is active and these arguments are motivated by the literature, we note that differences in control under different systems are an empirical question that our studies are designed to examine.

Bureaucratic control

Bureaucratic control systems emphasize specifying, monitoring, and enforcing rules. Bureaucracy fits well with "algorithmic management," in which rules encoded in software assign work, evaluate performance, and provide informational support (Lee et al., 2015). In contrast, some economists have argued that taxi drivers face a high level of bureaucratic control, while TNP drivers are relatively unencumbered. As an economics textbook notes:

> *If Adam Smith were alive today, he surely would have the Uber app on his phone... You have probably never lived in a centrally planned economy, but if you have ever tried to hail a cab in a major city, you have likely experienced a highly regulated market.* (Mankiw, 2016, p. 11).

City regulations restrict the supply of licensed taxis, set fares, and regulate grievance procedures. However, taxi drivers while on the road are relatively unencumbered by bureaucratic supervision. As discussed below in the section on market control, taxi drivers' on-the-job control system is more akin to a market control system. TNP platforms centralize information and control globally, a contrast with formerly localized markets (Beniger, 1989). TNP drivers, for example, must not decline too many rides while on the platform, are given a route to follow, and operate under automated processes for directing task outputs. The app acts as a performance management system, determining performance metrics based upon worker behaviors (Rosenblat, 2018).

Market control

Market systems are focused on outcomes such as profit. Taxi drivers have long been subject to market controls while on the job. Taxi drivers are independent contractors who are incentivized to maximize their income during their lease in a fashion that is the "economist's first-best solution" to the principal-agent problem (Farber, 2015). Taxi companies earn money only by leasing licensed vehicles to taxi drivers, typically for 12 h at a time. As Farber (2015, p. 1983) writes: "the driver internalizes the costs and benefits of working." While there are many rules related to becoming a taxi driver, once taxi drivers are on the road, there is little supervision or feedback except fares and tips.

In contrast, the way that TNP drivers are paid is opaque. For example, in October 2019, Lyft removed information from the platform that it had once provided drivers regarding how much money customers paid for each ride (Gordon, 2019). In many ways, remuneration for TNP drivers depends upon following behavioral rules, and thus control is more bureaucratic and less market-based than in the case of taxi drivers. In an experiment conducted by Uber, economists found that switching full-time drivers from Uber's remuneration system to a leasing system (like taxis) would increase driver earnings (Angrist et al., 2017).

Clan control

Kameswaran et al. (2018) find that drivers gain cultural and social capital through their interactions with passengers. Technology in the context of gig work can foster mutually beneficial exchanges of information between drivers and passengers, provide emotional support and companionship, and lead to instrumental helping behaviors as well. Such bonds occasionally become strong, as when drivers build independent relationships and friendships with customers outside of the app. While each ride may be transactional, an emphasis on getting along with customers acts as a form of clan control, potentially pushing out drivers who do not excel at customer service.

Hypotheses

Organizational control of taxi and limousine drivers operates through the market controls as described above, bureaucratic rules set by taxi companies and city regulations, and clan pressures to meet the expectations of a professional licensed chauffeur. In contrast, drivers for TNPs face a number of additional controls. Drivers accept the following as determined by the platform they work on: the fare, the terms and conditions (including mandatory arbitration), and a performance rating (Rosenblat, 2018). Gig drivers' location, speed, and each customer interaction, including declined rides, are monitored by the TNP, and are used in compensation decisions to reward and punish behaviors. Further, platforms hold arbitrary power to alter the terms and conditions at any time (e.g. Gordon, 2019). TNP companies have far more power than regulated taxi companies to set fares, pay drivers, and regulate disputes, and TNP drivers appear to confront greater monitoring and organizational control than taxi drivers under the traditional system.

Technological platforms enable gig companies to experiment with different managerial techniques to motivate driver performance and effort, and monitor and reward output (Scheiber, 2017). TNPs have experimented with more controlling, and more bureaucratic, HR practices. TNP firms set rules related to declined rides and handling low customer satisfaction ratings algorithmically (Rosenblat, 2018), which should increase bureaucratic control. Providing steady feedback on output metrics to drivers should increase market control. Tracking customer satisfaction on every ride should increase perceptions of clan control. Based on the above discussion, our first hypothesis is:

> *Hypothesis 1*: Supervision on technological platforms increases perceptions of control (bureaucratic, market, and clan) compared to traditional management systems.

We do not see a paradox of heightened control and motivation under platform management; rather, there are several ways platforms could increase both control and drivers' motivation, enjoyment, and satisfaction of needs. The absence of control for taxi and limousine drivers under a leasing structure increases risk and uncertainty for licensed drivers, while TNPs can provide income security protections and offer HR services through output-based market control systems. While marketing to drivers, Uber and Lyft frequently promote income guarantees (e.g. a guaranteed minimum $2100 over 4 weeks for 50 rides per week) and "boosts" for working needed shifts, hours, and providing dedicated levels of service (Calo & Rosenblat, 2017). Maximum flexibility for workers such as taxi drivers can lead to a "tyranny of the clock." Taxi drivers work long hours and search for fares in a process that cannot match the efficiency of ride-hailing apps (Cramer & Krueger, 2016). Formal workplace institutions such as shifts implemented by TNPs can free workers from idle procrastination and waiting (Lehdonvirta, 2018). HR policies and greater control can enhance scheduling autonomy, as bureaucratic rules regulate work flow to create scheduling flexibility (Briscoe, 2007). Such arrangements buffer both the driver and the firm from market whims: they provide adequate labor supply and reduce driver's risks of a negative income shock. By reducing idle time and introducing shift guarantees, platforms may make working as a driver more enjoyable and boost intrinsic motivations.

Before corporate HR bureaucracies existed to standardize management systems, supervision often left workers at the whim of arbitrary bosses (Jacoby, 1985). TNP companies' rationalization of the livery industry extends to HR practices: TNPs offer drivers training, and in some cases require it (see Edelman & Geradin, 2015). TNPs have added benefits, and provide concierge services at in-person company offices in Chicago, tax consulting, education benefits, and access to health insurance once drivers surpass a given level of rides per month (Uber, 2020). Prior studies of the taxi industry found that improved HR practices and benefits enhanced driver motivation and loyalty, reduced turnover, and ultimately, enhanced organizational performance (Sherer et al., 1998).

In addition to the above mechanisms, technological platforms may enhance intrinsic motivation through enabling and institutionalizing feedback. Adler and Borys (1996) propose that the effects of monitoring and control on workers' intrinsic motivation depends upon whether workers perceive control efforts as enabling or coercive. Digital supervision in the gig economy could be consistent with enhanced intrinsic motivation if it helps individuals meet needs, or increases enjoyment through "auto-gamification," when workers turn quantified metrics into a personal game (Ranganathan & Benson, 2020). Motivation on platforms may be higher if controls are institutionalized and normatively accepted, and become built into taken-for-granted routines, (Zucker, 1987). Finally, the combination of "effectance-promoting feedback, and freedom from demeaning evaluations" typical of platform-based management enhances intrinsic motivation (Deci & Ryan, 2000). Thus, we hypothesize that:

> *Hypothesis 2*: Supervision on technological platforms increases workers' intrinsic motivation, enjoyment of the work, and satisfaction of intrinsic needs (autonomy, competence, and relatedness) compared to traditional management systems.

Research context

Uber entered Chicago in 2011 with a focus on "Black Cars" and used existing licensed limousine drivers with a licensed vehicle under its UberBlack brand. UberX's entry in April 2013 represented a significant change in Uber's strategy and expansion into gig work. With UberX, any person could become an Uber driver with their own private vehicle, initially with no supervision from the city. This service was illegal under existing law but was tolerated as the city began discussions to regulate the TNPs.

City regulations initiated in 2014 required TNP companies to pay $25,000 to register with the city, and $25 for a license for each driver and car. Rasier LLC (UberX) was issued a license on February 17, 2015. While taxi drivers must clear a state-run background check that includes all past arrests, TNP companies run a criminal background check against a commercial conviction database. TNP companies apply for chauffeur licenses on behalf of their drivers, who supply vehicle and license information to the TNP companies, which then forward this information to

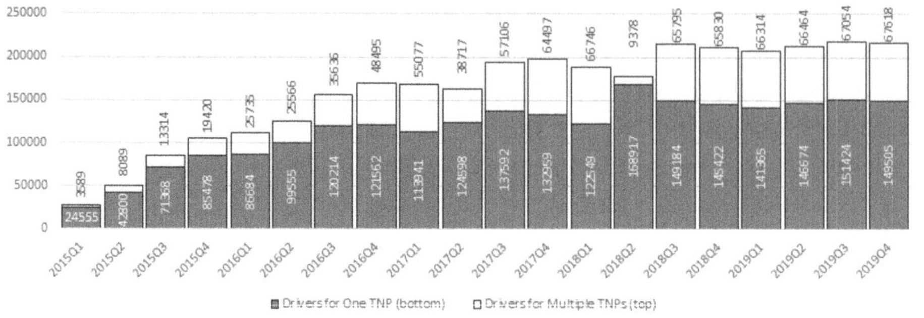

Source: (Chicago Data Portal, 2020)

Figure 1. Number of licensed TNP chauffeurs in Chicago active (quarterly). Source: (Chicago Data Portal, 2020).

the city (see Eidelson, 2019). Taxi drivers must take a city-required training course and pass an exam, pay associated costs, submit to a physical exam, and pass a drug test.

Figure 1 shows quarterly totals of the number of drivers with a city TNP chauffeur license who drove at least one passenger each month since registration data began being collected in March 2015, and details how many drivers work for multiple TNP companies as opposed to a single company. In March 2015, 16,025 TNP drivers completed at least 1 ride, compared to 72,797 in December 2019. Indicating the growing importance of full-time TNP drivers who work on multiple apps, the number of drivers working on multiple platforms increased from approximately 20% of drivers to over 30% of drivers between 2015 and 2019. City data shows that those licensed to drive for multiple TNPs averaged 154 rides per month in December 2019, compared to 113 for those who worked on only one platform (Chicago Data Portal, 2020). In December 2019, TNP drivers made just under 9 million passenger trips, 37% of which were completed by drivers on multiple platforms.

Research methods

We adopted a "full-cycle" methodological approach, moving between observation, interviews, surveys, and manipulated experiments. Interviews impressed upon us the importance of institutional and historical context for this research. The online Appendix more fully describes the context of the Chicago livery industry, and presents details of the qualitative and inductive analysis leading to our study design. We believe our detailed discussion of the methodology might be useful for future scholars studying this or related subjects.

We obtained IRB approval for all portions of our study: to conduct a field survey of taxi drivers and Uber drivers with student research assistants (RAs), to conduct a field experiment, and to conduct structured and unstructured interviews with drivers. Research began in the Fall of 2015 with open-ended questions for taxi, Lyft, and UberX drivers. Structured qualitative interviews of taxi, limousine, and TNP drivers were conducted from Fall 2016-2017. We provide additional details on participants, procedures, measures, and analyses below the description of each study.

Study 1: UberX vs. taxi

A between-subjects study of taxi drivers and UberX drivers was conducted in May 2016. This study draws from the OB literature to examine differences in perceptions of control and intrinsic motivations between incumbent taxi drivers and UberX drivers. Taxi drivers and UberX drivers perform the same task and were asked the same items from a questionnaire.

Participants

We recruited 14 graduate and undergraduate RAs who regularly traveled by hired vehicle to interview a total of 60 taxi and UberX drivers using a structured questionnaire. All RAs were volunteers from a pool of student RAs and engaged voluntarily in the research. While risks were involved, no adverse incidents occurred. RAs received training on study procedures and IRB protocols, and were debriefed after their participation. Driver response rates were high. Only one driver declined to participate in the survey. However, nine surveys were not completed before the ride ended. In debriefing our RAs, we learned that in these cases, the taxi or Uber ride was shorter than they had planned for, or the driver spoke slowly, was chatty, or had difficulty understanding the questions. Surveys not completed prior to the conclusion of the ride were discarded. In total, 50 surveys were completed, of which 26 were interviews of taxi drivers and 24 were interviews of UberX drivers.

Procedures

The RAs hired a passenger vehicle, read drivers an oral informed consent script, and obtained driver consent before reading drivers survey questions from an online Qualtrics survey accessed through their mobile phones. Driver names were not collected. At the conclusion of the ride, RAs left a physical flyer containing study and consent information and the first author's contact information. The survey took approximately 15 minutes to complete. RAs saved receipts and were reimbursed for the

Table 1. Variable descriptions.

Variable	Description
Bureaucratic Control—1	Company monitors rule following
Bureaucratic Control—2	Success at company is determined by rule following
Bureaucratic Control—3	Company emphasizes need to follow rules
Clan Control—1	Company monitors how well workers *get along* with customers
Clan Control—2	Company emphasizes need to *get along* with customers
Clan Control—3	Success at Company is determined by *get along* with customers
Market Control—1	Co. monitors individual performance
Market Control—2	Whether I succeed or not at Co. is largely determined by my level of individual performance.
Market Control—3	As a driver for Co., I spend most of my time working to achieve my individual performance goals and targets
Autonomy—1	While driving for Co., I feel like I can be myself.
Autonomy—2*	I often feel like I have to follow the Co.'s instructions.
Autonomy—3*	If I could choose, I would do things differently with regard to how the Co. works
Competence—1	I have really mastered the tasks required to be a driver for Co.
Competence—2	I am good at the things I do when I drive for Co.
Relatedness—1 *	I don't really feel connected with other people while driving for Co.
Relatedness—2	When I drive for Co. I can talk with people about things that really matter to me
Relatedness—3	I feel like some passengers are friends
Intrinsic—1	For the satisfaction I experience when driving
Intrinsic—2	Because I derive pleasure from driving
Enjoyable—1	Driving is enjoyable
Enjoyable—2	I like doing the things I do as a driver
Rating	What is your Uber rating?

Except for rating, each item was formulated as a statement. Participants were asked the extent to which they agreed with the statement on a 1–7 strongly disagree-strongly agree Likert scale. In studies 1 and 2, the only difference in the questionnaire was to vary the company ("Co." in the above) in each item directing the participant to respond for a taxi company, Uber, or a limousine company.
*Item is reverse-scored.

fare and compensated for their time; taxi drivers and UberX drivers were given a $5 gift card for voluntary participation. Each RA was initially assigned to hire either an UberX ride or a taxi, and to alternate ride source thereafter. We debriefed RAs at the conclusion of their participation with a standard questionnaire, as described more fully in the Appendix.

Measures

The survey instrument adapted items from Long et al. (2011) related to perceived organizational control, needs satisfaction at work items from Kasser et al. (1992), and motivation items from Tremblay et al. (2009). Table 1 presents the items that constitute each scale.

Results

Table 2 presents Bonferroni-Holm adjusted correlational analysis and descriptive statistics. The scales for bureaucratic control ($\alpha = 0.77$), clan control ($\alpha = 0.69$), competence ($\alpha = 0.60$), intrinsic motivation ($\alpha =$

Table 2. Study 1: Taxi vs. UberX: correlation table and descriptive statistics.

	Bur	Clan	Mar	Auto	Comp	Rel	Intr	Enj	Rating	Mean	SD	α
Bureaucratic	1									5.23	1.53	0.77
Clan	0.65***	1								5.07	1.47	0.69
Market	0.59***	0.54***	1							5.23	1.24	0.28
Autonomy	−0.30	−0.16	−0.17	1						1.92	1.24	0.29
Competence	0.26	0.09	0.32	−0.01	1					6.22	1.03	0.60
Relatedness	0.14	0.10	0.11	0.30	0.28	1				2.30	1.16	0.27
Intrinsic	0.26	0.12	0.41*	−0.06	0.3	0	1			4.89	1.9	0.8
Enjoyable	0.21	0.18	0.35	0.01	0.38	0.13	0.79***	1		5.56	1.38	0.58
Rating	0.43	0.00	−0.08	0.18	0.47	0.46	−0.04	0.06	1	4.77	0.08	–

Bonferroni-Holm adjusted significance indicated by $^{*}p < 0.10$, $^{**}p < 0.05$, and $^{***}p < 0.01$.

Table 3. Study 1: Taxi vs. UberX: group means and standard deviations.

	Taxi drivers		UberX drivers	
	Mean	SD	Mean	SD
Bureaucratic	4.67	1.77	5.87	0.94
Clan	4.54	1.43	5.58	1.34
Market	4.88	1.25	5.65	1.14
Autonomy	1.93	1.26	1.92	1.24
Competence	6.04	1.26	6.42	0.69
Relatedness	2.22	1.06	2.39	1.28
Intrinsic	4.69	2.04	5.27	1.57
Enjoyable	5.50	1.48	5.75	1.14

0.80), and enjoyable work ($\propto = 0.58$) demonstrated fair to good reliability. Higher perception of market control was correlated with greater intrinsic motivation ($r[49], = 0.41$, $p < 0.10$).

Table 3 reports Study 1 group means and standard deviations for all measures for both taxi and UberX drivers. Significant two-tailed t-test statistics at the $p < 0.10$ are described below. UberX drivers experienced significantly ($t[49] = 2.84$, $p < 0.01$, $d = 0.84$) greater bureaucratic control than taxi drivers, and significantly ($t[49] = 2.81$, $p = 0.01$, $d = 0.75$) greater clan control than taxi drivers. While the market control scale was unreliable ($\propto = 0.28$), UberX drivers experienced significantly greater market control ($t[49] = 2.15$, $p = 0.03$, $d = 0.65$) than taxi drivers. There were no significant differences in intrinsic motivation, needs satisfaction, or enjoyment of the work. Self-reported competence, relatedness, intrinsic motivation, and enjoyment of work were higher among UberX drivers, although these differences were not statistically significant. As a robustness check, we confirm that our results are robust to inclusion or exclusion of participants with missing observations.

Discussion

UberX drivers perceived more organizational control than taxi drivers on market, clan, and bureaucratic control measures, consistent with Hypothesis 1. We did not find that UberX drivers experienced significantly greater intrinsic motivation, needs satisfaction, or enjoyment compared to taxi drivers, contrary to Hypothesis 2.

Our finding of additional control of gig workers on platforms and no differences in intrinsic motivation, work satisfaction, or enjoyment, challenges the view that greater control decreases autonomy or increases alienation. UberX drivers appear unperturbed by the more controlling environment. A significant limitation of this study was that UberX and taxi drivers draw from different populations. Differences in driver perceptions of control and motivation are quite possibly related to selection effects. To address concerns about selection, a second study was devised.

Study 2: (Black car) limousine vs. (Uber black) limousine

We conducted a randomized field experiment to examine how the Uber platform affects driver perception of organizational control and motivation. To address selection effects, the study was designed for limousine drivers who work on both Uber and traditional limousine systems. We experimentally manipulate belief in whether the study is about perceptions while driving for Uber or for a limousine company, and randomize within-person, to identify causal effects of working on a technological platform.

Participants

The sample participants ($n = 79$) in Study 2 were limousine (black car) drivers who used the UberBlack app while owning or leasing their limousine vehicle. Only limousine drivers who reported using the Uber app were recruited to complete the survey. Approximately 34% of limousine drivers approached used Uber and were thus eligible for participation in the study. Of those eligible to participate, approximately 90% completed surveys. These numbers are approximate and based on first author and student RAs' tallies of contacts with potential study participants.

Procedures

The research site was the airport waiting lot at Chicago's O'Hare International Airport, which hosts a large number of idling drivers. The research team members clearly identified themselves as independent researchers in our introduction script, and by wearing Loyola University Chicago apparel. We randomly assign eligible drivers to an "Uber" or "Limousine" driver condition in which the survey alternatively asked for their perceptions while driving for Uber, or a limousine company. The cover page of the survey alternatively stated in a large font that it was an

Table 4. Study 2. Limo vs. Uber: correlation table.

	Bur	Clan	Mar	Auto	Comp	Rel	Intr	Enj	Rating	Mean	SD	α
Bureaucratic	1									5.41	1.18	0.61
Clan	0.40***	1								5.49	1.21	0.59
Market	0.47***	0.31	1							5.48	1.16	0.61
Autonomy	0.02	−0.31	0.05	1						−1.49	1.39	0.15
Competence	0.16	−0.07	0.10	0.18	1					5.8	1.35	0.62
Relatedness	0.08	0.11	0.17	0.21	0.22	1				1.68	1.13	0.00
Intrinsic	0.37**	0.18	0.34*	0.08	0.14	0.14	1			5.01	1.56	0.83
Enjoyable	0.30	−0.06	0.31	0.24	0.35*	0.29	0.54***	1		4.89	1.82	0.91
Rating	−0.17	−0.07	0.02	0.11	−0.09	0.04	0.26	0.38*	1	4.73	0.54	

Bonferroni-Holm adjusted significance indicated by $^{*}p < 0.10$, $^{**}p < 0.05$, and $^{***}p < 0.01$.

"Uber Driver" survey, or a "Limousine Driver" survey. Participating drivers were instructed to answer questions about either a) "the black car limo company you drive for" ($n = 41$) or b) "Uber" ($n = 38$). The questions are the same as in Study 1 and listed in Table 1, with variation in the putative employer. For example, drivers in the Uber condition were asked how strongly they agree with the statement: "Uber emphasizes the need to follow rules." In the limousine driver condition, drivers were presented with the statement: "The limousine company you drive for emphasizes the need to follow rules." Respondents were blind to this manipulation at the study outset, but this was revealed in a debriefing document given to drivers upon survey completion. We collected data on three dates: in October 2016, November 2016, and November 2017. RAs and the first author approached limousine drivers waiting for passengers to arrive. Drivers completed a consent form, received a $5 gift card for participation, and completed paper copies of the survey. The survey took approximately 15 minutes to complete.

Measures

Table 4 presents Bonferroni-Holm adjusted correlational analysis and descriptive statistics. The following scales had fair to good reliability: bureaucratic control ($\alpha = 0.61$), clan control ($\alpha = 0.59$), market control ($\alpha = 0.61$), competence ($\alpha = 0.62$), intrinsic motivation ($\alpha = 0.83$), and enjoyable work ($\alpha = 0.91$).

Results

Table 5 reports group means and standard deviations in the Uber and limousine driver conditions in Study 2. Drivers randomly assigned to the Uber condition perceive significantly more ($t[77] = 1.92$, $p = 0.06$, $d = 0.43$) market control than those in the limousine condition. While not significant at the $p < 0.10$ level, drivers in the Uber condition also reported higher bureaucratic and clan control. Drivers in the Uber

Table 5. Study 2. Limo vs. Uber: group means and standard deviations.

	Limousine company condition		Uber Black condition	
	Mean	SD	Mean	SD
Bureaucratic	5.29	1.08	5.53	1.28
Clan	5.33	1.18	5.67	1.23
Market	5.24	1.26	5.74	1.00
Autonomy	1.29	1.61	1.69	1.11
Competence	5.68	1.19	5.92	1.50
Relatedness	1.58	1.29	1.79	0.94
Intrinsic	4.81	1.66	5.22	1.45
Enjoyable	4.50	1.96	5.30	1.58

condition reported their work more enjoyable than in the limousine company condition ($t[76] = 1.98$, $p = 0.05$, $d = 0.45$). While not significant at the $p < 0.10$ level, drivers in the Uber condition also reported higher intrinsic motivation. As a robustness check, we confirm that our results are robust to inclusion or exclusion of participants with missing observations.

Seventy-five percent of limousine drivers in the sample owned their vehicles, while only 25% leased. We consider this group of owner-operators especially interesting because these drivers are their own boss. Comparing only the limousine owner-operators randomly assigned to either think about "Uber" ($n = 27$) or "the company you drive for" ($n = 31$) when working, owner-operators in the Uber condition reported greater perceived market controls ($t[56] = 1.68$, $p = 0.09$, $d = 0.44$), and greater clan controls ($t[56] = 1.91$, $p = 0.06$, $d = 0.50$) than those in the limousine condition. Even though acting as their own boss, owner-operators randomly assigned to think about driving for Uber rate their work as more enjoyable ($t[56] = 1.99$, $p = 0.05$, $d = 0.52$) than driving for their own company.

Discussion

Consistent with hypotheses 1 and 2, limousine drivers perceived significantly more market control and more enjoyment on the job in the Uber condition. Owner-operators also experience elevated market control and enjoyment of the work, as well as greater clan control, under Uber. Contrary to our hypotheses, there were not significant differences in bureaucratic or clan control, intrinsic motivation, or needs satisfaction. Higher levels of market control on Uber do not reduce intrinsic motivation and needs satisfaction.

To characterize effect sizes, we follow Funder and Ozer (2019) in interpreting these in comparison to one another (as smaller or larger). Where effect sizes in perceived control and motivation in Study 1 are relatively large, the differences reported in Study 2 are consistently smaller. This suggests that some of the strongly stated contrasts between Uber drivers and taxi or limousine drivers are driven by worker selection into each system, and not by platform management per se. Large differences between workers on the Uber platform and those in traditional management systems diminish among workers who operate on both systems.

Limitations

While our studies offer new insights into platform work in the gig economy, there are several limitations. First, we collected data in one city, which might limit the generalizability of our findings. Next, the sample sizes are small—future scholars could replicate our model with larger sample sizes. It would have been interesting to include the experiences of independent riders of Uber and Lyft, rather than relying on RAs. In addition, by comparing gig workers to incumbent independent contractors in an occupation of moderate complexity and an industry that lacks formalized institutions (such as unions) to strengthen their power, we may understate differences in other contexts.

Measures, originally designed for other contexts, may need to be further adapted and validated in the context of the gig economy. A few participants reported discomfort answering questions about the nature of control, when they felt little was there. In particular, the clan control measures may need further adaptation for the gig economy, in which gig workers and customers interact directly, but workers do not necessarily form a tight community typical of co-worker bonds in an environment with high clan control.

General discussion

In two studies contrasting gig work on platforms with workers in a comparison group, we advance knowledge of how gig workers perceive control and motivation under technological supervision. We find that technological platforms increase gig workers' perceptions of control. This finding suggests that gig workers on platform systems are more likely to fail the independent contractor control test than gig workers in traditional management systems. In Study 1, we find that UberX drivers have higher control perceptions than taxi drivers. In Study 2, we find that limousine drivers who use Uber report greater control, and greater enjoyment, when prompted to answer questions about driving for Uber as opposed to a limousine company. Several conclusions can be drawn from these studies.

First, comparisons between Uber and taxis related to the effects of the platform on drivers' perceptions of control and intrinsic motivation are easily overstated and are likely selection effects. The large effect sizes on bureaucratic and clan control measures found in Study 1 were not replicated in Study 2. There are significant differences between the people who work on platforms like Uber and those who work under the traditional taxi and limousine system. The causal effect of platforms seems limited to increases in market control perceptions, and work enjoyment.

Second, Uber creates a more controlling environment for its drivers than licensed drivers face in Study 1 and Study 2. In both studies, the mean control levels are higher in the Uber case than in the taxi or limousine case. There is a significant increase in work enjoyment in Study 2, which suggests platform-based management systems can both increase perceived control and enjoyment of work. Third, additional control does not diminish the intrinsically motivating aspects of the job. Differences in intrinsic motivation, although higher in the Uber condition in both studies, were insignificant in both studies.

Future directions

Much remains to be learned about control and motivation in technologically supervised platform work, and how innovations that replace traditional systems of control impact gig workers. Research on the inconsistent effects of monitoring has found important intervening variables, such as the complexity of work (Ranganathan & Benson, 2020). Likewise, personality factors matter, such that extroverts and those who are more emotionally stable are more likely to accept monitoring (Zweig & Webster, 2003). The causal effects of platforms we find in Study 2, when contrasted to the findings of Study 1, suggest additional studies should explore whether selection effects are related to the people opting-in to gig work, or by attrition.

Future work can also improve upon measurement and causal identification issues. In terms of the causal impact of control environments on motivation, more tightly controlled within-subjects experiments can explore small variations in the control environment in online gig work environments. Community expectations and norms are changed with the introduction of management by technological platform. The rise of, and importance of, community norms as a control mechanism among passengers and drivers, unregulated explicitly by the app, but apparent to those who work for both Uber and Lyft, could be explored in future work.

Implications for theory

Nearly all management theories are based upon an implicit or explicit assumption of human interaction. Our finding that platform-based supervision increased perceptions of organizational control, but did not negatively impact motivation, runs contrary to predictions in job characteristics theory and self-determination theory that greater control and extrinsic factors decrease intrinsic motivation. Some theorists of the gig economy contend that greater control and supervision through technology recreate demeaning and alienating management styles of the past. Focusing on the managerial aspect of working on app-based platforms, technological supervision over gig workers appears to offer many of the benefits of greater control, with few of the costs.

Technological mediums of organizational control likely impact how workers experience supervision and calls for greater theory. Due to the proliferation of technology as a means of relating to others, facilitating exchange, and providing instructions, workers and observers may accept more control when working under algorithmic systems of management, and can even experience it as enjoyable. Rather than being coercive, a system involving high levels of institutionalized organizational control could appear to observers, and be experienced by workers, as enabling. Can technological supervision be theorized as an enabling bureaucracy (Adler & Borys, 1996)? The resulting system is both highly controlled, and a result of the intrinsically motivated actions of workers. For example, the economics textbook that refers to taxis as a centrally planned economy, while highlighting Uber as a free market system, entirely misses the central planning and heightened control that workers experience under the algorithmic management system. An "invisible hand" constructed of code challenges many theoretical traditions. It might be interesting for future scholars to re-visit some of the classic management, motivation, and needs theories in light of the growing acceptance of technological supervision.

Further, theorized relationships between the various facets of control, motivation, flexibility, and freedom can be more usefully elaborated upon when imagining management on a technological platform compared to under human supervision. The high degree of precision in the design of technological platforms enables massive, low-cost experimentation in management systems, and theories are needed to guide the development of better systems and test the validity of old assumptions about, for example, how control affects motivation. While often implemented in conjunction with degradations of work, platforms could hold liberating potential for workers. As a research site that can be a test bed of ideas, management theorists should offer new and better ideas for design and experimentation, especially for applications designed with a long-term employment relationship in mind.

Implications for the employment relationship and HR systems

Platform management raises many ethical, legal, and practical challenges, and our research has implications for both employment relations and HR in this moment. In the employment relations area, policy makers have awakened to the challenge of regulating gig work. In October 2019, labor auditors from New Jersey's Department of Workforce Development surveyed drivers to better apply their existing independent contractor test (Opfer, 2019). Our research methods demonstrate a potential for comparing control under traditional and platform-based management systems that can be applied widely. Our results suggest that such surveys will indicate that control on platforms is greater than traditional management systems.

A growing divergence in employment relations in the United States increases the risk of non-compliance and the complexity of HR operations (Norlander, 2019). Perhaps platform management's centralization of activity will lead to a new convergence of both management systems and regulations. If one or two platforms come to dominate an industry, worker resistance to control efforts, and attempts to regulate the platforms, may find a focal point. For example, proposals to revise gig workers' rights under federal law may address the unbalanced assignment of power between gig companies and their workers and allow gig workers a voice in shaping platform technologies (see Paul, 2019).

For HRM, as technological supervision pioneered in the gig economy moves into traditional organizations, the transition from human supervisors to technology-based systems is an important development. While this appears to be a major transformation, our results suggest modest causal impacts on perceptions of control and motivation. Human beings develop relationships of various degrees with their supervisors based on a social exchange involving feelings, emotions, and affect (see, e.g. Wang & Varma, 2020). When human supervisors are replaced with digital systems, the "supervisor" is inhuman, which could have a long-term negative impact on multiple dimensions.

Finally, as scholars have noted (e.g. Veen et al., 2019), traditional performance management systems may be ill-equipped to handle platform-based work. The rise of big data and information processing systems to handle HRM can undermine the role of traditional HR departments (Angrave et al., 2016). HRM in the gig-economy has been likened to governance of an ecosystem, involving customers, gig workers, and platforms in a co-creation of value (Meijerink & Keegan, 2019). HR departments need to be involved with information systems design to remain relevant in this context. Traditional companies are likely to continue to rely on clan control systems that are difficult to monitor electronically, and yet have a powerful role in shaping workers' perceptions and performance. An information processing perspective to performance management can aid HR's adaptation (Norlander & Varma, 2019).

Optimistically, by subjecting software "supervisors" to engineering analysis that aims to keep workers logging in, platforms may develop into sophisticated HRM systems that enable high worker performance and motivation. The use of a balanced mix of market, bureaucratic, and clan controls is likely to be required for the long-run stability of these technological platforms (Cardinal et al., 2004). Our finding that Uber increases enjoyment of work is promising regarding the potential for platforms to improve the work environment through technological innovation. Although there is a risk that excessive control and power imbalances will lead to worker discontent, through experimentation and optimization methods, these systems may discover and spread successful HRM practices.

Acknowledgements

The authors wish to acknowledge Robert Hall, Ramya Madhurapantula, Anushi Shrivastava, Ramakanth Tallapragada, and Yuqi Zhang for their help with research for this project. We also thank Lindsey Cameron, Bori Csillag, Meg Lewis, Chris Long, Peter Sherer, three anonymous reviewers, the editors of the special issue on the gig economy, and participants at the Wharton People and Organizations Conference, the Organization Science Winter Conference, and the Academy of Management conference for encouragement and helpful comments. All errors are the authors' own.

ORCID

Peter Norlander http://orcid.org/0000-0001-8347-7653

Data availability statement

The data that support the findings of this study are available from the first author, Peter Norlander, upon reasonable request.

References

Adler, P. S., & Borys, B. (1996). Two types of bureaucracy: Enabling and coercive. *Administrative Science Quarterly*, *41*(1), 61–89. https://doi.org/10.2307/2393986

Angrave, D., Charlwood, A., Kirkpatrick, I., Lawrence, M., & Stuart, M. (2016). HR and analytics: Why HR is set to fail the big data challenge. *Human Resource Management Journal*, *26*(1), 1–11. https://doi.org/10.1111/1748-8583.12090

Angrist, J., Caldwell, S., & Hall, J. V. (2017). *Uber versus taxi: A driver's eye view*. NBER working paper #23891. Cambridge, MA: National Bureau of Economic Research.

Azevedo, E. M., & Weyl, E. G. (2016). Economics. Matching markets in the digital age. *Science (New York, N.Y.), 352* (6289), 1056–1057. https://doi.org/10.1126/science.aaf7781

Beniger, J. (1989). *The control revolution: Technological and economic origins of the information society*. Harvard University Press.

Briscoe, F. (2007). From iron cage to iron shield? How bureaucracy enables temporal flexibility for professional service workers. *Organization Science, 18*(2), 297–314. https://doi.org/10.1287/orsc.1060.0226

Calo, R., & Rosenblat, A. (2017). The taking economy: Uber, information, and power. *Columbia Law Review, 117*, 1623.

Cappelli, P., & Keller, J. (2013). A study of the extent and potential causes of alternative employment arrangements. *Industrial and Labor Relations Review, 66*(4), 874–901. https://doi.org/10.1177/001979391306600406

Cardinal, L. B., Sitkin, S. B., & Long, C. P. (2004). Balancing and rebalancing in the creation and evolution of organizational control. *Organization Science, 15*(4), 411–431. https://doi.org/10.1287/orsc.1040.0084

Cardinal, L. B., Sitkin, S. B., Long, C. P., et al. (2010). A configurational theory of control. In A. Sitkin (Ed.), *Organizational control* (pp. 51–79). Cambridge University Press.

Chicago Data Portal. (2020). Transportation network providers – drivers. https://data.cityofchicago.org/.

Collier, R. B., Dubal, V. B., & Carter, C. (2017). *Labor platforms and gig work: the failure to regulate*. IRLE Working paper no. 106-17. Berkeley, CA: Institute for Research on Labor and Employment, UC Berkeley.

Cramer, J., & Krueger, A. B. (2016). Disruptive change in the taxi business: The case of Uber. *American Economic Review, 106*(5), 177–182. https://doi.org/10.1257/aer.p20161002

Deci, E. L., Koestner, R., & Ryan, R. M. (1999). A meta-analytic review of experiments examining the effects of extrinsic rewards on intrinsic motivation. *Psychological Bulletin, 125*(6), 627 https://doi.org/10.1037/0033-2909.125.6.627

Deci, E. L., & Ryan, R. M. (2000). The 'what' and 'why' of goal pursuits: Human needs and the self-determination of behavior. *Psychological Inquiry, 11*(4), 227–268. https://doi.org/10.1207/S15327965PLI1104_01

Deterding, S. (2015). The lens of intrinsic skill atoms: A method for gameful design. *Human-Computer Interaction, 30*(3-4), 294–335. https://doi.org/10.1080/07370024.2014.993471

Duggan, J., Sherman, U., Carbery, R., & McDonnell, A. (2020). Algorithmic management and app-work in the gig economy: A research agenda for employment relations and HRM. *Human Resource Management Journal, 30*(1), 114–132. https://doi.org/10.1111/1748-8583.12258

Edelman, B. G., & Geradin, D. (2015). Efficiencies and regulatory shortcuts: How should we regulate companies like Airbnb and Uber. *Stanford Technology Law Review, 19*, 293.

Eidelson, J. (2019, September 3). Uber argues driver names are 'closely guarded trade secrets. *Bloomberg News*.

Farber, H. S. (2015). Why you can't find a taxi in the rain and other labor supply lessons from cab drivers. *The Quarterly Journal of Economics, 130*(4), 1975–2026. https://doi.org/10.1093/qje/qjv026

Funder, D. C., & Ozer, D. J. (2019). Evaluating effect size in psychological research: Sense and nonsense. *Advances in Methods and Practices in Psychological Science*, *2*(2), 156–168. https://doi.org/10.1177/2515245919847202

Gagné, M., & Deci, E. L. (2005). Self-determination theory and work motivation. *Journal of Organizational Behavior*, *26*(4), 331–362. https://doi.org/10.1002/job.322

Gordon, A. (2019). 'I wonder what they are hiding:' Lyft drivers can no longer see how much riders paid for each trip. https://jalopnik.com/i-wonder-what-they-are-hiding-lyft-drivers-can-no-long-1839224300

Richard, H. J., & Oldham, G. (1976). Motivation through the design of work: Test of a theory. *Organizational Behavior and Human Performance*, *16*(2), 250–279.

Harris, B. (2017). Uber, Lyft, and regulating the sharing economy. *Seattle University Law Review*, *41*, 269.

Jacoby, S. M. (1985). *Employing bureaucracy: Managers, unions, and the transformation of work in American industry, 1900-1945*. Columbia University Press.

Jabagi, N., Croteau, A. M., Audebrand, L. K., & Marsan, J. (2019). Gig workers' motivation: Thinking beyond carrots and sticks. *Journal of Managerial Psychology*, *34*(4), 192–213. https://doi.org/10.1108/JMP-06-2018-0255

Kalleberg, A. L. (2009). Precarious work, insecure workers: Employment relations in transition. *American Sociological Review*, *74*(1), 1–22. https://doi.org/10.1177/000312240907400101

Kameswaran, V., Cameron, L., & Dillahunt, T. R. (2018, April). Support for social and cultural capital development in real-time ridesharing services. In *Proceedings of the 2018 CHI conference on human factors in computing systems* (pp. 342). ACM.

Kasser, T., Davey, J., & Ryan, R. M. (1992). Motivation, dependability, and employee-supervisor discrepancies in psychiatric vocational rehabilitation settings. *Rehabilitation Psychology*, *37*, 175–187.

Kirven, A. (2018). Whose gig is it anyway: Technological change, workplace control and supervision, and workers' rights in the gig economy. *University of Colorado Law Review*, *89*, 249.

Kuhn, K. M., & Maleki, A. (2017). Micro-entrepreneurs, dependent contractors, and instaserfs: Understanding online labor platform workforces. *Academy of Management Perspectives*, *31*(3), 183–200. https://doi.org/10.5465/amp.2015.0111

Lee, M. K., Kusbit, D., Metsky, E., & Dabbish, L. (2015). Working with machines: The impact of algorithmic and data-driven management on human workers [Paper presentation]. In Proceedings of the 33rd annual ACM conference on human factors in computing systems (pp. 1603–1612). ACM.

Lehdonvirta, V. (2018). Flexibility in the gig economy: Managing time on three online piecework platforms. *New Technology, Work and Employment*, *33*(1), 13–29. https://doi.org/10.1111/ntwe.12102

Leighton, P. (2016). Professional self-employment, new power and the sharing economy: Some cautionary tales from Uber. *Journal of Management & Organization*, *22*(6), 859–874.

Long, C. P., Bendersky, C., & Morrill, C. (2011). Fairness monitoring: Linking managerial controls and fairness judgments in organizations. *Academy of Management Journal*, *54*(5), 1045–1068. https://doi.org/10.5465/amj.2011.0008

Mankiw, G. (2016). *Principles of microeconomics*. Cengage Learning.

Marquis, E. B., Kim, S., Alahmad, R., Pierce, C. S., & Robert, L. P., Jr. (2018, October). Impacts of perceived behavior control and emotional labor on gig workers. In *Companion of the 2018 ACM conference on computer supported cooperative work and social computing* (pp. 241–244). ACM. https://doi.org/10.1145/3272973.3274065

Mayer-Schönberger, V., & Cukier, K. (2013). *Big data–A revolution that will transform how we live, think and work*. Houghton Mifflin Harcourt.

McGaughey, E. (2018). Taylorooism: When network technology meets corporate power. *Industrial Relations Journal*, *49*(5-6), 459–472. https://doi.org/10.1111/irj.12228

Meijerink, J., & Keegan, A. (2019). Conceptualizing human resource management in the gig economy: Toward a platform ecosystem perspective. *Journal of Managerial Psychology*, *34* (4), 214–232. https://doi.org/10.1108/JMP-07-2018-0277

Möhlmann, M., & Zalmanson, L. (2017, December 10–13). Hands on the wheel: Navigating algorithmic management and Uber drivers' autonomy [Paper presentation]. In Proceedings of the international conference on information systems (ICIS 2017), Seoul, South Korea.

Mollick, E. R., & Rothbard, N. (2014). Mandatory fun: Consent, gamification and the impact of games at work. The Wharton School Research Paper Series.

Mollick, E., & Werbach, K. (2015). Gamification and the enterprise. In *The Gameful world: Approaches, issues, applications* (pp. 439–538). MIT Press.

Norlander, P. (2019). The growing divergence in US employee relations: Individualism, democracy, and conflict. In P. Manzella, K. Koch ,& E. Elgar *(Eds.), International comparative employee relations: The role of culture and language*. London, UK: Edward Elgar.

Norlander, P., & Varma, A. (2019). Performance information. In A. Varma & P. Budhwar *(Eds.), Performance management systems: An experiential approach*. Sage.

Opfer, C. (2019). *Uber, Lyft being probed in new jersey on misclassifying drivers*. Bloomberg Law: Daily Labor Report. October 17, 2019.

Paul, S. (2019). Fissuring and the Firm Exemption. *Law and Contemporary Problems*, *82*(2), 65–87.

Ranganathan, A., & Benson, A. (2020). A numbers game: Quantification of work, accidental gamification, and worker productivity. *American Sociological Review*, *85* (4), 573–609. 10.1177/0003122420936665 https://doi.org/10.1177/0003122420936665

Rosenblat, A., & Hwang, T. (2016). Regional diversity in autonomy and work: A case study from Uber and Lyft drivers. *Intelligence and Autonomy*, 1–15.

Rosenblat, A., & Stark, L. (2016). Algorithmic labor and information asymmetries: A case study of Uber's drivers. *International Journal of Communication*, *10*, 3758–3784.

Rosenblat, A. (2018). *Uberland: How algorithms are rewriting the rules of work*. University of California Press.

Scheiber, N. (2017, April 2). How Uber uses psychological tricks to push its drivers' buttons. *The New York Times*. https://www.nytimes.com/interactive/2017/04/02/technology/uber-drivers-psychological-tricks.html

Shapiro, A. (2018). Between autonomy and control: Strategies of arbitrage in the "on-demand" economy. *New Media & Society*, *20*(8), 2954–2971.

Sherer, P. D., Rogovsky, N., & Wright, N. (1998). What drives employment relationships in taxicab organizations? Linking agency to firm capabilities and strategic opportunities. *Organization Science*, *9*(1), 34–48. https://doi.org/10.1287/orsc.9.1.34

Sitkin, S. B., Cardinal, L. B., and Bijlsma-Frankema, K. M. (Eds.). (2010). *Organizational control*. Cambridge University Press.

Spreitzer, G. M., Cameron, L., & Garrett, L. (2017). Alternative work arrangements: Two images of the new world of work. *Annual Review of Organizational Psychology and Organizational Behavior*, *4*(1), 473–499. https://doi.org/10.1146/annurev-orgpsych-032516-113332

Tremblay, M. A., Blanchard, C. M., Taylor, S., Pelletier, L. G., & Villeneuve, M. (2009). Work extrinsic and intrinsic motivation scale: Its value for organizational psychology research. *Canadian Journal of Behavioural Science/Revue Canadienne Des Sciences du Comportement*, *41*(4), 213–226. https://doi.org/10.1037/a0015167

Uber. (2020). Introducing Uber-Pro. https://www.uber.com/us/en/drive/uber-pro/

Veen, A., Barratt, T., & Goods, C. (2020). Platform-capital's 'app-etite'for control: A labour process analysis of food-delivery work in Australia. *Work, Employment and Society*, *34*(3), 388-406. https://doi.org/10.1177%2F0950017019836911

Wang, C. H., & Varma, A. (2020). Supervisor subordinate relationships. In A. Varma & P. Budhwar (Eds.), *Performance management systems: An experiential approach*. Sage.

Weil, D. (2014). *The fissured workplace*. Harvard University Press.

Wood, A. J., Graham, M., Lehdonvirta, V., & Hjorth, I. (2019). Good gig, bad gig: Autonomy and algorithmic control in the global gig economy. *Work, Employment & Society*, *33*(1), 56–75. https://doi.org/10.1177/0950017018785616

Zuboff, S. (2015). Big other: Surveillance capitalism and the prospects of an information civilization. *Journal of Information Technology*, *30*(1), 75–89. https://doi.org/10.1057/jit.2015.5

Zucker, L. G. (1987). Institutional theories of organization. *Annual Review of Sociology*, *13*(1), 443–464. https://doi.org/10.1146/annurev.so.13.080187.002303

Zweig, D., & Webster, J. (2003). Personality as a moderator of monitoring acceptance. *Computers in Human Behavior*, *19*(4), 479–493. https://doi.org/10.1016/S0747-5632(02)00075-4

Fair's fair: psychological contracts and power in platform work

Genevieve Shanahan and Mark Smith

ABSTRACT

Platform work can be understood as a particularly acute instance of the individualization of economic risk. Responding to the broader trends of labour commodification and decline of the standard employment relationship, psychological contract theory emerged as a way to conceptualize fairness in individualized work arrangements. In this paper, we draw out the critical potential of psychological contract theory by mobilizing Lukes' theory of power. We apply this lens to 12 semi-structured interviews with platform-mediated food delivery couriers, supplemented by both online and offline participant observation, to identify ways in which platform firms use decision-making, nondecision-making and ideological power to encourage the acceptance of platform work as fair: through the unilateral modification of exchange terms, through the nondecisions of communication and technology design, and through the ideological power of neoliberalism and tribalism. In so doing, we also identify coping strategies deployed by couriers in response to violations by platform firms of perceived exchange terms, variously resistant to and reinforcing of these forms of platform power. In this way, we uncover mechanisms by which firms present risk individualization as a fair exchange of worker security for worker autonomy, as well as more and less effective ways workers can resist this framing.

1. Introduction

In platform work, digital technology is deployed by a firm to mediate market demand for services and worker supply (Gandini, 2019). The design of the labour process implies a staccato engagement between the worker and platform firm, discouraging imputations of an employment relationship, with its attendant rights and benefits for workers (Goudin,

Supplemental data for this article is available online at https://doi.org/10.1080/09585192.2020.1867615.

2016). These platform firms present themselves as harbingers of the "future of work" (Kalanick, 2015), responding to workers' needs in a way that disrupts labour regulation and demands that it catch up (Shu, 2018). Central to this vision is the maximization of flexibility, allowing the under-employed, students and those with caring responsibilities to pick up extra work at will in ways that improve their quality of life. Yet ongoing protests demonstrate that not all platform workers see this as a fair exchange. Tassinari and Maccarrone (2020, p. 44) identify the "perceived dissonance between the rhetoric of 'flexibility' promoted by the companies and the reality of the work process" as a key source of grievance. The development of expectations, and their degree of fulfilment and disappointment, is a relevant avenue for investigating the dark side of "new" forms of work (Daudigeos *et al.*, 2019; Picard & Islam, 2020) and the normalization of precarious and commodified labour (Rubery *et al.*, 2018).

The psychological contract (PC) can be understood as an employee's perception of a "fair" deal with their employer. PC theory holds that employees (and workers more generally, McLean Parks *et al.*, 1998; Guest, 2004) tend to develop beliefs about the obligations that obtain between themselves and the firm, beyond the terms of the employment contract (Rousseau, 1989). This implicit exchange draws on assumptions regarding fairness (Guest, 2004; Rousseau, 1989; Rousseau *et al.*, 2018): what a firm can reasonably demand of a worker for a certain level of pay, what autonomy a worker can reasonably expect, etc. These perceptions in turn condition worker consent to the exchange – whether that be enthusiastic, grudging, withdrawn or withheld (Wilkens & Nermerich, 2011).

While useful in analysing worker-employer expectations, PC theory has been critiqued for its tendency to rationalize and normalize employment relationships as they currently exist, and abstract from power structures, presenting labour relations as individualized and voluntarist (Cullinane & Dundon, 2006; Dick & Nadin, 2011). The *psychological* focus of the theory is core to this individualization, inquiring into workers' *subjective perceptions* of the terms of the exchange. This arguably contributes to a concern for managing worker perceptions of fairness rather than actually achieving fairness in work (Fortin & Fellenz, 2008). This focus on perceptions can serve to obscure the reality of the underlying exchange (Chai & Scully, 2019), thereby serving the interests of management against those of workers. Yet given that the PC is already concerned with perceptions of fairness, approaches that account for such power structures and embed the PC "within a deeper political economy of capitalism" (Cullinane & Dundon, 2006, p. 125) can uncover the critical potential of this framework, offering insights regarding the real fairness or unfairness of the exchange, and going some way towards explaining the accuracy or otherwise of workers' perceptions.

In this paper, therefore, we use the PC framework to ask: *how do platform workers navigate the divergent promises and realities of platform work?* In platform work, a new exchange of worker autonomy for market flexibility is presented as fair and discontinuous with the exchanges that have come before, framed in terms of a post-capitalist sharing economy (Acquier *et al.*, 2017; Papadimitropoulos, 2019; Peticca-Harris *et al.*, 2020). Yet the insecurity of this work is perhaps greater than anticipated (Rosenblat & Stark, 2015; Tassinari & Maccarrone, 2020) and the purported autonomy offered in exchange "often appears more limited than advertised," leading to "potential psychological contract breach" (Duggan *et al.*, 2020, p. 126). Platform work thus offers an appropriate site for the exploration of consent to "new" forms of work, and the power wielded by capital (Boltanski & Chiapello, 2017). Indeed, platform work can be seen as an extension of the individualization of risk (Duggan *et al.*, 2020; Friedman, 2014) and of worker relations which drove PC theory development, attended by claims that the old rules of labour management are no longer relevant (Chai & Scully, 2019). We attempt to realize the critical potential of PC theory by exploring the degree of success achieved by capital in convincing workers of the fairness of the exchange proposed by platform work, specifically mobilizing Lukes' (2005) theory of power to explore how explicit, implicit and ideological mechanisms of power affect what workers are prepared to accept as a "fair" exchange.

2. Psychological contracts and power

The concept of the PC emerged from social exchange theory as a way to describe the various exchanges and agreements – both explicit and implicit – that workers and employers believe they have with one another (Robinson *et al.*, 1994; Rousseau, 1990; Rousseau & McLean Parks, 1993). While developed in the context of the employment relationship, existing scholarship has shown the utility of applying PC theory to alternative arrangements, such as consultants, independent contractors, temporary workers and agency workers (McLean Parks *et al.*, 1998). Duggan *et al.* (2020) thus endorse the application of PC theory to platform work, despite the lack of an on-paper employment relationship between the platform firm and the worker.

Platform work also differs from the traditional employment contexts for which PC theory was originally developed in that it generally involves some degree of algorithmic management. This form of management relies on remote surveillance by "an assemblage of computational processes, which automatically generate data, evaluate worker behaviour and assign labour activities" (Newlands, 2020, p. 5). In this way, direct human interaction with platform firm representatives is minimized, with at least two *a priori* implications for the psychological contracts of platform workers. First, the platform engages not with the worker directly but with an abstracted representation of the worker in data (Newlands, 2020). This arguably excludes engagement with the worker as a whole person, characteristic of relational psychological contracts (Rousseau, 1990). Second, the discretion of the platform firm in its treatment of the worker is somewhat concealed, as the decisions made by the algorithm are imbued with a veneer of objectivity (Duggan *et al.*, 2020). The societal perception of algorithms as objective obscures the choices of the human managers and programmers who design such algorithms (Feenberg, 2002; Pasquale, 2015). In this paper we are particularly interested in this second implication of algorithmic management for how workers perceive their exchanges with platform firms as fair or otherwise.

Given their subjective nature, workers develop idiosyncratic PCs based on the information available to them and the background assumptions and beliefs that inform how they interpret that information (Conway & Briner, 2005; Rousseau, 1989). The algorithmic mediation of the relationship between the worker and platform firm entails a high degree of standardization of communication and treatment, which might give us reason to expect limited divergence in platform workers' PCs. However, PC theory identifies a plethora of influences on PC formation (Sherman & Morley, 2015) and studies of platform work do indeed find heterogeneity and ambiguity in workers' understanding of their mutual obligations with platform firms (Berg, 2016). These workers each construct their PCs from various and not necessarily coherent sources, using "their own experiences with [Community Support Representatives], media reports, company statements, written policies, notices from local markets, and their own advice in forums" (Rosenblat & Stark, 2015, p. 14). What is more, the PC is informed by broader ideologies and is thus "inextricably bound up with the political interests of power holders within organisations and society more generally" (Dick & Nadin, 2011, p. 296).

Further divergence is likely due to the dynamic nature of the PC. Rousseau *et al.* (2018) propose a dynamic model of the PC as developing across distinct phases. In the *creation phase*, which comprises the first few months of the employment relationship, the worker refines their pre-existing beliefs about the reciprocal obligations between themselves and the organization "based on environmental cues from observation and interaction with the organization and its members" (p. 1082). This fine-tuning continues through the *maintenance phase*, in which the worker's PC is stable but still responsive to "minor discrepancies that are assimilated effortlessly into the PC" (p. 1084). By contrast, the PC is *violated* when the worker perceives some major discrepancy between their

PC and the actual exchange, and this triggers reassessment of the PC. When the violation is due to under-fulfilment of the terms of the PC by the organization, the worker's PC enters the *repair phase*, whereby the worker attempts "to reduce negative affect and reestablish a functional or goal-consistent PC" (p. 1091).

This decomposition is important for our purposes, as it makes space for the evolution of the worker's PC over time (Conway & Briner, 2005), and thus captures workers' evaluations of the extent to which the firm holds up its side of the bargain. Tomprou *et al.* (2015) also attend to the agency of workers, detailing four categories of coping strategies workers may deploy to deal with PC violations: *problem-focused coping*, where the worker attempts to resolve the discrepancy by directly engaging the firm; *emotion-focused coping*, where the worker instead attempts to dilute the negative emotions associated with the discrepancy by venting or positively reinterpreting the situation; *mental disengagement*, where the worker becomes cynical, reduces their expectations of the firm and reduces their psychological investment in their relationship with the firm; and *behavioural disengagement*, where the worker either resigns or withdraws above-and-beyond efforts. These coping strategies are differentially associated with PC outcomes: *PC reactivation*, where the original exchange terms are reinstituted; *PC thriving*, where exchange terms more advantageous to the worker are implemented; *PC impairment*, where the new exchange terms are less advantageous to the worker; and *PC dissolution*, where the worker "is unable to accept the altered circumstances as a basis for a new psychological contract, choosing to remain instead in a chronic and dysfunctional state of felt violation" (Tomprou *et al.*, 2015, p. 562). When a worker "chooses" to continue a dysfunctional exchange without a functional PC on which to rely "to decide on his or her contributions and investments to the employer" (Solinger *et al.*, 2016, p. 496), we are prompted to consider the structures that inform that choice.

Lukes' (2005) account of power is instructive here, as it allows us to recognize the role of overt power relations in such choices, but also the more covert and insidious ways prevailing power structures inform and shape workers' consent, perceptions of fairness, and conceptions of what is possible. Moreover, his framework allows us to get 'below' pure behaviour to the beliefs and subjectivities that condition that behaviour – precisely the subjective individual level the PC approach attempts to theorize. Lukes' first face of power, decision-making power, involves the overt conflict and obvious political behaviour covered by traditional accounts of power. It focuses on clearly designated actors whose observable behaviour reveals their interests. Accounts that consider only this face of power are limited, however, as they conceive power to be relevant only to issues explicitly identified as political. Lukes builds on Bachrach and Baratz (1970) to define the second face of power, nondecision-making power, which addresses how issues come to be identified as political or otherwise. A 'nondecision' is defined as "a decision that results in suppression or thwarting of a latent or manifest challenge to the values or interests of the decision-maker" (Bachrach & Baratz, 1970, p. 44). These more indirect forms of power, inherent in agenda-setting and subtle silencing practices (Fortin & Fellenz, 2008), open up the possibility of latent conflicts of interest that are not manifested in behaviour (Lukes, 2005, p. 28). The third face, ideological power, follows this potential for latent conflict to the extreme, naming the operation of power that shapes "the conception of issues and [...] wants of others" (Fortin & Fellenz, 2008, p. 420). Here, hegemonic ways of understanding the world, including the requirements of the prevailing socio-economic system and what we owe to one another, inhibit the conception and articulation of grievances (Lukes, 2005, p. 11). This ideological power can range from total and enthusiastic internalization of this hegemony to reluctant acceptance that there is no alternative (Lukes, 2005, p. 8, 28). This form of power operates to defend and entrench the interests of the dominant in society, and thus need not be actively deployed by a given powerful actor, though specific actors may make efforts to increase the salience of a given ideology in contexts of potential ideological conflict. It is through this face of power that the possibility of distance between subjective interests and real interests – false consciousness or misrecognition (Dick & Nadin, 2011) – emerges. Ideological power is thus particularly useful for understanding platform workers' maintenance of apparently dysfunctional exchanges.

In this paper, we show how Lukes' three faces of power complement the dynamic phase model of the PC described by Rousseau *et al.* (2018), specifically by demonstrating the complex interaction between platform firms' power and workers' means of coping with PC violation (Tomprou *et al.*, 2015). The testimony of platform workers presented here reveals the sleight of hand by which platform firms, through these three faces of power, conceal the real terms of the exchange. We also identify in their accounts some of the ways in which workers can cope with this discrepancy and continue the exchange without necessarily endorsing these terms as "fair".

3. Methods

Following Duggan *et al.* (2020), we consider in this paper the subset of platform work they call "app-work": location-specific service work performed on-demand, controlled and mediated by a platform's proprietary algorithm. More specifically, we focus on food delivery couriers for platforms such as Deliveroo, Uber Eats, Foodora, Glovo, Just Eat, Take Eat Easy and Stuart. We chose this population due to the strong focus on worker autonomy in delivery firms' promotion of this work, and high-profile, sustained protests by couriers regarding these claims (Cant, 2020; Tassinari & Maccarrone, 2020). Our analysis is rooted in 12 semi-structured interviews, supplemented by participant observation. We focused our data collection on the UK and France, with this case study approach allowing us to locate platform worker experiences within different institutional settings (Tassinari & Maccarrone, 2020).

Our methodological approach can be understood in the frame of critical grounded theory (Belfrage & Hauf, 2017). We chose this approach as we are interested in exploring how platform work reproduces neoliberal conceptions of worker autonomy in terms of risk individualization, how such conceptions "become reified or naturalized and thus expelled from the realm of what appears to be discursively negotiable" (2017, p. 260), as well as discursive and material resistance to such naturalization. We thus follow the steps outlined by Belfrage and Hauf, beginning with a period of sensitization to operant discourses and theoretical approaches through participant observation, followed by a 'gentle' testing of initial conceptualizations through semi-structured interviews, and concluding with reflexive revision of the initial pre-concepts.

To begin, the first author engaged in an extensive period of participant observation, both in-person and online, to gain familiarity with couriers' concerns and lived, embodied experiences (Finlay, 2005). The first author created a courier account with platform 2 (henceforth P2), and completed deliveries part-time over a period of three months in Grenoble, France, thereby gaining something of an insider perspective on the difficulties and pleasures of the job, the functioning of the app, the incentives it creates, and the social dynamics of interactions with restaurants, customers and other couriers. The insider identity this engagement afforded (Cunliffe & Karunanayake, 2013) eased entry to physical courier hangouts in Grenoble and Glasgow, where informal conversations informed the authors' theorizing in the early stages. The insider identity also allowed for access to online spaces, such as social media and instant messaging groups, both platform-moderated and private (see Table 1 for details). The first author consciously adopted a "lurker" role (Paechter, 2013) for the majority of her time in these groups, simply reading posts and conversation threads to gain an understanding of couriers' priorities and the variety of discourses invoked by couriers and platform representatives. Through this exploration of couriers' concerns and discursive constructions of their working conditions, the question of the fairness of the exchange between themselves and the platform firms emerged as

Table 1 . Participant observation.

	France	UK	Cross-border
Participant observation: in-person	3 months (Grenoble)	2 days (Glasgow)	
Participant observation: online groups	3 general support groups 2 protest/union groups	5 general support groups 3 protest/union groups	2 general support groups 3 protest / union groups

particularly salient. This led us to consider how these exchanges might fit within existing PC theorizing.

In a second step, we conducted semi-structured interviews with couriers in the UK and France to gain purchase on the PC specifically, on the understanding that such a cognitive phenomenon requires individual-level, interpretive analysis (Bankins, 2011; Conway & Briner, 2005; Gill, 2014). We developed an interview schedule with questions and prompts derived from existing interview- and survey-based studies of workers' PCs (Coyle-Shapiro & Kessler, 2000, 2002a, 2002b; Eisenberger *et al.*, 1986; Robinson & Morrison, 2000; Rousseau, 2008), which we adapted to the platform work context.[1] The schedule was refined as interviews were conducted to improve the data collection.

The majority of interviews were conducted in English; just one, with interviewee 4, was conducted in French and analysed in that language, with the quotations presented here translated by the first author. The interviews lasted between 40 and 90 minutes each. All but one of the participants consented to audio recording and transcription of their interviews, with interviewee 11 consenting to paraphrasing of his answers instead. The recruitment of participants was determined by the specific characteristics of this workforce, which renders systematic sampling of representative populations difficult (Chai & Scully, 2019). Since platforms do not employ couriers directly, a conventional strategy of approaching the firm to negotiate access to workers was inapplicable. Instead, it was necessary to approach couriers in informal gathering places, both physical and virtual. A convenience sampling strategy was adopted in the first round to access as many participants as possible in this dispersed and hard-to-reach population, with recruitment targeting physical hotspots and general support groups (returning 10 participants). A second round was more purposeful, focusing on activists encountered in the course of participant observation (returning one participant from each country). We are mindful that the couriers interviewed are not representative of the wider courier population, with our sample biased in favour of those who, for instance, have the capacity and inclination to spend their downtime interacting with other couriers. Indeed, we do not aim at representativeness, but rather useful cases for refining and enhancing the analytic

Table 2. Participant attributes and characteristics.

Age range	Experience level (months)	Financial dependence	Platform	Activist?	Status (Part-time: PT; full-time: FT; self-employed: SE)	Vehicle	Int #
France							
26–30	15	Dependent	1 and 2	No	PT, student, SE	Bike	1
20–25	10	Relatively dependent	1, then 2	No	PT, student, SE	Bike	2
20–25	3	Relatively dependent	2	No	PT, student, SE	Bike	4
20–25	<1	Relatively dependent	1	No	PT, student, SE	Bike	6
20–25	<1	Not dependent	2	No	PT, student, SE	Bike	7
20–25	1	Not dependent	2	No	PT, student, SE	Bike	8
26–30	18	Dependent	1 and 3	Yes	PT, student, SE	Bike	11
UK							
26–30	2	Dependent	1 and 2	No	FT, SE	Bike	3
20–25	4	Dependent	1	No	FT, SE	Bike	5
26–30	9	Dependent	1 and 2	No	FT, SE	Bike	9
36–40	10	Dependent	1, then 2 and 4	No	FT, SE	Car	10
31–35	18	Dependent	1 and 2	Yes	FT, SE	Bike	12

frame of PC theory through retroduction (ten Have, 2004), in line with our emancipatory research agenda (Amis & Silk, 2008).

In a third and final step, we revised our understanding of PC theory as it applies to platform workers in light of this fieldwork. We did so by iteratively coding the interview transcripts in NVIVO (version 11) and deliberating over our findings and interpretations (McCarthy *et al.*, 2018), refining our coding approaches as we progressed (Fereday & Muir-Cochrane, 2006) in a process of retroduction informed by our exploration of both the existing literature and our data (Belfrage & Hauf, 2017; Dick & Nadin, 2011). We thus progressively coded for courier expectations, PC violations, accounts of platform power, discourses explicitly or implicitly invoked in couriers' expressions of satisfaction or dissatisfaction with the exchange, and moments of resistance (Fairclough, 2005). We chose to code and analyse these interviews in an inclusive manner, in acknowledgement of the ambivalence of workers' interpretations of their situation, as well as their multiple and sometimes contradictory responses to violations.

4. Findings and analysis

In this section, we first explore the operation of platform firms' power as revealed through participants' attempts to make sense of their reciprocal obligations with these businesses. In the subsequent sub-section, we identify how couriers deal with these forms of power, revealed through the coping approaches they deploy in response to PC violations (Tomprou *et al.*, 2015).

4.1. Platform firms' power

In our interviews with couriers, we were surprised to find some workers continuing to attest to the fairness of their exchanges with platform firms, despite experiencing the same conditions as their dissatisfied colleagues, often accounting for broken promises in the language of fair interaction between businesses. This finding sensitized us to the possible operation of covert and ideological power in this case. We thus reviewed the interview transcripts to identify points where workers explicitly or implicitly identified platform firms' exercises of power, and categorized these according to Lukes' (2005) faces of power.

4.1.1. The first face of platform firms' power

The exercise of decision-making power by the platform firms was perhaps the most obvious from the outset, revealed in instances of platform firms' *unilateral modification of exchange terms,* which necessitated couriers' reappraisal of their PCs. The three most prominent subcategories of this type of power are detailed with sample evidence in Table 3:

Platform firms unilaterally *reduced pay*, both by reducing the pay offered per-delivery, and by reducing and suppressing hourly wages and incentive rates (e.g., for periods of high demand or adverse weather conditions). Couriers' take-home pay was also negatively affected by platform firms' *increasing demands on couriers*, including expanding delivery zones, such that the effort and time necessary to complete each order increased even as pay-per-order decreased. At the same time, our interview participants identified discrete actions platform firms took to *limit courier autonomy* in manners incongruous with the purported flexibility of the work. Interviewee 2, for instance, recounted booking some time off on P2's scheduling platform for a holiday, only to receive a text to inform him his contract had been terminated by the platform firm.

A number of our interviewees explicitly framed this deterioration in conditions in terms of normative obligations. In the table above, Interviewee 1 recounts the progressive pay decreases he had experienced over his time with P1, alluding to the violation of "an implied promise." Interviewee 12, describing a P1 software update that restricted couriers' ability to use multiple delivery platforms simultaneously, similarly frames this action as breaching "a sort of contract" that allowed couriers to accept reduced workers' rights in exchange for greater flexibility and autonomy.

4.1.2. The second face of platform firms' power

Many couriers' perceptions of the terms of the exchange morphed over time as they discovered, through the labour process, ways in which

Table 3. Platforms' decision-making power.

Vectors of power	Techniques	Supporting quotations
Unilateral modification of exchange terms	Reducing pay	"There are also premium rates offered for working Friday, Saturday and Sunday. And those have reduced over the 15 months that I've been working there. So I've been paid progressively less and less right from the beginning, which is quite different to most jobs. [. . .] I think that there's an implied promise that you won't be paid less and less as your time goes on with the company, which they have done." I1
	Increasing demands on couriers	Conditions at P3 have deteriorated significantly over the course of Interviewee 11's engagement. The maximum delivery distance has increased from three to five kilometres. This has been accompanied by massive recruitment, meaning it is now quite common to spend several hours without any orders.
	Limiting courier autonomy	"I think that's one of the reasons why people are so angry about these changes is that it feels like a breach of the sort of the contract we had with them, which was about 'we accept that we don't have these certain rights, but we do have these freedoms' and to have those taken away. Yeah. It hits people and they feel it in that, in that level of that kind of breach of an unspoken contract kind of thing, yeah." I12

platform firms' decisions regarding *technology and communication design* undermined couriers' interests and the terms of the exchange initially presented. These are not explicitly political decisions (Feenberg, 2002), and their execution by impersonal algorithms can give the impression of impartiality. Yet these decisions were found to undermine the interests of our interviewees to the advantage of the platform firms. This second face of platform firms' power, nondecision-making power, thus encouraged a certain perception of the terms of the exchange for outsiders and newcomers, constituting a PC that was then experienced as breached in delivery by more experienced couriers.

Nondecision-making power is particularly concerned with communication and the way some issues come to be understood as political. Our interviews revealed three main mechanisms by which communication design disrupted couriers' identification of their own interests, the interests of the platform firm, and their potential conflicts: *impeding comparison*, *blocking communication*, and *excluding critique*. This in turn affected the development of each couriers' PC and their assessment of the degree to which it is upheld.

When asking couriers about their conditions and how these had developed over time, we were surprised to find a degree of uncertainty despite the apparent simplicity of the app-mediated economic exchange. This we traced to the ways in which platforms *impede comparison*. Complex and inconstant systems of pay tied to distance, demand, weather conditions and short-term incentives made it difficult for couriers to say with certainty how their remunerative opportunities had changed over time.

Table 4. Platforms' nondecision-making power.

ectors of power	Techniques	Supporting quotations
Communication design	Impeding comparison	"Personally, it's really hard to tell because it's quite opaque. [...] So this feeds into our statistics, which are about the priority for booking shifts. And I can see what my statistics are, but what the cut-off is to get into the top group is [...] fluid, and it's adjusted sort of dynamically both like over time and in different cities." I12
	Blocking communication	"You just don't want a complaint against your name because [P1]'s sort of firing policy ... you hear a lot of stories but there's very little out there to find out how people get in trouble or how to avoid getting in trouble. There's no sort of written warning or verbal warning system, like in a normal job. So, you're not really sure about how you're doing." I9
	Excluding critique	"There is no trust because we know that at the slightest fault they can fire us. It happens. And I know there are people who – either they protest or they complain about [P2] – and it happens. It's true because I saw the emails." I4
Technology design	Hidden incentives	"It's a bit tricky because when you say this is my last one and you're done with it, the app is gonna ask you 'Are you really sure you want to stop there?' And, one time, I was like ... ok, let's continue, just one last one and I had the biggest delivery of ... I guess it was like six kilometres each way. So yeah [laughs]! So now when I'm done, I'm done! I'm getting tricked by the application. That's why it really feels like a game." I8
	Excluding worker interests	"I'm sat in the restaurant waiting for food for say fifteen minutes [...] I'm getting paid zero for that time waiting. [...] Because the restaurants hasn't got the food ready and as far as I'm aware, there's no real procedure in place there to make the restaurant hurry up." I9

Similarly, in the above quotation, we can see that P1's performance requirements are perceived by couriers as opaque and ever-changing. Each courier is granted visibility on only a portion of their own performance statistics, leaving them guessing as to their vulnerability to sanction.

Uncertainty is compounded by *blocked communication*, whereby couriers experience the platform firm as "a black box" (I12) that does not explain or account for its unilateral decisions. In the above quotation, interviewee 9 explains that he is anxious to avoid provoking client complaints due to fear that he could lose his job without warning. Interviewee 2 indeed attested to being dismissed from P1 without warning or explanation. Similarly, interviewee 4 recounted losing a week of work when his P2 account was mistakenly blocked and repeated attempts to contact support were met with only automated responses. In this way, couriers' sense of vulnerability is exacerbated by lacking communication.

What is more, certain couriers we spoke to attribute some such dismissals to their own or others' criticism of the platforms. In the above quotation, interviewee 4 claims to have seen proof that a colleague was fired for protesting against P2. During the first authors' participant observation in Glasgow, couriers discussed dismissals they presumed to be connected to their activism, but highlighted the difficulty of proving such grounds when, for instance, P2's service contract claims the right to

Table 5. Platforms' ideological power.

Vectors of power	Techniques	Supporting quotations
Neoliberalism	Identification with capital	"It's not a lot of money either, but it can be if you put the effort into it. So it's all based on yourself. If you want to make money, it's there for you. If you don't want to make money and you're just lazy – well, not lazy, but if you don't give it 100% then you're not going to get much out of it to be honest. Which is fine for a lot of people." I3 "Without the platform you can't make that money. […] So for me it's legit and it's fair. They made the work, they should get paid for it." I7
	There is no alternative	"if they pay more, there will be more delivery people, and they will lower their prices. [laughs] it's impossible! Mechanically, economically speaking, it is impossible." I4
Tribalism	Scapegoating	"sorry, I don't want to be racist or anything - but these Romanian guys coming, signing up with the bicycle and they drive around in the car illegally delivering food. And I went into [P2]'s office and I said, like […] I'm almost the only driver with proper insurance in [city] and I see like all of these guys in the cars, […] and nothing, no one cares about it." I10

end the service relationship without explanation. These activist couriers also pointed to platforms' *exclusion of critique* by framing protestors and unions as radical external actors, illegitimate as representatives of couriers.

Nondecision-making power is also regularly wielded through the purportedly non-political design of technological tools (Stirling, 2008). Our data revealed two broad mechanisms by which technological design quietly undermined couriers' interests: *hidden incentives* and *excluding workers' interests*. Again, these operations shaped couriers' experience of their work, and thus their PCs with the platform firms.

We were struck by the high expectations our participants had of themselves, given the minimal obligations implied by the exchange as presented in the platform apps. Through the interviews we identified *hidden incentives* in the design of the platform apps, which can be experienced as obligations when couriers are financially dependent on platform work. The couriers we spoke to reported maintaining high work intensity to maximize their delivery speed and order acceptance rates, and avoiding taking time off, since the apps afford couriers only a limited window of visibility on their own performance statistics, and the platforms' algorithms for assigning work and determining sanctions are kept hidden. Interviewee 12 thus noted that "it's not like you have a hard target you're aiming for. You just have to aim for 100% and see how close you get." The platform apps' use of game dynamics to motivate work, or "gamification" (Woodcock & Johnson, 2018), additionally encourages prolonging working time and intensity, as illustrated by the above quotation from interviewee 8, who describes "getting tricked by the application," somewhat obscuring how this design specifically serves the platform firms' interests.

While the design of the applications perhaps conceals their service to platform firms' interests, our interviews point to a number of ways in which they simultaneously *exclude workers' interests*. In the above quotation from interviewee 9, we see that the interest workers have in prompt food preparation by restaurants, to minimize their unpaid waiting time, is perceived by some to be ignored in the design of the platform algorithms. Others highlighted how the app interface can induce customers and restaurants to forget the human labour behind the delivery: "because on a map it doesn't look that we're going fast. […] the app, I guess, disconnects people from the reality" (I8).

4.1.3. The third face of platform firms' power

Despite perceiving violations *via* the first and second faces of platform firms' power, however, some couriers continued to judge the terms of the exchange to be fair and to trust the platform firms to deliver these terms going forward. These couriers' accounts revealed the operation of the third face of power, ideological power, which conditioned workers' assessments of their own interests. We found two broad categories of ideological power in our data: *neoliberalism* and *tribalism*. These ideologies are widely prevalent in both UK and French discourse, and served to further the interests of the platform firms, whether or not they were intentionally mobilized by the firms themselves.

The force of neoliberal ideology in defending platform owners' interests amongst couriers is perhaps most obvious in cases of courier *identification with capital*. Some of our interviewees strongly identified as entrepreneurs, bolstered by their official work status as autoentrepreneurs, in France, and self-employed contractors, in the UK. These couriers thus tended to conceive of their relationship with platform firms as that between businesses, rather than employee and employer, arguably obscuring the relationship of power between these two parties. Interviewee 12, a union activist, noted the difficulty of organizing this subset of workers who identify as self-employed contractors and attribute great legitimacy to platforms' presentations of the economic rationality of their pay and conditions. The algorithmic management of the workers perhaps encouraged the view that platform apps afford delivery couriers direct access to the free market, with interviewee 7, for instance, describing P2 as "just an application in a smartphone that you can use to get some money."

Another set of couriers less inclined to see their interests and those of the platform as fully aligned nevertheless espoused a view, near-hegemonic in the UK and French contexts, that *there is no alternative*. The quotation from interviewee 4 above is particularly explicit on this point. Others came to this conclusion through considering what changes they might like to see in the exchange between themselves and the platforms, arguing, for instance, that any increase in support or security for couriers would necessarily require a return to the employment relationship and an end to valued flexibility (I6). Interviewee 8 sounded a particularly defeated note here, claiming "it's not right [...] but really, it's how the system works so you can't really do anything about it," and arguing against his protesting colleagues that "it's better to have a job with less security than every job than to not have a job."

Finally, animosity between courier groups – on the basis of ethnicity, immigration status or other forms of *tribalism* – arguably spared platforms some critique due to scapegoating of particular subsets of workers. For instance, some of our participants felt aggrieved that other workers were violating rules they themselves adhered to, presented in racialized terms in the above quotation from interviewee 10. Similarly, interviewee 6 expressed concern regarding "foreign" delivery workers operating in France without correct working visas. The UK union organizer acknowledged this divide, and noted that "the nature of the way the work's set up, and particularly the vehicle priority system, encourages that" (I12).

4.2. Couriers' coping strategies

How, then, do platform workers exercise agency in response to these forms of platform firms' power in shaping the terms of the exchange and how it is understood by both couriers and the general public? Withdrawal of labour is of course a key basis of power for workers in the individualized market interaction framework posited by platform firms (Cowen, 2017). It has certainly been reported that turnover for these jobs is high (Prassl, 2018). For this study, however, we focus on the coping strategies of those couriers who choose to continue with the exchange, interviewing only active platform workers.

We have seen that some interviewed workers, especially relatively new hires, accepted the fairness of the exchange as presented by the platform firms. Yet others, especially the more experienced in our sample, resisted the above-identified operations of power, calling out attempts at overt domination, masking of worker interests, and shaping of worker subjectivities. In this way couriers invoked, implicitly or explicitly, a standard of fairness against which to assess the PC.

4.2.1. Coping with the first face of platforms' power

In reviewing our interview data through the post-violation coping choices lens, we noticed that the majority of the strategies identified by

Tomprou *et al.* (2015) were deployed in response to platform firms' unilateral modification of exchange terms.

Under the category of *problem-focused coping*, we can identify couriers' direct attempts to repair the PC by asking platform firms to reverse explicit decisions and reinstate lost exchange terms. Whereas ordinarily a worker may approach a direct manager or other superior to voice their grievance and attempt to negotiate a return to the original exchange terms or the establishment of acceptable new terms, this problem-solving route is largely closed to platform workers. In Table 6, for instance, we see interviewee 1 recounting his frustrated attempts to communicate directly with the platform firm to achieve the pay increase he believed to be part of their exchange terms. In the absence of functioning direct communication channels, a few of the couriers we interviewed (I11, I12) became involved in protest actions, some of which were successful in reinstituting the original exchange. However, these successes were often limited and temporary, prompting couriers to attempt to rebalance the exchange in other ways.

Aligning with the category of *emotion-focused coping*, we observed numerous instances of couriers rationalizing violations of their PCs. In some cases, this was attributable to a short period of experience – interviewees 3, 6, 7 and 8 had not been working for their respective platforms long enough to personally encounter a modification of terms, though interviewee 6 had few illusions entering the exchange as his brother had lost a month's pay when another delivery platform fell into bankruptcy without warning the year before. Other couriers (I2, I5 and I9) presented decreases in pay and increases in demands as adjustments to a fair exchange from an overly generous and economically unsustainable initial offering. Justifying P2's increase of the supply of couriers, reducing each courier's earning abilities, interviewee 8 argued:

> *"It would be better if [P2] were restricting the amount of riders. But they don't really mind because for them, the more riders they have, the better it is because they will never have a time when there is a delivery and no one will take it. I mean, I guess it's the fact that we are really free in our work."*

In this way, these couriers modify their original understanding of what a fair exchange would be so as to accommodate the discrepancy between the PC and the actual exchange.

Yet others acknowledged that their original PC had been violated, and described responses aligning with *behavioural disengagement*. This can be realized as exit intention, which we identified in interviewees 10 and 12. However more common amongst the couriers we spoke to was balancing, or withdrawal of effort (Tomprou *et al.*, 2015). This can be understood as a means of repairing the PC by rebalancing the worker's side of the exchange directly. Interviewee 10, for instance, describes colleagues making themselves available for work on multiple platforms

Table 6. Couriers' responses to platform firms' decision-making power.

Coping approach	Specific strategy	Supporting quotations
Problem-focused coping	Direct appeals	"So recently I've tried to negotiate my contract up to six euro per delivery instead of five. But since there's no office I can call I'm met with the normal shield of, just, delayed responses. Like they use Zendesk or something like that, so immediately when you send a message they say 'great, we're going to get working on this' and then you hear nothing about it. And then sometimes after a couple of weeks the ticket is obviously closed cause you get a 'how satisfied were you with our response?' but nothing has happened." – I1
	Protest	Involved in wildcat strikes which temporarily stalled Delivery P1's announced elimination of couriers' shift-based hourly pay – I11
Emotion-focused coping	Accommodation	"I guess I've had a few invoices [where] there's a few missing or they've got it wrong, but it only takes one email to say this is my record and this is yours and this is where I think you're wrong." – I3 "You could say it's great being self-employed, it's great coming to work whenever you want. But it's much better to have a rough idea of how many are gonna be on the road and then hopefully [Delivery Platform 1] can get the right number of riders out there to make enough money that we aspired to make that day." – I9
Behavioural disengagement	Exit intention	"the bad bit is you don't get holiday payment [...], which really annoys me, and that's why I start looking for a job again because I think I'm going to go back managing coffee shops." I10
	Balancing	"I started being more relaxed with it and also doing things that would possibly not be seen very well in the eyes of the company. Like faking my location and signing up for shifts that I knew I wasn't going to have to work but I would get paid for, things like this. [...] Because they have shown no loyalty to me so I've become disillusioned with them, and I wasn't very illusioned in the beginning [laughs]." I1

simultaneously "because no one of the platforms are guaranteed for you – no guaranteed wage per hour, per day, even per week." Alternatively, withdrawal of effort can be an expression of rejection of a perceived unfair exchange. In the above table, interviewee 1 speaks of his perception that P1 showed him no loyalty, and uses this to justify exploiting loopholes in the design of the platform app. This perception of unfairness can be rooted in platform firms' explicit decisions – the unilateral modifications of exchange terms we reviewed in relation to the first face of power – or the more implicit technological and communication design decisions we argue belong to the second face of power.

4.2.2. Coping with the second face of platforms' power

Some couriers indeed cope with perceived violations rooted in platform firms' nondecision-making power by exploiting the communication and technology design itself. Through trial and error, interviewee 1 claimed to have "worked out how the algorithm works" and recounted tricks he used to maximize his earnings while minimizing effort. Others, like

Table 7. Couriers' responses to platform firms' nondecision-making power.

Coping approach	Specific strategy	Supporting quotations
Behavioural disengagement	Balancing	"There are ways of circumventing the system [...] so the way the app works, if you've used it for a while you figure out how you can get around things." I1 "Often what people do is they use a scooter – they take a photo of a bicycle, sent it to [P2] and after use the scooter." I4
Unveiling political interests	Unveiling platform interests behind nondecisions	"I think that's part of the advantage for the company because they can have this sort of panopticon effect, this self-policing effect, because you don't know how you're doing – it makes you paranoid." I1 "pay has been steadily going down - every few months, they'll update their pay calculations, and they'll be updated downwards. But it's always a little bit complicated. So [...] they've adjusted the pay system so as to pay us more for the longer journeys but to pay us less for the shorter journeys. And most people fear that overall they're seeing their pay go down as a result, and like right from the start that was the assumption, that that was what they were playing at." I12

interviewee 4, noted the possibility of flouting rules due to the limitations of algorithmic surveillance. This subversion was in part facilitated by forums that allowed for the pooling of experience and sharing of tricks among vast numbers of couriers, though discussion in porous online spaces perhaps also facilitated platform firms in identifying and closing such loopholes. Activist couriers noted the importance of comparisons between cities and countries in identifying platform firms' upcoming moves in this arms race.

The coping strategies we could observe were much more circumscribed in relation to this face of power, however. This is unsurprising, as nondecision-making power is precisely power that operates by obscuring the fact that a particular decision is political, that the design serves one party's interests over another's (Lukes, 2005). However we did identify a response to this second face of power in our participants' accounts that was not accounted for within the post-violation coping framework put forward by Tomprou *et al.* (2015): *unveiling political interests* behind the "nondecisions" of communication and technology design. Many of the couriers we spoke to expressed suspicion or outright cynicism regarding the platform interests underlying their communication and technology designs. Above, we see interviewee 1 identifying a "panopticon effect" of the opacity of platform algorithms, requiring couriers to self-police to the platform firms' advantage. Interviewee 12 similarly suggests that the complex and ever-changing systems for determining courier pay amount to intentional obfuscation which fails to hide from the majority of couriers the reality of declining rates. The activist couriers we spoke to worked to disabuse their colleagues of the belief that failures to pay bonuses or full fees were honest mistakes, arguing that, while platform firms present themselves as "bumbling, naive

Table 8. Couriers' responses to platform firms' ideological power.

Coping approach	Specific strategy	Supporting quotations
Unveiling political interests	Unveiling platform interests behind self-employed status	"the very nature of being self-employed these guys have chosen those flexible jobs. And suddenly it's not so flexible anymore because you have to work Friday, Saturday, Sunday night [laughs] - it's just really hard! It's really hard isn't it?" I9 "They don't say how many riders they have, they don't want to tell anything about this but they have huge amounts of riders. So, if one rider gets injured, they don't care. Because they don't have to give us anything if we get injured [...] they don't have to give us money for the time we can't work." I8
	Identifying alternative possibilities	"I think they should adjust when we are in the period of underpay, because when we have no orders we wait in the streets and we're still in the job. [...] so I think they should address the moments when we have no orders [...] like, uh, if we have no orders in one hour we can be paid 5 per hour and it can be adjusted with the moment when we work a lot." I2
	Unveiling platform interests behind tribalism	"I don't know how to say this, but people who are much less malleable – there are people of foreign nationality coming in and they are ready to work for two or three euros an hour, so it suits [P2] a lot." I4
	Fostering resistant solidarity	"the nature of our work puts us up against restaurant staff quite a lot. And the frustrations of waiting for orders. But I feel like when there are discussions about organizing strikes, we've successfully sort of put forward that argument that we don't take it out on the workers and that we seek solidarity with them." I12

start-ups" (I12), these supposed software errors are to be viewed with scepticism. In this way, couriers attempted to unveil the platform firms' interests underlying supposedly non-political decisions regarding software and communication design, identifying points of conflict with couriers' interests, and exposing the managing algorithms' partiality.

4.2.3. Coping with the third face of platforms' power

The *unveiling political interests* response was particularly prominent regarding platform firms' ideological power, with many of our participants discursively resisting, to varying degrees, the ideologies invoked and depended upon by the platform firms.

The issue of employment status was one key entry point here, with objections raised ranging from tentative questioning, as in interviewee 9's consideration of the implications of limited flexibility, to outright rejection: "them sending me payslips that're called invoices, calling me a partner, all these things – just an obvious attempt to obscure the fact that I'm an employee" (I1). Interviewee 8, while generally enthusiastic about his work for P2, recognizes the platform firms' interest in using the independent contractor relationship to deny responsibility for couriers' health and safety. This line of inquiry was perhaps assisted by multiple contemporaneous legal challenges to this designation in both countries (Butler, 2018; Jacqué, 2018), pointing to the availability of an alternative understanding and undermining the ideological force of the couriers' self-employed status.

Some of the couriers we spoke to did resist the *no alternative* ideology by identifying possible improvements to the exchange, even those not yet provided for in either of the two legal contexts here studied. Interviewee 2, above, highlights his dissatisfaction with the risk borne by couriers for periods of low demand, and suggests potential ways for mitigating the individualization of risk. Interviewee 10 expressed concern regarding the financial burden borne by couriers in periods of sickness or incapacity, and proposed platform firms might provide some income support during these times, pegged to couriers' work for the platform.

Finally, in opposition to the ideologies of tribalism that pit workers against one another, we found evidence of both spontaneous and cultivated worker solidarity. Couriers like interviewee 4 recognized, for instance, the difficult position of migrant workers, and the platform interest in fostering a race to the bottom in terms of courier pay. From the labour organizing perspective, interviewee 12 highlighted successful efforts of unions to foster solidarity amongst different subsets of couriers (bicycle and scooter, migrant and non-migrant) and with other workers, such as restaurant staff. This view is at least partly corroborated by the degree of support shared amongst couriers, who often expressed surprise at the solidarity amongst couriers: "No one has to do that, we are all self-employed, they don't have to help – but people do and I'll do it the same for them" (I5).

5. Discussion

In line with our aim of exploiting the critical potential of PC theory to disentangle the power relations underlying platform work, we consider how the coping approaches here identified variously reify and resist the naturalization of risk individualization advanced by platform firms. Figure 1 offers a simplified illustration of how couriers' coping approaches interact with platform firms' three faces of power.

In terms of coping approaches that tend to reinforce platform firms' power, *accommodation* is the least ambiguous. This approach involves "reframing or rationalizing the breach event" (Bankins, 2015, p. 1075), thereby drawing within the realm of fair exchanges both platform firms' unilateral modifications of the terms of the exchange and design choices that disadvantage platform workers. In contrast, coping approaches that unambiguously resist platforms' power include *direct appeals* and *protests*,

	Platform firms' power			
	Decision-making power	Nondecision-making power	Ideological power	
Couriers' coping approaches	Unilateral modification of exchange terms	Communication and technology design	Neoliberal ideology	Tribalism
Direct appeals	–	–		
Protest	–			
Accommodation	+	+		
Balancing	+/–	+/–	+	
Exit intention	–	–	+	
Unveiling platform interests		–	–	–
Identifying alternative possibilities		–	–	
Fostering resistant solidarity		+	–	–

Resistance: –
Reinforcement: +

Figure 1. Couriers' resistance to platform firms' ideological power.

which address platforms' decision-making power head-on. In contrast to accommodation, these approaches require that the worker identify PC violations, generally articulated in terms of fairness, referring to a normative standard at odds with that advocated by the platform firms.

Furthermore, by leading couriers to uncover the political interest behind platforms' purportedly neutral communication and technology designs, direct appeals also undermine platform firms' nondecision-making power. As our interviews portray, couriers' communications with platform firms were quite effectively blocked, with queries regarding payment or problems routed through the app or contact centres that often offered only automated responses. Couriers therefore turned to one another, especially *via* online forums, to compare experiences and thereby deduce the effects and interests behind nondecisions. The coping approach of direct appeals thus tended in this context to lead to the *unveiling of platform interests*. As Duggan *et al.* (2020, p. 121) note, algorithmic management "facilitates asymmetric information in the working relationship," impeding fairness assessments. Furthermore, platforms' communication designs arguably aim at hiding information from couriers, thereby reinforcing "unbalanced power relations in the labor process, because capital can track what labor is doing while labor may not see capital's designs" (Chai & Scully, 2019, p. 948). Couriers undermined this power by rendering such nondecisions visible and subject to critique, thereby enabling more accurate fairness assessments.

Couriers' *identification of alternative possibilities* similarly demonstrates the political interest behind nondecision-making power, and also undermines hegemonic ideology. By internalizing worker demands for autonomy, but tying the delivery of this condition to the undermining of worker income and job security, platform firms "repurpose" the idea of autonomy (Gandini, 2019, p. 1051) and thus "disarm critique by depriving it of its argument" (Daudigeos *et al.*, 2019, p. 1). The classification of couriers as self-employed or "autoentrepreneurs" aides the internalization of this ideology and is a core mechanism of the third face of power, supporting the individualization of risk (Duggan *et al.*, 2020). Studies of other platform workers, such as Uber taxi drivers, have found evidence of internalization of this discourse of individual responsibility as a way to claim control in an economic context of precarity (Peticca-Harris *et al.*, 2020). A precondition of recognizing their political interests as workers is thus for couriers to identify alternative possible configurations – of communication and technology design, and of economic relations – that resist the false dichotomy of autonomy and security.

By contrast, some coping approaches are arguably ambivalent towards platform firms' power. In *balancing*, couriers modify their efforts to rebalance the terms of the exchange, thereby claiming greater autonomy than platform firms officially permit. As we saw in our above findings, this is often facilitated by revealing lacunae in supervision and loopholes in platform apps that couriers can exploit to their own advantage. The limited reach of algorithmic surveillance at once renders algorithmic management less accurate and fair because it cannot account for "contextual and embodied information about the experiences of working" (Newlands, 2020, p. 2), and *yet al*so permits scope for resistance given the practical constraints on how effectively platforms can utilize "the mountain of monitoring information with which they are now provided" (Brown & Korczynski, 2010, p. 406). Nevertheless, by rebalancing the exchange in these ways, couriers do the work of rendering palatable what is often otherwise an unfair exchange. What is more, these workers make themselves vulnerable to sanctions thereby enhancing the risk they bear individually.

Exit intention, similarly, can be understood as a form of resistance, while simultaneously aligning with an ideology of labour exchange as free contracting between equals. Through exit, or the intention to exit, workers communicate their dissatisfaction with the terms of the exchange, as set down through platform firms' decision- and nondecision-making power. Yet this "vote with your feet" approach to labour relations is itself an aspect of neoliberal ideology, which obscures the structural inequality of the contracting parties (Anderson, 2017).

Fostering resistant solidarity also arguably displays this dual character. This coping approach is indeed resistant to the individualizing ideologies of neoliberalism and tribalism. Recent research has highlighted the unexpected ways in which the labour process of food delivery platform work, in particular, facilitates the solidarity needed to counter discourses of individualized responsibility (Tassinari & Maccarrone, 2020). Many of our participants assist and support one another despite self-identifying as independent entrepreneurs, materializing resistance to a discourse of competition between individual economic units. Yet by filling the gaps in platform firms' provisions of support to couriers, it too can function to smooth the exchange.

As we have seen from our findings above, individual couriers utilize multiple coping approaches, both sequentially and simultaneously. Of course these coping approaches are not selected by workers on purely political grounds, but in response to a pragmatic need to (re)institute a functioning PC to enable a continuing economic exchange (Bankins, 2015). Figure 2 illustrates the coping approaches adopted by each of our participants[2], placing these within the repair phase of the dynamic PC model (Rousseau *et al.*, 2018), and connecting each to the consequences for the PC predicted by that literature.

Our findings suggest that many ordinary routes towards violation resolution, such as negotiation of remedies or promises of substitute benefits (Rousseau *et al.*, 2018), are blocked *a priori*. Tomprou *et al.* argue that, in cases where a worker "fails to perceive any opportunities toward re-engaging in a new agreement with the employer," PC dissolution is likely (2015, p. 572). However, whereas workers with "[n]on-work resources such as alternative job opportunities […] and external funds" (Tomprou *et al.*, 2015, p. 574) may respond to PC dissolution by exiting the exchange, the couriers we spoke to who perceived PC violation nevertheless continued the exchange. This continuation seemed to be attributable to the paucity of acceptable alternative work options consistent with their requirements for autonomy and the flexibility to focus on extra-work interests, including political organizing and education.

For some, such as interviewees 2, 5 and 9, the felt necessity of continuing the exchange arguably motivated rationalization of PC violation, ultimately aligning the couriers' views of what counts as a fair exchange with the accounts advanced by platform firms. For others, such as interviewee 10, it led to short-term acceptance of limited violation resolution and a new, impaired PC, with the intention to pursue alternative work opportunities. Yet for a final group, including interviewees 1, 11 and 12,

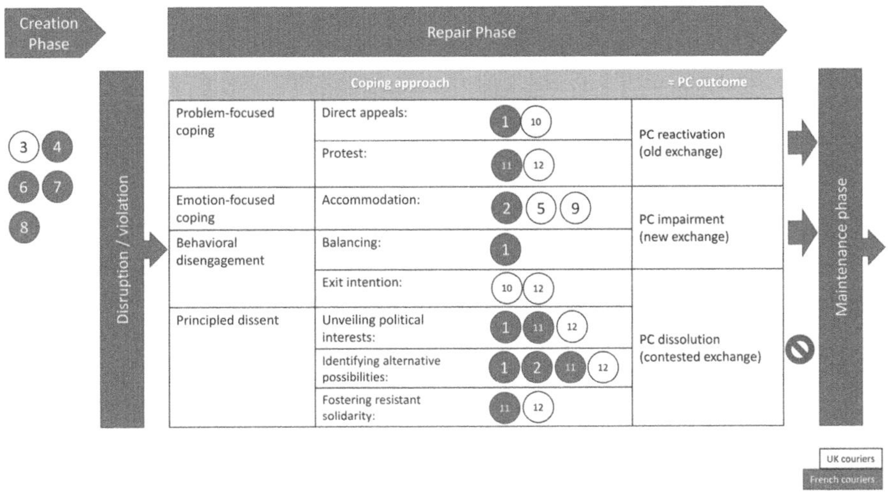

Figure 2. Couriers' coping strategies.

the fact that exchange with these platform firms continued to be the best of their options did not lead them to conclude that the exchange was fair. This response mirrors the "principled dissent" observed by Krause and Moore (2018). In place of the pure mental disengagement posited by Tomprou *et al.* (2015), principled dissent combines the cynical attitude characteristic of mental disengagement with nevertheless earnest attempts "to restore the company to its prior operating practices" (Krause & Moore, 2018, p. 274), including strategies such as "direct resistance, confrontation, and/or 'back door' ways of working" (p. 269). In this response, the worker does not really anticipate reactivation of the original PC – whether because the violation has endured for multiple years, as in the case presented by Krause and Moore (2018), or due to a recognition of or cynicism regarding the broader strategy adopted by the firm, as in the case of food delivery platform firms. Instead, it is an ideological commitment that motivates these workers to resist discursive constructions of the new exchange terms as "fair" and to push for realization of the promised exchange where possible. Rousseau *et al.* (2018, p. 1083) note that the perceived obligations that constitute a worker's PC are rooted in expectations, and these expectations can be either probabilistic or normative. The idea of simultaneous PC dissolution and maintenance, suggested by Krause and Moore (2018) and again indicated in our analysis of principled dissent amongst the couriers studied here, implies the potential for fruitful inquiry into the possibility of multiple simultaneously held PCs as a tool for resisting firms' construction of risk individualization as a normatively valid realization of worker autonomy, while nevertheless achieving what autonomy is possible amongst the presently available options through a functioning pragmatic PC, based on probabilistic expectations.

6. Conclusion

In this paper, we have drawn on 12 semi-structured interviews with food delivery couriers, supplemented by both online and offline participant observation, to identify ways in which platform firms use decision-making, nondecision-making and ideological power (Lukes, 2005) to encourage the acceptance of this form of work as fair. We examine how platform workers cope with violations of their PCs, and how these coping approaches are variously resistant to and reinforcing of platform firms' power. We identify one coping approach, principled dissent (Krause & Moore, 2018), which arguably allows workers to continue the exchange so as to achieve the limited worker autonomy available within the current configuration without necessarily endorsing as "fair" the terms proposed by platform firms. In so doing, we highlight the potential of PC theorizing as a form of critique.

This paper responds to calls for a more critical approach to PC theorizing (Cullinane & Dundon, 2006; Dick & Nadin, 2011), and adds to recent literature regarding how workers cope with PC violations, actively adjusting their expectations and behaviour in response (Bankins, 2015; Krause & Moore, 2018; Tomprou *et al.*, 2015). In addition, by adopting an insider position as a food delivery courier in the sensitization step, the first author generated within herself some of the cognitive tensions of trying to make sense of these exchanges, and was thus able to mobilize introspection as a tool for identifying avenues for more robust investigation. This arguably mitigated, if imperfectly, the othering risks associated with theorizing regarding ideology and false consciousness (Žižek, 1989). At the same time, this insider identity was moderated by the outsider perspective of the second author, permitting a degree of "critical distance from insider assumptions" (Reedy *et al.*, 2016, p. 1559).

We also contribute to the sub-stream within the PC literature that applies the PC framework to relationships beyond those of direct employment (Bankins *et al.*, 2020; Guest, 2004; Marsden, 2004; McLean Parks *et al.*, 1998; Sherman & Morley, 2020; Wilkens & Nermerich, 2011). We have here suggested how some qualitative measures of a worker's PC can be modified (see Annex 1). Nevertheless, the specific context of internet- and app-mediated labour exchange relationships calls for further refinement of PC measurement tools and theorizing, following cues from, for example, Sherman and Morley (2020).

We acknowledge that our small sample size limits the generalisability of our claims within the set of platform workers, and we recognize its bias towards the perspectives of young, non-migrant, able-bodied men with limited caring responsibilities. These characteristics moderate the types of discourses our participants bring to bear on questions of the fairness of their work. However, a close reading of particular workers' subjective interpretations of these exchanges and their development is an important element in critically evaluating the fairness claims of new forms for work, alongside other avenues of investigation (Dick & Nadin, 2011). Future research might fruitfully address the perspectives of atypical platform workers, as well as those who have exited platform work, to augment the perspectives presented here and shed light on how platform work experiences shape workers' expectations in future exchanges.

Another area for future research highlighted by this paper's findings is the possibility of multiple simultaneously operational PCs, based on normative obligations and probabilistic expectations. Rousseau *et al.* (2018, p. 1083) note that "[t]his distinction has not been a focus in PC research [although] it is relevant to understanding how obligations and expectations are interrelated." Both the findings presented here and those of Krause and Moore (2018) suggest that this separability may be a result of the labour exchange continuing subsequent to PC dissolution on the basis of principled dissent. Yet more focused research would be necessary to confirm this possibility, and explore whether it is limited to cases of post-dissolution engagement.

This study has focused on the relationship between the delivery courier and the platform firm, yet app-work is importantly characterized by multi-party relationships, as the platform mediates interaction between the worker, the end-customer, and often also suppliers (i.e. restaurants, in the case of food delivery platforms) (Duggan *et al.*, 2020). Marks (2001) proposed that employees in traditional organizations, too, generally maintain PCs with multiple exchange partners, including superiors, work groups, unions and customers. Sherman and Morley (2020) have emphasized the importance of this expansion of the PC concept in the platform work context specifically, given that each party to the platform-mediated exchange must relate with two or three independent parties. They highlight interactions between these relationships as an important topic of study, noting how, in the case of food delivery platform work, "the courier's relationship with Deliveroo is significantly contingent on the customer being happy with how the restaurant has prepared the food, [and] the restaurateur's psychological contract with Deliveroo is contingent on them recruiting and managing competent couriers, and so on" (2020, p. 4). The present study suggests that these various relationships will be marked by explicit and implicit operations of power, and these various power relations will similarly overlap and intersect. We would thus welcome future research applying the above power framework to these multiple relationships.

Finally, while our findings are specific to food delivery app-work, and thus cannot be easily generalized to other forms of app-mediated labour exchange, we submit that the discourses regarding flexible work advanced in this context are influential in broader societal conversations regarding the status of platform work, the individualization of risk and what counts as a fair exchange between workers and firms. The implications of these discourses are not limited to platform work, but indeed extend to more traditional employee-employer relationships that are becoming increasingly precarious and digitally-mediated, connected to the wider adoption of algorithmic management elements (Andonova, 2019; Petriglieri *et al.*, 2019). Our findings regarding the operation of nondecision-making power through these apparently impartial technological tools is therefore of broader relevance to HRM practitioners. By drawing attention to the politics of such seemingly neutral technology and communication design, our findings may assist those practitioners who wish to develop tools that are fairer and more transparent, thereby fostering greater alignment between workers and firms regarding the content and fulfilment of exchange obligations.

Notes

1. See Annex 1 for a full list of interview questions, sources and modification rationales.
2. For this analysis, we separated out those participants arguably still establishing their initial conception of the exchange, having three or fewer months of experience with food delivery platform work at the time of interview (based on the contention that the PC creation phase lasts for three months, Rousseau et al., 2018). While these couriers – I3, I4, I6, I7 and I8 – do demonstrate some of the above-discussed coping responses, this can be understood as part of the PC calibration process. The remaining seven participants had longer tenure at the time of interview, and thus were able to detail clear moments of PC violation and their responses, corresponding to the repair phase of the dynamic model of the PC (Rousseau et al., 2018).

Acknowledgements

We would like to thank wholeheartedly the study participants who generously shared their time and insights regarding their work. We are also thankful to participants of the International Working Party on Labour Market Segmentation conference at the University of Manchester (2017), the MOTI seminar at the Grenoble Ecole de Management (2017), the Insecurity for One is Insecurity for All colloquium organized by the Work, Labour and Globalisation network at Strathclyde Business School (2018), and the SASE conference at the New School, New York (2019), for their feedback on earlier versions of the paper. Finally, we thank the guest editors and the three anonymous reviewers for their invaluable suggestions, guidance, and encouragements.

Disclosure statement

No potential conflict of interest was reported by the author(s).

Funding

This work was supported by the European Union's Seventh Framework Programme for Research, Technological Development and Demonstration under Grant Agreement no. 613256 (http://www.style-research.eu).

Data availability statement

The data that support the findings of this study are available from the first author upon reasonable request.

References

Acquier, A., Daudigeos, T., & Pinkse, J. (2017). Promises and paradoxes of the sharing economy: An organizing framework. *Technological Forecasting and Social Change*, *125*, 1–10. https://doi.org/10.1016/j.techfore.2017.07.006

Amis, J. M., & Silk, M. L. (2008). The philosophy and politics of quality in qualitative organizational research. *Organizational Research Methods*, *11*(3), 456–480. https://doi.org/10.1177/1094428107300341

Anderson, E. (2017). *Private Government: How Employers Rule Our Lives (and Why We Don't Talk about It)*. Princeton University Press.

Andonova, Y. (2019). Algorithmic management, organizational changes and the digitalization of hr practices: A critical perspective. In È. George (Ed.), *Digitalization of Society and Socio-political Issues 1* (pp. 27–37). ISTE Ltd and John Wiley & Sons, Inc. https://doi.org/10.1002/9781119687177.ch3

Bachrach, P., & Baratz, M. S. (1970). *Power and Poverty: Theory and Practice*. Oxford University Press.

Bankins, S. (2011). Tracking employees' twists and turns: Describing a mixed methods approach to assessing change in the psychological contract. *International Journal of Multiple Research Approaches*, *5*(3), 351–366. https://doi.org/10.5172/mra.2011.5.3.351

Bankins, S. (2015). A process perspective on psychological contract change: Making sense of, and repairing, psychological contract breach and violation through employee coping actions. *Journal of Organizational Behavior*, *36*(8), 1071–1095. https://doi.org/10.1002/job.2007

Bankins, S., Griep, Y., & Hansen, S. D. (2020). Charting directions for a new research era: Addressing gaps and advancing scholarship in the study of psychological contracts. *European Journal of Work and Organizational Psychology*, *29*(2), 159–163. https://doi.org/10.1080/1359432X.2020.1737219

Belfrage, C., & Hauf, F. (2017). The gentle art of retroduction: Critical realism, cultural political economy and critical grounded theory. *Organization Studies*, *38*(2), 251–271. https://doi.org/10.1177/0170840616663239

Berg, J. (2016). *Income security in the on-demand economy: Findings and policy lessons from a survey of crowdworkers. ILO Conditions of work and employment series.* Retrieved from https://www.ilo.org/travail/whatwedo/publications/WCMS_479693/lang–en/index.htm

Boltanski, L., & Chiapello, E. (2017). *The New Spirit of Capitalism* (G. Elliott, Trans.). Verso.

Brown, K., & Korczynski, M. (2010). When caring and surveillance technology meet: Organizational commitment and discretionary effort in home care work. *Work and Occupations*, *37*(3), 404–432. https://doi.org/10.1177/0730888410373875

Butler, S. ((2018)., June 28). Deliveroo couriers win six-figure payout in employment rights case. *The Guardian*. Retrieved from https://www.theguardian.com/business/2018/jun/28/deliveroo-couriers-win-six-figure-payout-in-employment-rights-case

Cant, C. (2020). *Riding for Deliveroo: Resistance in the New Economy*. Polity Press.

Chai, S., & Scully, M. A. (2019). It's about distributing rather than sharing: Using labor process theory to probe the "sharing" economy. *Journal of Business Ethics*, *159*(4), 943–960. https://doi.org/10.1007/s10551-019-04210-y

Conway, N., & Briner, R. B. (2005). *Understanding Psychological Contracts at Work: A Critical Evaluation of Theory and Research*. Oxford University Press.

Cowen, T. (2017). Work Isn't So Bad After All. In E. Anderson (Ed.), *Private Government: How Employers Rule Our Lives (and Why We Don't Talk about It)* (pp. 108–118). Princeton University Press.

Coyle-Shapiro, J., & Kessler, I. (2000). Consequences of the psychological contract for the employment relationship: A large scale survey. *Journal of Management Studies*, *37*(7), 903–930. https://doi.org/10.1111/1467-6486.00210

Coyle-Shapiro, J., & Kessler, I. (2002a). Contingent and non-contingent work in local government: Contrasts in psychological contracts. *Public Administration*, *80*(1), 77–101. https://doi.org/10.1111/1467-9299.00295

Coyle-Shapiro, J., & Kessler, I. (2002b). Exploring reciprocity through the lens of the psychological contract: Employee and employer perspectives. *European Journal of Work and Organizational Psychology*, *11*(1), 69–86. https://doi.org/10.1080/13594320143000852

Cullinane, N., & Dundon, T. (2006). The psychological contract: A critical review. *International Journal of Management Reviews*, *8*(2), 113–129. https://doi.org/10.1111/j.1468-2370.2006.00123.x

Cunliffe, A. L., & Karunanayake, G. (2013). Working within hyphen-spaces in ethnographic research: Implications for research identities and practice. *Organizational Research Methods*, *16*(3), 364–392. https://doi.org/10.1177/1094428113489353

Daudigeos, T., Edwards, T., Jaumier, S., Pasquier, V., & Picard, H. (2019). Elusive domination and the fate of critique in neo-participative management: A French pragmatist approach. *Organization Studies*, (OnlineFirst), 017084061985602–017084061985638. https://doi.org/10.1177/0170840619856027

Dick, P., & Nadin, S. (2011). Exploiting the exploited: The psychological contract, workplace domination and symbolic violence. *Culture and Organization*, *17*(4), 293–311. https://doi.org/10.1080/14759551.2011.590306

Duggan, J., Sherman, U., Carbery, R., & McDonnell, A. (2020). Algorithmic management and app-work in the gig economy: A research agenda for employment relations and HRM. *Human Resource Management Journal*, *30*(1), 114–132. https://doi.org/10.1111/1748-8583.12258

Eisenberger, R., Huntington, R., Hutchison, S., & Sowa, D. (1986). Perceived organizational support. *Journal of Applied Psychology, 71*(3), 500–507. https://doi.org/10.1037/0021-9010.71.3.500

Fairclough, N. (2005). Discourse analysis in organization studies: The case for critical realism. *Organization Studies, 26*(6), 915–939. https://doi.org/10.1177/0170840605054610

Feenberg, A. (2002). *Transforming Technology: A Critical Theory Revisited.* Oxford University Press.

Fereday, J., & Muir-Cochrane, E. (2006). Demonstrating rigor using thematic analysis: A hybrid approach of inductive and deductive coding and theme development. *International Journal of Qualitative Methods, 5*(1), 80–92. https://doi.org/10.1177/160940690600500107

Finlay, L. (2005). Reflexive embodied empathy: A phenomenology of participant-researcher intersubjectivity. *The Humanistic Psychologist, 33*(4), 271–292. https://doi.org/10.1207/s15473333thp3304_4

Fortin, M., & Fellenz, M. R. (2008). Hypocrisies of fairness: Towards a more reflexive ethical base in organizational justice research and practice. *Journal of Business Ethics, 78*(3), 415–433. https://doi.org/10.1007/s10551-006-9330-z

Friedman, G. (2014). Workers without employers: Shadow corporations and the rise of the gig economy. *Review of Keynesian Economics, 2*(2), 171–188. https://doi.org/10.4337/roke.2014.02.03

Gandini, A. (2019). Labour process theory and the gig economy. *Human Relations, 72*(6), 1039–1056. https://doi.org/10.1177/0018726718790002

Gill, M. J. (2014). The possibilities of phenomenology for organizational research. *Organizational Research Methods, 17*(2), 118–137. https://doi.org/10.1177/1094428113518348

Goudin, P. (2016). *The Cost of Non-Europe in the Sharing Economy.* European Parliamentary Research Service. https://doi.org/10.2861/26238

Guest, D. (2004). Flexible employment contracts, the psychological contract and employee outcomes: An analysis and review of the evidence. *International Journal of Management Reviews, 5-6*(1), 1–19. https://doi.org/10.1111/j.1460-8545.2004.00094.x

Jacqué, P. (2018). December 1). Uber, Deliveroo… Cet arrêt de la Cour de cassation qui inquiète les plates-formes numériques. *Le Monde.* Retrieved from https://www.lemonde.fr/economie/article/2018/12/01/uber-deliveroo-cet-arret-de-la-cour-de-cassation-qui-inquiete-les-plates-formes-numeriques_5391259_3234.html

Kalanick, T. (2015). October). The Future of Work: Independence and Flexibility. *Pacific Standard.* Retrieved from https://psmag.com/economics/the-future-of-work-independence-and-flexibility

Krause, A. J., & Moore, S. Y. (2018). Working in imbalance: How employees revise their psychological contracts in a post-breach environment. *Employee Responsibilities and Rights Journal, 30*(4), 253–278. https://doi.org/10.1007/s10672-018-9321-0

Lukes, S. (2005). *Power: A Radical View.* (2nd Edn). Palgrave Macmillan.

Marsden, D. (2004). The "network economy" and models of the employment contract. *British Journal of Industrial Relations, 42*(4), 659–684. https://doi.org/10.1111/j.1467-8543.2004.00335.x

McCarthy, L., Touboulic, A., & Matthews, L. (2018). Voiceless but empowered farmers in corporate supply chains: Contradictory imagery and instrumental approach to empowerment. *Organization, 25*(5), 609–635. https://doi.org/10.1177/1350508418763265

McLean Parks, J., Kidder, D. L., & Gallagher, D. G. (1998). Fitting square pegs into round holes: mapping the domain of contingent work arrangements onto the psychological contract. *Journal of Organizational Behavior, 19*(S1), 697–730. https://doi.org/10.1002/(SICI)1099-1379(1998)19:1+<697::AID-JOB974>3.0.CO;2-I

Newlands, G. (2020). Algorithmic surveillance in the gig economy: The organisation of work through Lefebvrian conceived space. *Organization Studies*, (OnlineFirst). https://doi.org/10.1177/0170840620937900

Paechter, C. (2013). Researching sensitive issues online: Implications of a hybrid insider/outsider position in a retrospective ethnographic study. *Qualitative Research, 13*(1), 71–86. https://doi.org/10.1177/1468794112446107

Papadimitropoulos, E. (2019). Beyond neoliberalism: Digitization, freedom and the workplace. *Ephemera, 19*(3), 565–589.

Pasquale, F. (2015). *The Black Box Society.* Harvard University Press.

Peticca-Harris, A., DeGama, N., & Ravishankar, M. N. (2020). Postcapitalist precarious work and those in the 'drivers' seat: Exploring the motivations and lived experiences of Uber drivers in Canada. *Organization, 27*(1), 36–59. https://doi.org/10.1177/1350508418757332

Petriglieri, G., Ashford, S. J., & Wrzesniewski, A. (2019). Agony and Ecstasy in the Gig Economy: Cultivating Holding Environments for Precarious and Personalized Work Identities. *Administrative Science Quarterly, 64*(1), 124–170. https://doi.org/10.1177/0001839218759646

Picard, H., & Islam, G. (2020). Free to Do What I Want'? Exploring the ambivalent effects of liberating leadership. *Organization Studies, 41*(3), 393–414. https://doi.org/10.1177/0170840618814554

Prassl, J. (2018). *Humans as a Service: The Promise and Perils of Work in the Gig Economy.* Oxford University Press.

Reedy, P., King, D., & Coupland, C. (2016). Organizing for Individuation: Alternative Organizing, Politics and New Identities. *Organization Studies, 37*(11), 1553–1573. https://doi.org/10.1177/0170840616641983

Robinson, S. L., Kraatz, M. S., & Rousseau, D. M. (1994). Changing Obligations and the Psychological Contract: A Longitudinal Study. *Academy of Management Journal, 37*(1), 137–152.

Robinson, S. L., & Morrison, E. W. (2000). The development of psychological contract breach and violation: A longitudinal study. *Journal of Organizational Behavior, 21*(5), 525–546. https://doi.org/10.1002/1099-1379(200008)21:5<525::AID-JOB40>3.0.CO;2-T

Rosenblat, A., & Stark, L. (2015). Uber's Drivers: Information Asymmetries and Control in Dynamic Work. In *Labour in the on-demand economy* (pp. 1–17). Centre for European Policy Studies (CEPS). https://doi.org/10.2139/ssrn.2686227

Rousseau, D. M. (1989). Psychological and implicit contracts in organizations. *Employee Responsibilities and Rights Journal, 2*(2), 121–139. https://doi.org/10.1007/BF01384942

Rousseau, D. M. (1990). New hire perceptions of their own and their employer's obligations: A study of psychological contracts. *Journal of Organizational Behavior, 11*(5), 389–400. https://doi.org/10.1002/job.4030110506

Rousseau, D. M., Hansen, S. D., & Tomprou, M. (2018). A dynamic phase model of psychological contract processes. *Journal of Organizational Behavior, 39*(9), 1081–1098. https://doi.org/10.1002/job.2284

Rousseau, D. M., & McLean Parks, J. (1993). The contracts of individuals and organizations. *Research in Organizational Behavior, 15*, 1–43.

Rousseau, D. M. (2008). *Psychological Contract Inventory: Employee and Employer Obligations*. Technical Report, CCER, Heinz School of Public Policy,.

Rubery, J., Grimshaw, D., Keizer, A., & Johnson, M. (2018). Challenges and Contradictions in the 'Normalising' of Precarious Work. *Work, Employment and Society*, *32*(3), 509–527. https://doi.org/10.1177/0950017017751790

Sherman, U. P., & Morley, M. J. (2015). On the formation of the psychological contract: A schema theory perspective. *Group & Organization Management*, *40*(2), 160–192. https://doi.org/10.1177/1059601115574944

Sherman, U. P., & Morley, M. J. (2020). What do we measure and how do we elicit it? The case for the use of repertory grid technique in multi-party psychological contract research. *European Journal of Work and Organizational Psychology*, *29*(2), 230–242. https://doi.org/10.1080/1359432X.2019.1668844

Shu, W. ((2018)., July 22). We want Deliveroo riders to have flexibility and the benefits of employment. *The Telegraph*. Retrieved from https://www.telegraph.co.uk/business/2018/07/22/want-deliveroo-riders-have-flexibility-benefits-employment/

Solinger, O. N., Hofmans, J., Bal, P. M., & Jansen, P. G. W. (2016). Bouncing back from psychological contract breach: How commitment recovers over time. *Journal of Organizational Behavior*, *37*(4), 494–514. https://doi.org/10.1002/job.2047

Stirling, A. (2008). Opening up" and "closing down": Power, participation, and pluralism in the social appraisal of technology. *Science Technology and Human Values*, *33*(2), 262–294. https://doi.org/10.1177/0162243907311265

Tassinari, A., & Maccarrone, V. (2020). Riders on the Storm: Workplace Solidarity among Gig Economy Couriers in Italy and the UK. *Work, Employment and Society*, *34*(1), 35–54. https://doi.org/10.1177/0950017019862954

ten Have, P. (2004). *Understanding Qualitative Research and Ethnomethodology*. SAGE Publications. https://doi.org/10.1017/CBO9781107415324.004

Tomprou, M., Rousseau, D. M., & Hansen, S. D. (2015). The psychological contracts of violation victims: A post-violation model. *Journal of Organizational Behavior*, *36*(4), 561–581. https://doi.org/10.1002/job.1997

Wilkens, U., & Nermerich, D. (2011). Love it, change it, or leave it"– Understanding Highly-skilled Flexible Workers' Job Satisfaction from a Psychological Contract Perspective. *Management Revu*, *22*(1), 65–83. https://doi.org/10.5771/0935-9915-2011-1-65

Woodcock, J., & Johnson, M. R. (2018). Gamification: What it is, and how to fight it. *The Sociological Review*, *66*(3), 542–558. https://doi.org/10.1177/0038026117728620

Žižek, S. (1989). *The Sublime Object of Ideology*. Verso.

Job quality, fair work and gig work: the lived experience of gig workers

Katie Myhill, James Richards and Kate Sang

ABSTRACT

Despite growing interest in the concept of gig work, the nature and quality of gig work is not well understood. The article builds on recent research by exploring gig work through an application of notions of job quality associated with Scotland's Fair Work Convention. Further, in recognising the multidimensional nature of job quality and the divide between objective versus subjective approaches to job quality, the article adopts a checklist or job characteristics approach, focusing on objective aspects of quality work, whilst drawing on subjective experiences to capture lived experience of gig work. A key finding is, in spite of a deficit in objective characteristics of Fair Work, the subjective experience varies between platforms as well as in accordance with individual worker characteristics, such as between those undertaking gig work as a primary or supplementary source of income. A further key finding suggests the growth in gig work reflects the normalisation of what in the past would constitute poor working conditions. Taken together, the findings highlight limitations of theoretical models of job quality due to an emphasis on traditional employment.

Introduction

Gig work is defined by Flanagan (2017) as: 'platform-based employment which uses digital technology to mediate the process of commissioning, supervising, delivery and compensating work performed by workers on a contingent, piece-work basis' (p. 2). The UK gig economy has grown rapidly and in 2018 an estimated four percent of the adult population received 50 percent or more of their monthly income through platform work (Persole et al., 2018). However, despite high-profile media attention and association with raising employment levels (e.g. see Edwards, 2017; O'Connor, 2017), a growing concern is the association of gig work with 'low quality' jobs and low/stagnating levels of pay. Indeed, early studies indicated problems with employment rights, limited autonomy, career opportunities and job security (REC, 2016). Such problems appear reflected in high levels of labour turnover (Field & Forsey, 2017) and challenges to the legalities of gig work on a global scale.

Growing concern over low-pay and precarity has led to a resurgence of debate about the quality of work in contemporary and advanced industrialised societies (Kelly, 2017; Warhurst et al., 2012). The rise of 'digital platforms', such as Uber, has led to renewed interest in what constitutes job quality or 'good' work. In 2016 the Fair Work Convention published the Fair Work Framework outlining the vision and framework for Fair Work in Scotland (FWC, 2016). A Fair Work Action Plan was announced by the Scottish Government in February 2019 with a commitment to provide additional support services to assist employers to adopt fairer workplace practices and to address challenges to delivering Fair Work within specific sectors, including the gig economy (Scot Gov, 2019).

Despite growing political interest, research exploring job quality and gig work remains in its infancy. Available evidence fails to frame empirical findings within the context of broader debates regarding job quality and what makes a job 'good or bad' (see e.g. ILO, 2018). A key concern is gig work differs markedly from traditional employment (Duggan et al., 2020), with key commentators critiquing a lack of debate surrounding the nuances to gig work (Kalleberg & Dunn, 2017). As highlighted by Kalleberg and Dunn, gig work varies in terms of the level of control exerted by platform operators, as well as the wages paid and duration of tasks. Further, differences exist in the legal classification of gig workers and the consequential access to employment and social security benefits with some digital platforms classifying such workers as employed and others as self-employed (Forde et al., 2017). To better understand novel forms of work and the consequences of growth in the demand for gig work it is necessary to move beyond polarised assessments of such work. Doing so ensures recommendations to improve working lives are rooted in the lived experiences of gig workers.

The study presented responds to calls for greater emphasis on the quality of nonstandard forms of work (Ashford et al., 2007) and builds upon an emerging literature on job quality and good work through an exploration into the subjective experiences of so called 'gig work'. To this end, the article contributes to broader debates on the complexity of worker experiences in contemporary employment and considers the extent to which gig work represents an inferior equivalent to the standard model of full time, open-ended employment.

To achieve such aims, the article begins with an overview of the gig economy, examining the growth of the gig economy in the UK and current evidence relating to the quality of gig work. Secondly, to allow the positioning of the study within existing literature, a review of concepts related to job quality and 'fair work' is provided. Following on from this, the methodological approach is described and discussed with the findings presented and analysed in the fourth section. The paper concludes in the final section with a discussion of key findings and the implications for practices as well as some of the directions for future research.

Gig economy and gig work

The term 'gig economy' emerged in the aftermath of the 2007-2008 Financial Crisis, where growing numbers of workers turned to 'gigging', undertaking a number of short-term, casual jobs, to make a living (Hook, 2015). The concept has since evolved to encompass a range of digital online platforms connecting workers with tasks, both online and offline, in 'digital' marketplaces (Minter, 2017). The notion of digital, irregular, task-based work or 'gig work' can be applied to a range of different functions, across a range of different industries, making the concept itself imprecise (Stewart & Stanford, 2017).

A lack of conceptual clarity has led to 'gig work' being used as a catch-all statement for non-standard work (e.g. see, MGI, 2016; TUC, 2016). Whilst many of the core characteristics of gig work are not necessarily new, with features such as piece based work, precarious contractual conditions and irregular scheduling evident throughout the history of capitalism (Stanford, 2017), key differences exist between gig work and other forms of nonstandard work such as agency work, including in the influence of technology and the absence of a physical work location (Duggan et al., 2020).

Indeed, despite variations in the conceptualisation of gig work, a number of distinguishing features have been identified including: the employment contract and the engagement of workers on an ad hoc/task-by-task basis, the exploitation of low cost-labour, algorithmic control and a reliance upon digital rating systems, and, the organisation of work through a digital mediator, web based platform or digital smartphone application (Howcroft & Bergvall-Kåreborn, 2019; Minter, 2017; Stewart & Stanford, 2017). A further distinction can be made between gig work, involving work conducted locally, requiring the individual to be physically present, and virtual or crowd work, delivered remotely and undertaken anywhere (Huws et al., 2018). While the latter includes the provision of a variety of digital tasks, such as data entry or software development, the former is more commonly associated with 'lower skilled' service provision, including food delivery and transport services (Goulden et al., 2018). It is the latter category, work conducted through local labour-based platforms, which provides the focus for the current study.

Job quality and gig work

Recently, organisational use of digital, online platforms has accelerated, showing little sign of slowing, with a quarter of young people indicating interest in such work (Balaram et al., 2017). While an estimated three million UK workers earn more than 50 percent of their earnings through platforms (Persole et al., 2018), gig work is expected to become the norm for new entrants to labour markets, while many gig workers struggle to secure traditional forms of employment.

The continued rise of gig work represents new opportunities and challenges for workers. While some see gig work as an opportunity for entrepreneurship and innovation, allowing flexibility and work-life balance (Burtch et al., 2018), many see gig work as a 'platform for exploitation' (Kessler, 2018), questioning the sustainability and fairness of working conditions. As such, concerns about labour standards and employment regulation regularly arise, typically related to 'sham' contracting arrangements, enabling gig organisations to disguise employment, avoid national insurance contributions, and deny basic employment rights (Field & Forsey, 2017). Prior research indicates gig workers share experiences with other non-standard workers, including a risk of falling outwith the scope of existing employment and social protections (Forde et al., 2017). Further, the media report gig workers living in poverty, bearing high levels of financial and personal risk, and being subject to intrusive surveillance and non-consensual data collection (Funnell, 2016).

Research specifically on the quality of gig work is limited. Where it exists, it emphasises online 'virtual' or 'crowd work' (e.g. Wood et al., 2018), which, as highlighted above, is conceptually different from localised, service-based gig work. In addition, existing research is often based on official survey data, which fails to reveal nuances or lived experience of such employment. What qualitative research exists tends to suggest gig workers choose to work in such a manner and are on the whole satisfied with working conditions (Broughton et al., 2018). That may be true to a point, but such research tends to take gig worker views at face value and rarely deploys a critical conceptual framework.

Job quality and Scotland's fair work framework

This section provides a discussion of how job quality has been defined and explored, including what is meant by job quality and in commentary of the key dimensions of quality work identified by Scotland's Fair Work Framework (FWF).

What is job quality?

Job quality represents a core issue in HRM and is associated with employee satisfaction and motivation (Grote & Guest, 2017). Despite considerable research, there remains little consensus on defining and conceptualising a good job (Findlay et al., 2013; Kalleberg, 2016). This has resulted in a range of approaches to the study and measurement of job quality.

A core debate relates to the focus upon objective versus subjective accounts of job quality (Royuela et al., 2008). While job quality has been measured historically in accordance with the presence or absence of certain objective criteria, such as job security and safe working conditions, the emergence of psychological needs based theories during the 1950s, saw a marked trend towards an increasingly subjective conceptualisation of job quality, with job satisfaction used as a proxy for good work (Martel & Dupuis, 2006). However, while addressing the limitations of the objective approach by recognising what makes a good job for one individual may not be the same as for another (e.g. Brown et al., 2007), the subjective approach faces criticism for understating the importance of key extrinsic measures, such as wages and benefits (Rose, 2003). As such, an increasingly common approach incorporates aspects of both, including objective features of jobs, while drawing upon workers subjective evaluations to capture personal experience (Kalleberg & Vaisey, 2005).

Although there is no consensus reflecting a best way to measure job quality, there is a view that the relevance of the concept arises from its impact, whether on the employer, the company, the individual or broader society. There is also growing recognition that a notion as fluid and multidimensional as job quality, cannot be measured against a single characteristic, such as job security or wage levels, with each job comprising a complex culmination of negative and positive characteristics, which together, determine job quality (Smith, et al., 2008; Burgess & Connell, 2008; Clark, 2005). Furthermore, it is increasingly recognised subjective evaluations of job quality are influenced by individual and contextual factors, including worker characteristics and preferences (Brown et al., 2007; Loughlin & Murray, 2013), as well as the broader labour market context (Gaillie, 2007). Thus, context as well as content must be considered in any analysis of job quality.

With a lack of consensus on the definition and characteristics of 'good work' (Ashford et al., 1989; Munoz-Bustillo et al., 2009), a range of perspectives have been noted within the literature (Burchell et al., 2014). The most recognised approach is provided by the International Labour Organisation (ILO) who define good work as:

> Opportunities for work that are productive and deliver a fair income, security in the workplace and social protection for families, better prospects for personal development and social integration, freedom for people to express their concerns, organise and participate in the decisions which affect their lives and equality of opportunity and treatment for all men and women (ILO, 2017).

This approach, underpinned by eleven dimensions of decent work, ranging from wages and time at work, to social dialogue and equality, represents the ILO's policy agenda to raise labour standards across Member States (ILO, 2017); a strategy-for-action which, itself, is promoted by the European Commission (EurWork, 2012) and underpins the development of a number of domestic initiatives for improved monitoring and measuring of job quality, including Scotland's Fair Work Framework.

Emergent forms of nonstandard and digital forms of work have received limited attention within the job quality literature, leading to calls for a greater emphasis on the aspects of work quality for those in nonstandard forms of work (Ashford et al., 2007). Indeed, theories of job quality have traditionally been associated with features of 'standard' jobs, such as level of earnings or job security. However, with growing diversity in modern working arrangements and increased recognition the term 'standard' does not necessarily equate with good, it has been said such classifications are no longer useful (Cappelli & Keller, 2013). Further, it is increasingly recognised the ability to choose the type and nature of work, and thus the existence of alternative working arrangements, represents a key aspect of job quality (Bamberry, 2011). As such, quality of work arrangements and conditions under which such work may be experienced as good or bad, represents a key area of interest in need of further research. To this end, countries, including the UK, have begun to consider how job quality can be protected and enhanced. One example is Scotland's Fair Work Framework, based on principles backed by the Scottish Government, yet untested in terms of reflecting the growth of gig work. Specifically, the FWF responds to calls for a more integrated approach to research and policy on job quality (Grote & Guest, 2017), enhancing the impact of the evidence through the integration within a broader Fair Work agenda.

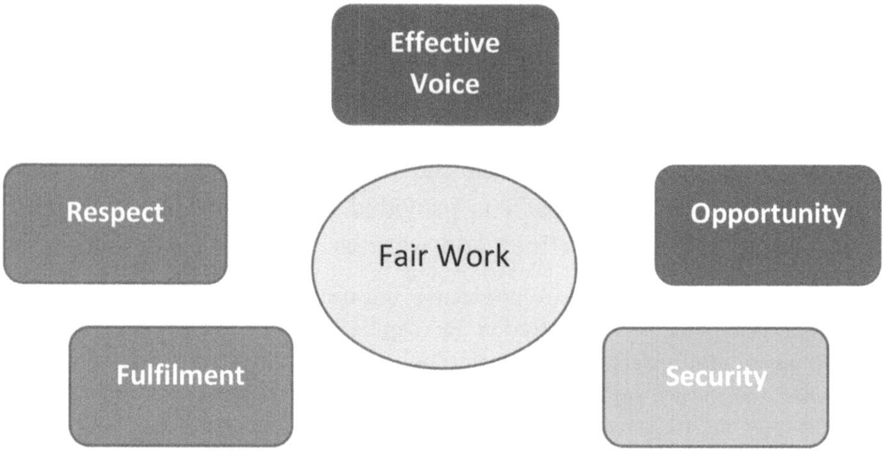

Figure 1. Fair Work Framework (adapted from FWC (2016)).

Scotland's fair work framework

Scotland's FWF was established in 2015, aiming to promote 'Fair Work' and embed such principles into Scotland's workplaces and economy (FWC, 2016). Within the FWF, Fair Work is defined as 'work that offers effective voice, opportunity, security, fulfilment and respect; that balances the rights and responsibilities of employers and workers and that can generate benefits for individuals, organisations and society' (FWC, 2016, p. 5). There are five dimensions to Fair Work - effective voice, opportunity, security, fulfilment and respect[1]. These dimensions reflect existing notions of job quality and workplace relationships drawing upon national and international research and identified good practice, within each dimension, and with a focus upon positive outcomes for individuals, organisations and society. Details of the FWF are presented in Figure 1.

The first dimension of the FWF (see Figure 1) is defined as 'the creation of a safe environment where dialogue and challenge are dealt with constructively and where employee views are sought out, listened to and can make a difference' (FWF, 2016). Employee voice and participation feature widely in the job quality literature, principally as they enhance well-being (Holman, 2013). However, with the long-term decline of trade unions, denial of representation and voice for gig workers represents an area of concern in need of further investigation (Croft, 2018). Similarly, the second dimension of the FWF, opportunity for career advancement, is a common feature of the broader job quality literature (e.g. see Clark, 2005), yet such opportunities appear to be lacking in the gig economy due to the absence of traditional organisational structures, further raising concerns regarding the quality of gig jobs. In considering the third dimension of the FWF, 'Security', which incorporates stability of employment, security of income and predictability of work commitment (FWC,

2016), the quality of gig work can again be questioned due to its association with precarious employment (MacDonald & Giazitzoglu, 2019).

In the case of the fourth dimensions of 'Fulfilment' (see Figure 1), the emphasis is on psychological aspects of jobs and aspects of worker autonomy (FWC, 2016). Within the FWF, fulfilling work is defined by opportunities to use and develop skills, as well as allowing autonomous working (ibid). In the case of gig work, whilst debate increases regarding the extent to which such work can be described as autonomous and the impact of digital control mechanisms upon individual levels of autonomy at work (Duggan et al., 2020; Healy et al., 2017) the workers voice remains largely absent. In addition, there remains some ambiguity over the extent to which the seemingly repetitive nature of such task based work can be equated with the broader definition of fulfilling work highlighting the need for further research exploring the experiences and perceptions of those undertaking this type of work. The final dimension of the FWF relates to respect at work (see Figure 1), including dignity at work, social support and trusting relationships (FWC, 2016). Whilst respect is key to health, safety and well-being, reflecting core principles of fair and decent work (ILO, 2017), it is an aspect of job quality often underrepresented within alternative frameworks, representing a potential strength in the FWF which may help to provide a more comprehensive understanding of work life in the gig economy.

While the FWF has been widely promoted by the Scottish Government, representing a key feature of Scotland's labour market strategy to deliver a fair work economy (Scottish Government, 2016), its relevance to gig work remains untested. This article aims to contribute to such an assessment, exploring the subjective experience and perception of key dimensions of fair work in relation to gig work. The next part considers research methodology as a means to explore fair work and job quality in the gig economy.

Methodology

To explore the lived experience of gig workers (Boylorn, 2008), a qualitative approach using semi-structured interviews was adopted. The study sought to explore subjective experiences of gig work through interviews. These testaments assist in exploring the quality of gig work in relation to the FWF. In addition, interviews helped to build knowledge of worker experiences of app-based employment and their views of traditional aspects of job quality.

The study received ethical approval from the authors' institution and participants were informed of the purpose of the study and of a right to

Table 1. Participant details.

Name (pseudonym)	Platform	Age range	Source of Income (Primary, Exclusive or Supplementary)
Jonny	Taxi	51-60	Supplementary
Gavin	Taxi	51-60	Supplementary
Leo	Taxi	21-30	Exclusive
David	Courier	21-30	Exclusive
Hamish	Courier	16-20	Supplementary
Kevin	Courier	21-30	Primary
Billy	Courier	21-30	Supplementary
George	Taxi	21-30	Supplementary
Jill	Courier	21-30	Supplementary
Joe	Taxi	51-60	Supplementary
Jenny	Courier	21-30	Exclusive
Michael	Taxi	41-50	Exclusive
Tony	Taxi	41-50	Supplementary
Peter	Taxi	51-60	Primary
Allan	Courier	21-30	Primary
Chris	Hospitality	21-30	Exclusive
Jay	Hospitality	21-30	Exclusive
Craig	Hospitality	31-40	Supplementary
Sam	Hospitality	21-30	Primary
Liam	Hospitality	31-40	Exclusive
Paul	Taxi + Courier	31-40	Primary
Josh	Hospitality	16-20	Supplementary
Wendy	Courier	21-30	Exclusive
Jacob	Hospitality	31-40	Primary
Alex	Hospitality	21-30	Primary
Will	Hospitality	21-30	Supplementary
Simon	Hospitality	31-40	Primary
Amy	Hospitality	21-30	Supplementary
John	Taxi	51-60	Supplementary
Sarah	Hospitality	21-30	Primary
Kirsty	Courier	16-20	Primary
Phil	Taxi	51-60	Supplementary

withdraw. In addition, all respondents were assured of anonymity, with interview transcripts anonymised to protect participants' identities. Table 1 summarises participant details, with all names pseudonymised.

Interviews were conducted face-to-face by the lead author. In total, 32 gig workers located in central Scotland were interviewed (see Table 1). All participants were working *via* digital app-based platforms undertaking hospitality, courier and taxi driving employment. Given the exploratory nature of the study, a purposive sampling was deemed appropriate, to maximise chances of capturing experiences of hard to reach workers. Wherever possible, participants were recruited on the basis of gathering a sample allowing for variance in age range and gender (see Table 1). This variation allowed for a range of perspectives, maximising opportunities to explore differences and inequities in experience for different groups of workers.

Participants were initially recruited through social media platforms populated by gig workers (for example, through gig worker self-organised *Uber* and *Deliveroo* forums on *Facebook*). Participants were also recruited through recruitment flyers around 'hot spots' such as city centre areas where gig workers congregate. A further recruitment strategy involved snowball sampling - asking interviewees to recommend study participation to fellow gig workers. Gig workers were also recruited directly from a platform app. The strategy involved posting a call for participants directly on a hospitality work app.

As Table 1 notes, 10 interviews were conducted with workers employed *via* courier delivery platforms, such as *Deliveroo*; 11 with workers employed *via* taxi platforms, such as *Uber*; and, 11 gig workers undertaking hospitality work, through platforms such as *Gig*. Participants ranged in age from 18-60 years, with an average age of 34 years. The majority of participants were men ($n = 26$), reflecting an over-representation of men in gig work (Balaram et al., 2017). Of the sample, gig work was a supplementary source of income for 14 participants and a primary source for 18 participants, 8 of which relied upon gig work as their singular source of income. Table 1 provides details of gig work in relation to primary, exclusive or supplementary ways to earn.

Interviews were conducted in public, yet safe places such as a café, and were 30-90 min in length, averaging 51 min each. Permission to record interviews was attained in all cases with interviews transcribed verbatim. Given the low-pay element of gig work, participants were compensated with a £10 voucher. Interview questions were developed based on characteristics of job quality in addition to, reasons for working in the gig economy, perceptions of wages and conditions and the impact of gig work on broader aspects of working life (see Appendix 1).

Interviews were analysed using template analysis (King & Brooks, 2016) and a combination of priori and posteriori coding, developed in accordance with key components of job quality outlined in the FWF and ad hoc codes which emerged from data analysis including, for example, personal financial literacy or stage of career (see Appendix 2). Analysed findings are presented in the following section, based on comparing gig work to the FWF, as well as wider notions of job quality.

The lived experience of gig work in Scotland

Despite overlap between dimensions of FW, the findings are presented as per the FWF outlined in Figure 1. A subjective lens is applied, principally accounting for lived experience of job quality and gig work.

Gig work and voice

With voice, most participants reported little to no input in decision-making. A lack of voice was commonly linked to the size of platform operator and a sense of disposability, with several respondents referring to being 'just a number'. In addition, while respondents reported consultation *via* surveys, sent *via* email or through the app, a large proportion viewed them as 'box ticking' exercises, with little sense of how results would lead to changes in working. A lack of voice left participants feeling undervalued and distrustful of the platform operator. George, a taxi driver, demonstrates how a lack of voice leads to cynicism towards the gig organisation:

> Uber have their own agenda. Every time they introduce a change you see people getting nervous, even when it's a good change like with the tipping system. People are suspicious it is just going to be another way to swindle you out of more money (George, taxi, aged 21-30).

Opportunities for collective voice were also limited. Trade union membership was low among participants, with four participants reporting membership, and even then, it was unclear how membership could enhance voice. Those reporting trade union membership were 40 years old plus, with membership a legacy of a prior occupation. For non-members, an indifference towards trade unions was commonly reported. Further, many participants, particularly aged 16-31 years, were not aware of the role or purpose of trade unions.

Despite a lack of voice, participants did not believe the situation was unusual and, in some cases, struggled to envisage how it could be any different. To this end, the data suggests a lack of participation in decision-making was experienced as normal, with leaving to work for other platforms the most common response to work difficulties.

Gig work and career opportunity

A majority of participants reported limited opportunities for career progression, particularly in terms of promotion. In addition, with the exception of hospitality workers, who reported some opportunities for training[2], most participants reported no access to formal training, with a majority reporting ad hoc experiences of 'learning on the job'.

Despite an absence of training and development opportunities, participants referred to opportunities for personal development through, for example, entrepreneurial activity, networking and skill diversification. A specific example includes taxi drivers renting out their car at times when not driving, as a source of additional income. In addition, two respondents established businesses as a consequence of growth in the platform operator, buying, licensing and renting out multiple vehicles to other drivers registered with the platform. Joe exemplifies such opportunities:

> If you want to work through the platform but you don't have a car or much money, you come to me, rent a car and then you can save up and get your own car. Then maybe you can do what I did. Save up again and get another car, get someone driving that for you and you can keep going. I think that's progression. I couldn't have as many cars on the road if it wasn't for the platform (Joe, taxi, aged 51-60).

Three further participants, one running a consultancy business and two running independent private hire companies, reported growing pre-existing businesses as a consequence of gig work.

That said, opportunity differed according to the setting of gig work. For instance, whilst some taxi workers reported opportunities for entrepreneurship, courier workers reported a general absence of opportunity for career development. Hospitality workers however, remarked on networking and skill diversification, with further opportunities to gain experience hard to come by through traditional forms of employment. Craig, a hotel reception manager, described such opportunity whereby gig work enabled him to work in different hotels and the opportunity to gain experience of working in different departments:

> As part of the next 2-3 year plan I want to apply for the position of general manager. At my hotel we don't have a bar or a restaurant, so my sole focus is reception. With *Gig* I can do supervisor shifts in a food and drink scenario, I can do waiting, I can do bar work, I can hone the little bits and pieces which will make me a more well-rounded employee so that if I'm going for an interview, I can talk about the things I have done and it adds an extra string to the bow (Craig, hospitality, aged 31-40).

While the findings revealed limited career development opportunities, the extent to which such opportunities were perceived as important also varied. For example, whilst those new to the labour market, or who sought to gain experience in an unfamiliar area of work, valued opportunities available *via* gig work, a clear majority of participants reported aspirations unrelated to their current employment. This was particularly common amongst students working in the gig economy to support their studies and who hoped to secure a future career within their relevant disciplines. Similarly, participants also drawing on welfare benefits, showed little interest in career opportunities related to their current gig-work. Despite differing perceptions of career development, gig work overall, was not associated with a better future career. As Jay indicates, gig work is more of a temporary end in itself, rather than a means to base a career:

> This type of work it isn't really a career. Everybody is looking for a career, this type of job, it isn't really a career. It is great for the mean time but I'm really looking for something permanent that I can build on. Something that you invest in and can build up (Jay, hospitality, aged 21-30).

Gig work and security

All participants were contracted on a non-employee basis, receiving no job security or rights to holiday or sick pay. This lack of security leaves workers vulnerable to involuntary unemployment and exposed to high levels of financial risk related to fluctuations in demand, periods of ill-health, equipment and technological issues or, deactivation. A lack of security typically resulted in a sense of anxiety as demonstrated by Amy's experience of gig work:

> With gig work, there is that lack of stability and we all have bills to pay and you need to know what income you will be bringing in. The sort of person that I am I get very anxious about where the next wage is going to come from (Amy, hospitality, aged 21-30).

In addition to a lack of formalised job security, participants reported weekly variability in hours worked and money earned. Issues of income volatility are further compounded by the self-employed status of a large proportion of participants, in particular, those operating through courier and taxi platforms. Indeed, while the interviews suggest hospitality workers are less vulnerable to income volatility, as work was typically offered on a shift-by-shift basis, this was not the case with taxi and courier workers, who were paid only when completing a specific task, such as delivering a food order. In such instances, courier and taxi workers experienced income volatility within a shift as well as over lengthier periods. Thus, while headline pay rates compared favourably with work outside the gig economy, sub-minimum wage employment emerged from volatility in the supply of work.

How vulnerable workers were in such situations appeared to depend on the extent to which employment represents a primary or supplementary source of income. For example, some gig workers used gig work to supplement a steadier stream of income, while others relied on such work to cover key living expenses. As expected, primary gig workers reported most dissatisfaction in relation to insecurity of income, often retelling experience of 'keeping their head above water'. An example of the impact of job insecurity on well-being is demonstrated in the following excerpt from John who also experiences a health condition which can sometimes affect his ability to work:

> It can be quite depressing if you take a dip in earnings. Like 2 weeks ago I was having bother with my legs and I'm just feeling the effects of that now in my wages and it does get you down (John, taxi, aged 51-60).

Aside from impacting on well-being, a further dimension to income insecurity involves hidden work costs. Within taxi work, for example, costs related to licensing, maintenance and insurance were underwritten by the worker with some workers reporting costs of up to £900 a month, almost half their total revenue for that period. Even where taxi drivers could consolidate costs in rental agreements, such arrangements often came with hidden penalties including the need to work more hours to cover basic costs. Such gig workers could not work when they wanted, leading to a sense of exploitation and undermining of work-life balance goals commonly associated with nonstandard work. George details such a scenario:

> I started driving for Uber 6 months ago [because] I needed a day job and I wanted something that provided that flexibility and it seemed liked it could provide pretty decent money. But I felt misled to be honest. I'm earning ok money but the 'work when you want ethos' is just not true. You have to put the hours in, especially when you are renting (George, taxi, aged 21-30).

Courier and hospitality work also came with hidden costs. Courier workers, for example, incur costs for equipment, maintenance, additional data and battery chargers whilst for hospitality workers, travel costs lowered already minimal and variable income streams. Indeed, while transport was provided for 'large events', for smaller events workers were expected to cover their travel costs, which could involve long, expensive and unpaid journeys.

In many instances, a lack of security manifested in anxiety and concerns about sustainability of gig work. To this end, participants frequently retold plans to find 'reliable' and 'permanent' forms of employment. However, despite lacking security in a conventional sense, participants equated a regular flow of work with a sense of security. For example, Jill believed gig work to be as secure as traditional employment in certain sectors:

> The good thing about the gig economy is you don't have to worry about redundancy in a way. After seeing House of Fraser and all the stories in the media you can't help but feel a bit anxious if you work in retail. These apps aren't going anywhere (Jill, courier, aged 21-30).

Indeed, gig workers more widely contemplated the notion of security with the perceived opportunity to quickly and easily access work through an app during, for example, times of financial hardship, providing a broader sense of security. Furthermore, for some, gig work was a preference, with absence of contractual obligation and associated rights perceived as a worthwhile sacrifice in a quest for control and a sense of freedom.

Gig work and fulfilment

Autonomy and control over work was perceived to be a selling point of gig work, with many participants working remotely and without any direct supervision. Indeed, freedom over how and when to work was commonly cited as a benefit of gig work:

> One of the main benefits is that you can fully control your own schedule and you know exactly when you are working because you are volunteering in a sense, whereas sometimes in bar work you don't really have any control of when you are working or how you are working (Alex, hospitality, aged 21-30).

Having control over work schedules was widely welcomed by participants. However, the extract above belies the reality of control and autonomy for many gig workers. For instance, many participants could only acquire acceptable levels of work if prepared to work evenings and weekends, suggesting control is only possible if worker demands match that of consumers. Control and autonomy were further reduced because gig organisations had the power to 'deactivate' workers [remove from the system] if they rejected too many requests or received a negative customer review. Gig workers also reported a range of other restrictions. For example, taxi workers reported little say in the price of a fare as well as the route taken in fulfilling the fare whilst hospitality workers were often restricted by the client with the provision of specific task instructions. Courier workers also commented on restrictions to autonomy associated with the need to 'keep stats up' with one participant referring to the requirement to work a certain number of hours per week in order to maintain priority access for booking 'shifts' through the app.

Evidence was however, provided of different ways in which individuals resisted digital control mechanisms. Indeed, several respondents referred to the subversion of such mechanisms, with 'prohibited' practices such as working through multiple apps at one time (in some cases using multiple devices), accepting cash jobs/tips and stealing from/fiddling customers to make amends for unfair practices. An example of subversive activity is demonstrated in the following quote from a participant working through a courier and taxi platform:

> You aren't supposed to, but I do courier work at the same time as the taxi work. They don't employ you, so they can't stop me. There is no reason not to be dishonest with them because I never meet anyone from the company. It's not like you are lying to your boss, you are lying to an app (Paul, taxi and courier, age 31-40).

Therefore, while the autonomy of gig workers is constrained due to digital control mechanisms, many participants commented on the limitations of these mechanisms and the belief that, in spite of such mechanisms, their work was in fact defined by some degree of autonomy.

Furthermore, despite depictions of gig work as repetitive and unsatisfying (Parkinson, 2017), interviews provided positive accounts of fulfilment. Indeed, many participants reported high levels of 'enjoyment' from their work including, for example, in regard to the opportunity to 'keep fit' when undertaking courier work as well as in regard to the social aspect of gig work more generally. For example, Jonny, a full-time Uber driver, reflected on the social benefits of gig work through meeting new people:

> I enjoy chatting to different people around the world. It is used by international customers a lot and you meet a diverse group of people. Providing them good customer service can be very satisfying (Jonny, taxi, aged 51-60).

Such was the satisfaction attained from customer interactions, several participants believed they would continue to do gig work as a 'side hustle' even if they secured better terms of employment elsewhere. Further, for some participants, in particular those whom were working in the gig economy on an ad hoc basis to supplement income, gig work was seen as something beyond employment, comparable instead to a 'paid hobby' or taking part in a 'game'.

Gig work and respect

The perceived absence of work-related social support from the platform operator was commonly identified as a key downside to working through an app. Indeed, whilst some respondents preferred not having a 'traditional' manager, others reported a sense of abandonment following registration with a number of participants referring to feeling like they were 'just a number'.

A further yet similar concern raised relates to the repeated prioritisation of customers' interests over workers, including taking the customers' side in a dispute with such incidences typically resulting in the deactivation or suspension of the worker whilst complaints were investigated. Not only are workers denied income while this happens, heightening issues of job and income insecurity, but it also adds to a sense of disposability. Tony retells a story of customer-related deactivation and how he was left without income for several days:

> If the customer makes a complaint, [the platform] will take you off the system for days whilst they investigate it. If a driver says you need to put your seatbelts on or refuses 5 passengers in a car and the customer complains, the driver could be off the system for 2 or 3 days. They aren't an app for taxi drivers, they are an app for consumers (Tony, taxi, aged 41-50).

To this end, several respondents attributed 'unfairness' to the subjective customer-based rating systems designed to manage work accessed through the platform with concerns raised over the arbitrary nature of such mechanisms and the lack of transparency, for both consumers and workers, as to how this data is used. The perceived unfairness of such systems is retold by Peter:

> The customer rating system is just another stick to beat you with. You get a drunk customer at 2 a.m. and they can give you a 1 star because they maybe think it's funny but then that can affect your rating really badly. If you get too many you can get kicked off the platform… 4 stars seems like a good score so [customers] don't realise that it's a demerit and could result in drivers being deactivated (Peter, taxi, aged 51-60).

However, in spite of reports of an absence of work based social support, dignity and respect did feature in a range of new and novel ways. For instance, participants believed having an app as a 'manager' led to a sense of work being distributed on a non-discriminatory basis, as apps were perceived to be apolitical and have no wider aspirations or agenda.

Similarly, participants did report a sense of safety, mainly because of the abatement of the need to carry cash, but also in terms of avoiding many other downsides to traditional forms of employment. John, a taxi driver, exemplifies how platform technology can enhance job quality, simply because of the reduced chance of customer non-payment, receiving counterfeit money, or being robbed by a customer:

> The security is much better because it's the first to use all card payments. When you get cash jobs you don't know who the person is and if it's a no show you can spend half an hour getting to someone and waiting for them and they don't show up and you don't get any money. At least with Uber if someone cancels a job you get a cancellation fee. Everyone has to have an account, customers and drivers, so you don't get so many people running off and the people that do get in your cab, well they are a higher quality of customer (John, taxi, aged 51-60).

Discussion

Within a resurgence of interest in job quality and in the context of debates on the quality of gig work (Kalleberg & Dunn, 2017), this article makes a contribution *via* an analysis of gig work through the lens of Scotland's FWF. In comparing gig work to objective characteristics of job quality, the findings support the dominant view of gig work as 'bad' (Kessler, 2018; REC, 2016; TUC, 2016), suggesting gig work fails the criteria set out by FWF. Indeed, gig work is particularly problematic in terms of income volatility, hidden costs and penalties for workers, and, a lack of support and voice for workers.

However, despite falling short of the ideals of the FWF, the subjective experience, or lived experience of gig work, revealed a hidden, complex and nuanced side to such work. For example, despite apparent job insecurity, participants reported a sense of security due to a reliable supply of work, plus broader life security through opportunities to generate income at times of wider financial hardship or whilst in pursuit of longer-term career aspirations. Similarly, despite evidence to suggest gig work is tightly controlled, typically through tracking software and strict task designation, workers reported a perceived increased sense of control over when to work, important for wider life priorities. Such findings contrast with wider research based on tightly controlled call centre employment (e.g. Taylor & Bain, 1999), yet compare to research highlighting how algorithmic management techniques can facilitate higher levels of autonomy and favourable terms of flexible working for workers (Wood, et al., 2018). In addition, the findings are best summarised in terms of further, yet novel insights, into how jobs can be viewed as bad by external observers, yet experienced as good by those undertaking them (Hodson, 1991; Knox et al., 2015).

Furthermore, the findings reveal the impacts of the presence or absence of objective characteristics of fair work on individuals' experience and perception of gig work, were mediated by worker characteristics, including their individual preferences, ingenuity, expectations and personal circumstance. For example, the extent to which individuals were vulnerable to wage fluctuation and job insecurity were largely dependent on whether they relied upon gig work as a primary or supplementary source of income. Similarly, whilst opportunity for participation were limited, participants rarely rated participation as important due to few having long-term ambitions to remain a gig worker. For many gig work supplemented wider income and served wider aspirations, and many gig workers could switch platform if they faced a problem.

The variation in perceived importance of job quality dimensions and the impact of worker characteristics and preferences on individual experiences and perceptions of gig work, resonates with previous studies, recognising that where work can be defined on the surface as good or bad, the subjective experience often tells us something different (Brown et al., 2007; Holman, 2013; Loughlin & Murray, 2013). To this end, the findings help explain why, in spite of gig work viewed objectively as poor quality work, gig work can be associated with worker acceptance and satisfaction (Broughton et al., 2018; Mcdonald, et al., 2019). Indeed, a strength of the findings is how lived experience approaches allows insiders a chance to tell a story of how they come to frame work, sometimes quite differently, from those who have little or no experience of such work.

In addition, the divergence in experience, particularly as gig workers are drawn to such work for a wide-range of reasons, further reveals distinct limitations in observing gig work through a lens based on objective evaluations of job quality. The limitations are most notable in how traditional conceptions of job quality, such as with the FWF, fail to take into account why many workers choose to undertake 'inferior' work, how many workers make informed decisions when seeking gig work, and, how gig work impacts on broader aspects of life.

However, these limitations should not be used to underplay further key findings and contributions of the study. For instance, the findings show how low-quality work goes unchallenged by many workers, principally because many such workers have limited if no prior awareness of what a good job may look like. This aspect of the findings supports the view of increasing normalisation of precarious work (Rubery et al., 2018). Put differently, the findings give an indication of how easy it is for many workers, especially those with minimal or no experience of traditional forms of employment, to see gig work as normal or routine, therefore having few if any expectations of 'good' work.

Conclusions

The aim of the study was to explore an under-researched feature of contemporary work and employment, that of the quality of gig work. Part of the aim was to explore the quality of gig work through the lens of Scotland's emergent FWF. A further objective was to recognise the subjective side of job quality in exploring gig work. In doing so it is evident how an empirical contribution is made, as the study adds to knowledge on the basis of providing graphic, yet structured and meaningful details of the lived experience of gig work, highlighting how gig workers respond and react to the many challenges inherent in such situations. Importantly, a theoretical contribution is made in terms of highlighting the complex nature of job quality in the gig economy, through drawing attention to the difficulties in evaluating the quality of nonstandard forms of work, such as gig work, in accordance with principles of 'good' or 'fair' work, which in themselves remain based on notions of traditional employment. Indeed, the findings highlight the benefits of recognising worker lived experience when conceptualising job quality, thus offering greater recognition of the fluidity of job quality and the variations in the perceived importance of job quality dimensions for different groups of workers, at different points in time.

Through accounts of the lived experience of gig work, key contributions to come from the study include the following. First, determining the quality of gig work is not straightforward. The findings indicate how gig work is complex and nuanced, with no two workers experiencing gig work in the same way. Indeed, only through a lived experience lens was it possible to appreciate many hidden and important sides to gig work. For example, whilst in an objective sense gig work is evidently lacking in comparison with traditional notions of 'good work', the lived experience reveals a different and fuller picture of gig work, including benefits related to autonomy and flexibility. Thus, whilst it is unlikely gig work can be incorporated into traditional models of job quality, this is not to say such work can be described as unequivocally bad, as evidence produced in the current study suggests gig work can in some instances be viewed as good work, particularly for workers not seeking stable or permanent employment. As such, it seems models of job quality need to change to reflect the realities of gig work, as much as gig work may need to change to more closely comply with traditional models of job quality. Furthermore, while subjective evaluations and the use of job satisfaction as a proxy for job quality may be problematic due to the potential for such an approach to provide an oversimplified view of gig work, the subjective experience remains key in understanding how individual differences influence the relationship between determinants and outcomes of job quality and thus how they shape the overall quality of work experience.

The findings of the study also have potential use for policy makers, HRM practitioners and trade unions, seeking to improve the quality of gig work more generally. To this end, the findings highlight the deficits gig workers face when applying job quality dimensions to their jobs, particularly relating to aspects of security and respect. However, the findings also reveal some characteristics which may be considered positive for the quality of jobs in the gig economy and which should be maintained and protected, especially levels of flexibility, an attribute most appreciated by participants in this study.

Despite the positive features of gig work referred to in the current study, almost all participants viewed gig work as unsustainable or a 'dead-end-job', with many indicating intentions to seek more open-ended, stable forms of employment. Thus, a key challenge for HRM practitioners and platform operators is how best to mitigate against problems associated with 'short-termism', resulting in most instances, in misbehaviour and turnover. To this end, worker subversive techniques highlight a distinct and problematic side to algorithmic control mechanisms, principally based on diminished and degraded opportunities for mutual trust and confidence to emerge from the platform-worker relationship. As such, whilst algorithmic control mechanisms may lead to a short-term reduction in labour management costs, in the longer-term, the same mechanisms are likely to lead to problematic levels of worker demotivation and indifference, which in wider terms equates to declining customer satisfaction and brand reputation.

While the current study makes important contributions, it is not without limitations. For instance, the study is limited in terms of being based on a modest sample of gig workers, working in a limited range of industrial sectors, as well as located in a specific geographical location characterised by a unique political climate. The findings are also limited in terms of lacking insights into experiences of gig work over time. As such, priorities for follow up research includes longitudinal methods, larger samples, participants drawn from a wider range of industries and geographical locations, as well as more attention to workers dependent on gig work to make a living. A priority, as such, is to test out and develop models of job quality based on extended and detailed accounts of gig work.

Notes

1. Note this framework is distinct from the Five Pillars of Fair Work developed by the Fair Work Foundation.
2. The GIG Academy was established in 2019 providing apprenticeship opportunities and online training facilities.

Disclosure statement

No potential conflict of interest was reported by the author(s).

ORCID

James Richards http://orcid.org/0000-0003-3664-2884
Kate Sang http://orcid.org/0000-0003-1397-1116

Data availability statement: RIJH-2019-0416

The data that support the findings of this study are available from the corresponding author upon reasonable request.

References

Ashford, S., George, E., & Blatt, R. (2007). Old assumptions, new work: the opportunities and challenges of research on nonstandard employment. *Academy of Management Annals*, *1*(1), 65–117. https://doi.org/10.5465/078559807

Ashford, S., Lee, C., & Bobko, P. (1989). Content, causes and consequences of job insecurity: a theory-based measure and substantive test. *Academy of Management Journal*, *32*(4), 803–829. https://doi.org/10.2307/256569

Balaram, B., Warden, J., & Wallace-Stephens, F. (2017). *Good gigs: A fairer future for the UK gig economy*. RSA.

Bamberry, L. (2011). As disposable as the next tissue out of the box… casual teaching and job quality in new south wales public school education. *Journal of Industrial Relations*, *53*(1), 49–64. https://doi.org/10.1177/0022185610390296

Boylorn, R. (2008). Lived experience. In L M Given (ed.) *The sage encyclopedia of qualitative research methods* (Vol. 2). Sage.

Broughton, A., Gloster, R., Marvell, R., Green, M., Langley, J., & Martin, A. (2018). *The experience of individuals in the gig economy*. DBEIS.

Brown, A., Charlwood, A., Forde, C., & Spencer, D. (2007). Job quality and the economics of new labour: A critical appraisal using subjective survey data. *Cambridge Journal of Economics, 31*(6), 941–971. https://doi.org/10.1093/cje/bem028

Burchell, B., Sehnbruch, K., Piasna, A., & Agloni, N. (2014). The quality of employment and decent work: Definitions, methodologies and ongoing debates. *Cambridge Journal of Economics, 38*(2), 459–477. https://doi.org/10.1093/cje/bet067

Burgess, J. & Connell, J. (2008). Introduction to special issue. *International Journal of Human Resource Management, 19*(3), 407–418.

Burtch, G., Carnahan, S., & Greenwood, B. (2018). Can you gig it? An emperical examination of the gig economy and entrepreneurial activity. *Management Science, 64*(12), 5497–5959. https://doi.org/10.1287/mnsc.2017.2916

Cappelli, P., & Keller, J. R. (2013). Classifying work in the new economy. *Academy of Management Review, 38*(4), 575–596. https://doi.org/10.5465/amr.2011.0302

Clark, A. (2005). What makes a good job? Evidence from OECD countries. In S. Bazen, C. Lucifora & W. Salverda (Eds.) *Job quality and employer behaviour* (pp. 11–30). Palgrave Macmillan.

Duggan, J., Sherman, U., Carbery, R., & McDonnell, A. (2020). Algorithmic management and app-work in the gig economy: A research agenda for employment relations and HRM. *Human Resource Management Journal, 30*(1), 114–132. https://doi.org/10.1111/1748-8583.12258

Edwards, J. (2017). The Gig Economy Has Broken A Fundmental Link in Capitalism. [Online] Available at: http://uk.businessinsider.com/low-unemployment-wage-increases-gig-economy-2017-5 [Accessed 26 March 2019].

EurWork (2012)., Decent Work. [Online] Available at: https://www.eurofound.europa.eu/observatories/eurwork/industrial-relations-dictionary/decent-work [Accessed 12 April 2019].

Field, D., Forsey, A. (2017). Inside the Gig Economy: The Vulnerable Human Underbelly of the UK Labour Market. [Online] Available at: https://www.theguardian.com/inequality/2017/aug/24/inside-gig-economy-vulnerable-human-underbelly-of-uk-labour-market [Accessed 6 April 2019].

Findlay, P., Kalleberg, A., & Warhurst, C. (2013). The challange of job quality. *Human Relations, 66*(4), 441–451. https://doi.org/10.1177/0018726713481070

Flanagan, F. (2017). Symposium on work in the gig economy: Introduction. *The Economic and Labour Relations Review, 28*(3), 378–374. Volume https://doi.org/10.1177/1035304617724302,

Forde, C., Stuart, M., Joyce, S., Oliver, L., Valizade, D., Alberti, G., Hardy, K., Trappman, V., Umney, C., & Carson, C. (2017). *The Social Protection of Workers in the Platform Economy*. European Parliament.

Funnell, A. (2016). The contingent workforce and the growth of digital Taylorism. ABC, 28 August. Available at: https://www.abc.net.au/radionational/programs/futuretense/future-employment—going-back-to-square-one/7700584

FWC (2016). *Fair work framework 2016*. APS Group.

Gaillie, D. (2007). *Employment regimes and the quality of work* (1st ed.). Oxford University Press.

Goulden, H., Purvis, P., Coburn, J., Robinson, P., Mack, C., & Roughead, M. (2018). *Scottish Expert Advisory Panel on The Collaborative Economy - Final Report*. Scottish Government.

Grote, G., & Guest, D. (2017). The case for reinvigorating quality of working life research. *Human Relations, 70*(2), 149–167. https://doi.org/10.1177/0018726716654746

Healy, J., Nicholson, D., & Pekarek, A. (2017). Should we take the gig economy seriously? *Labour & Industry: a Journal of the Social and Economic Relations of Work, 27*(3), 232–248. https://doi.org/10.1080/10301763.2017.1377048

Hodson, R. (1991). *Dignity at work* (1st ed.). Cambridge University Press.

Holman, D. (2013). Job types and job quality in Europe. *Human Relations, 66*(4), 475–502. https://doi.org/10.1177/0018726712456407

Hook, L. (2015). FT: year in a word - Gig economy. [Online] Available at: https://www.ft.com/content/b5a2b122-a41b-11e5-8218-6b8ff73aae15 [Accessed 4 January 2019].

Howcroft, D., & Bergvall-Kåreborn, B. (2019). A typology of crowdwork platforms. *Work, Employment and Society, 33*(1), 21–38. https://doi.org/10.1177/0950017018760136

Huws, U., Spencer, N., Syrdal, D., & Holts, K. (2018). *Work in the European gig economy.* Research Results from the Foundation for European Progressive Studies; UNI Europa and; University of Hertfordshire.

ILO (2017). Decent Work. [Online] Available at: http://www.ilo.org/global/topics/decent-work/lang–en/index.htm [Accessed 01 April 2019].

ILO (2018). *Job Quality in the Platform Economy.* International Labour Organisation.

Kalleberg, A. (2016). Good Jobs, Bad Jobs. In: S. Edgell, H. Gottfried & E. Granter (Eds.). *The sage handbook of the sociology of work and employment* (pp. 111–128). Sage Publications.

Kalleberg, A. L., & Vaisey, S. (2005). Pathways to good job: perceived job quality amongst the machinists in North America. *British Journal of Industrial Relations, 43*(3), 431–454. https://doi.org/10.1111/j.1467-8543.2005.00363.x

Kalleberg, A., Dunn, M. (2017). Good Jobs, Bad Jobs in the Gig Economy. [Online] Available at: http://michael-dunn.org/wp-content/uploads/2017/05/ALK-MD.-JQ-in-Gig-Economy.pdf [Accessed 19 April 2019].

Kelly, G. (2017). FT: Trade Unions - Adapt to the Modern World or Die. [Online] Available at: https://www.ft.com/content/f65a8510-4626-11e7-8d27-59b4dd6296b8 [Accessed 27 March 2019].

Kessler, S. (2018). *Gigged: The Gig Economy, The End of The Job and The Future of Work* (1st ed.). Random House Business.

King, N., & Brooks, J. (2016). *Template Analysis for Business and Management Students* (1st ed.). Sage.

Knox, A., Warhurst, C., Nickson, D., & Dutton, E. (2015). More than a feeling: Using hotel room attendants to improve understanding of job quality. *The International Journal of Human Resource Management, 26*(12), 1547–1567. https://doi.org/10.1080/09585192.2014.949818

Loughlin, C., & Murray, R. (2013). Employment status congruence and job quality. *Human Relations, 66*(4), 529–553. https://doi.org/10.1177/0018726712460705

MacDonald, R. & Giazitzoglu, A. (2019). Youth enterprise and precarity: or, what is, and what is wrong with, the 'gig economy. *Journal of Sociology, 55*(4), 724–740.

Martel, J., & Dupuis, P. (2006). Quality of work life: Theoretical and methodological problems and presentation of a new model and measuring instrument. *Social Indicators Research, 77*(2), 333–368. https://doi.org/10.1007/s11205-004-5368-4

MGI (2016). *Independent Work: Choice, necessity and the gig economy.* McKinsey Global Institute.

Minter, K. (2017). Negotiating labour standards in the gig economy: Airtasker and unions in South Wales. *The Economic and Labour Relations Review, 28*(3), 438–417. https://doi.org/10.1177/1035304617724305

Munoz-Bustillo, R., Fernandez-Macias, E., Anton, J., & Esteve, F. (2009). *E pluribus unum? A critical review of job quality indicators*. International Labour Organisation.

O'Connor, S. (2017). Driven to despair - the hidden costs of the gig economy. [Online] Available at: https://www.ft.com/content/749cb87e-6ca8-11e7-b9c7-15af748b60d0 [Accessed 6 April 2019].

Parkinson, H. (2017). The Guardian: 'Sometimes you dont feel human' - how the gig economy chews up and spits out millenials. [Online] Available at: https://www.theguardian.com/business/2017/oct/17/sometimes-you-dont-feel-human-how-the-gig-economy-chews-up-and-spits-out-millennials [Accessed 20 September 2019].

Persole, A., Urzi Brancati, M. C., Fernandez-Macia, E., Biagi, F., & Gonzalez Vazquex, I. (2018). *Platform workers in Europe*. Publications Office of the European Union.

REC (2016). *Gig economy: The uberisation of work*. Recruitment and Employment Confederation.

Rose, M. (2003). Good deal, bad deal? *Work, Employment and Society, 17*(3), 503–530. https://doi.org/10.1177/09500170030173006

Royuela, V., Lopez-Tamayo, J., & Surinach, J. (2008). The institutional v academic definition of the quality of work life: What is the focus of The European Commission? *Social Indicators Research, 86*(3), 401–415. https://doi.org/10.1007/s11205-007-9175-6

Rubery, J., Grimshaw, D., Keizer, A., & Johnson, M. (2018). Challenges and contradictions in the 'normalising' of precarious work. *Work, Employment and Society, 32*(3), 509–527. https://doi.org/10.1177/0950017017751790

Scot Gov (2019). Overview of Actions: Fair Work Action Plan. [Online] Available at: https://economicactionplan.mygov.scot/fair-work/overview/ [Accessed 8 April 2019].

Scottish Government (2016). *Scotlands labour market strategy*. The Scottish Government.

Stanford, J. (2017). The resurgence of gig work: Historical and theoretical perspectives. *Economic and Labour Relations Review 28*(3), 382–401.

Stewart, A., & Stanford, J. (2017). Regulating Work in the gig economy: What are the options? *The Economic and Labour Relations Review, 28*(3), 420–418. https://doi.org/10.1177/1035304617722461

Taylor, P., & Bain, P. (1999). An assembly line in the head: Work and employee relations in the call centre. *Industrial Relations Journal, 30*(2), 101–117. https://doi.org/10.1111/1468-2338.00113

TUC (2016). *Living on the edge*. Trade Unions Congress.

Warhurst, C., Carre, F., Findlay, P., & Tilly, C. (2012). *Are bad jobs inevitable?. Trends, determinants and responses to job quality in the twenty first century* (1st ed.). Palgrave Macmillan.

Wood, A. J., Graham, M., Lehdonvirta, V., & Hjorth, I. (2018). Good Gig, Bad Gig: Autonomy and Algorithmic Control in the Global Gig Economy. *Work, Employment & Society: A Journal of the British Sociological Association, 33*(1), 56–75. https://doi.org/10.1177/0950017018785616

Appendix A: Interview guide

Topics Covered During Interview	Example of Questions Asked
Personal Background and Reasons for Undertaking Gig Work	1. Tell me a bit about your work history and how you ended up working for [platform]. 2. Did you apply for other jobs before you started working for [platform]? 3. Why are you still working for [platform] now?
Overall perception and Experiences of Gig Work	1. Tell me a bit about your current role and what an average day or week might be like for you. Is this consistent? 2. What aspects of gig work do you enjoy the most? 3. Do you see any disadvantages to working this way in comparison to other types of work? 4. Would you recommend working this way to a friend or family member?
Perception and Experiences of Key Job Quality Components	*Probing questions were used to explore subjective experiences of key job quality components including; wages and conditions; job content; wages; workplace demands; work-related risks; job security; social working environment; training; opportunities for career development; working hours; access to social benefits and; physical work conditions.*
Perceived Impact of Technology on Quality of Work Experience	1. Tell me about how the application works. 2. How do you feel about working through an app on your phone? 3. Do you think there are any benefits or downsides to working this way?
Future Ambitions of Gig Workers	1. What are your plans over the next 5 years? 2. Do you think you will continue to use the platform to find work?

Appendix A. Coding framework

Effective Voice	Opportunities for individual voice	Surveys
		Contact with platform
	Opportunities for collective voice	Union representation
		Informal collectivism
Career Opportunity	Training	Formal
		On the job
	Progression	Gaining experience
		Networking
		Entrepreneurship
		Skill development
Security	Formal job security	Contractual status
	Income security	Wage levels
		Wage volatility
		Hidden costs
	Perceived security	Accessibility
		Anonymity
Fulfilment	Psychological aspects	Repetitive
		Enjoyment
	Autonomy	Sense of freedom
		Flexible scheduling
		Restrictions on autonomy
Respect	Relationship with platform	Discrimination/favouritism
		Dignity
		Lack of trust
	Social support	Support from platform
		Support from co-workers
	Safety at work	Work-related risks
		Cashless system
External factors	Individual factors	Prior work experience
		Individual preference
		Dependence upon income from gig economy as primary/supplementary source
		Dependence upon gig work on short term v long term basis
	Contextual factors	Availability of labour market alternatives
		Employment regime (trade-off between security and flexibility)

Recruitment in the gig economy: attraction and selection on digital platforms

Penny Williams, Paula McDonald and Robyn Mayes

ABSTRACT

Digital platform work is undertaken as short term, temporary 'gigs' mediated by platform businesses that connect self-employed workers to clients *via* an app. Platforms manage and profit from labour-capital relations yet are not employers. This study explores the extent to which, and how, digital platforms implement human resource practices to attract and select self-employed platform workers. A qualitative, comparative analysis of the website content, and terms and conditions documents of 17 digital platforms offering virtual work in graphic design, and in-person care work in Australia was undertaken. The findings reveal how platforms combine traditional recruitment practices with new forms of algorithmic shortlisting that result in industry-specific risks for platform workers. More broadly, the study provides insights into the recruitment practices used by digital platform businesses and contributes to knowledge of how the roles and responsibilities of human resource management are reconfigured in digital platform work.

Introduction

Distinct from other forms of contingent work such as contracting or agency employment, online platforms digitally connect workers with individuals or businesses that require goods, services, or labour (Duggan *et al.*, 2020; Katz and Krueger, 2019). The number of people seeking work through digital platforms globally is currently estimated to be relatively small, ranging between 0.4% to 19% of the population within various countries (for a summary see Florisson & Mandl, 2018). However, strong growth is projected as digital platform work expands into new industries and as large multinationals, as well as individuals, turn to platforms to source contingent workers (Kässi & Lehdonvirta, 2018). As self-employed contractors or freelancers, platform workers are not committed to a single employer long-term, but rather undertake short term "gigs" sourced *via* an app that is neither an agency nor an employer, but regardless imposes terms and conditions and forms of control that govern the workers' access to work (Graham *et al.*, 2017; Veen *et al.*, 2020).

Digital platform work has been decried for driving down wages and exposing workers to greater levels of risk and precarity (Graham *et al.*, 2019) and current research suggests that few individuals engage in platform work on a full-time basis (Pesole *et al.*, 2018). Yet, platforms are emerging in greater numbers across new industries (Kässi & Lehdonvirta, 2018). Where they have been established for some time, competition for workers is fierce (Cook *et al.*, 2018). At the same time, platform work may be attractive to workers because it provides the flexibility to choose when and how often they work, and the autonomy to supplement or earn their entire income in this way. (McDonald *et al.*, 2020; Wood *et al.*, 2019). However, the autonomy and flexibility enjoyed by workers poses an inherent commercial risk for digital platform businesses because to be financially viable they must rely on the consistent availability of clients and workers willing to use the platform.

This fundamental challenge raises significant questions about the nature of HR practices, roles, and responsibilities as they apply to the three parties involved in platform work: the platform, the worker, and the client. To date, research addressing HR practices used by platform companies has been confined largely to the use of platform workers as a contingent workforce within traditional organisations, or to conceptual discussions. The extent to which, and how, digital platform companies implement human resource management (HRM) practices to attract or manage the quality of self-employed workers has rarely been empirically explored. This study addresses this paucity of evidence through an examination of the practices of attraction and selection in two distinct types of platform work in two different industries. The study asks: how do digital platforms attract and select workers to meet the needs of platform clients?

Before turning to the analysis, we firstly provide a synthesis of the literature on digital platform work, including the limited research that has specifically addressed HR practices in this context. Drawing on Schneider's (1987) attraction-selection-attrition (ASA) framework, we examine the website content, and terms and conditions documents of 17 digital platforms which offer aged/disability care work and graphic design work in Australia. The study contributes to the HR literature by addressing critical questions about the relevance of these fundamental HR concepts to digital platform work (Aguinis & Lawal, 2013; Duggan *et al.*, 2020; Kuhn & Maleki, 2017). It further enriches understandings of how platform businesses build and attempt to manage the demand for and quality of platform labour.

Digital platform work

Digital platform work is an emergent dimension of the labour market that is characterised by short term, temporary 'gigs' mediated by digital platform businesses that connect self-employed or independent contract workers to clients/consumers *via* a website or app. Digital platform businesses are not employers but rather labour market intermediaries or agents (Gramano, 2020; Kässi & Lehdonvirta, 2018; Meijerink & Keegan, 2019). The extant literature has attempted to distinguish between various types of work offered by platforms and the digital means through which work can now be accessed but there is no universal agreement about such categories of work or workers. Duggan *et al.* (2020) for example, identify three categories of work: capital platform work where individuals sell or lease assets *via* a digital platform; crowdwork where digitally-mediated work is completed remotely; and app-work where work is organised *via* the digital platform but completed locally. Howcroft and Bergvall-Kåreborn (2019) further distinguish crowdwork into four subcategories whereas Huws *et al.* (2018, p.1130) define crowdwork simply as "work managed by online platforms". Recent reviews further highlight the complexities associated with categorising platform work including that a single platform business may offer multiple types of work simultaneously (Florisson & Mandl, 2018; Riso, 2019). For example, graphic design platforms may concurrently facilitate online freelance work by connecting designers to clients; provide a venue for designers to share portfolios in the hope of obtaining work; and conduct design contests (Howcroft & Bergvall-Kåreborn, 2019). However, common across various typologies and central to the empirical focus of the current study, is the distinction between work that is 'virtual' or done wholly online, and in-person work completed locally (Drahokoupil & Fabo, 2016; Pesole *et al.*, 2018; Wood *et al.*, 2019). We explore this distinction in our examination of HR practices used by platform businesses on the basis that the organisation of virtual and physical platform work is likely to differ in terms of the potential labour pool available and the methods of sourcing this labour.

Platforms that offer 'in person' services mediate labour-capital relations in one of two ways; the platform assigns tasks to workers *via* an app, as occurs on platforms such as Uber or Deliveroo; or clients post jobs and worker profiles are 'matched' to those jobs *via* platform algorithms. Workers can choose to bid for the job and clients can select and pay their preferred worker *via* the platform, often only meeting when the task is being performed. This second approach is common to platforms offering household tasks, maintenance, or care work (Mandl, 2019). Similarly, virtual work can consist of micro-tasking or 'click work' such as on MTurk, where jobs are broken into small tasks and algorithmically assigned to an invisible pool of workers; or contests where speculative work is completed in response to a client brief and only the selected 'winner' is paid; or online freelance work *via* platforms such as Upwork or Freelancer, where workers post their profile and bid for jobs posted by clients (Howcroft & Bergvall-Kåreborn, 2019; Taylor & Joshi, 2019). Some digital platforms offer more than one type of work.

Both virtual and in-person digital platform work are fundamentally different to traditional models of allocating labour to tasks. Firstly, digital platforms broker the labour hire relationship yet are rarely defined as an employer, labour hire firm, or employment agency. Platforms instead define themselves as a 'technology company', 'website', 'meeting place', or other (self-selected) category. These definitions create symbolic boundaries (Ticona & Mateescu, 2018) that arguably deny the platform's role in providing employment services. Work proceeds through registration and active engagement with a website or app governed by terms and conditions of use, rather than being defined by an employment contract (Degryse, 2016; Gramano, 2020). Workers are typically independent contractors or freelancers who sometimes pay the platform to receive work opportunities, and who are usually in control of their place of work, their equipment, and their time and availability. The frequency and extent of participation in digital platform work is at the discretion of the worker, and workers can participate concurrently in different types of work across multiple platforms (Pesole *et al.*, 2018).

Although platform workers are generally self-employed freelancers, the intermediary role played by the platform is distinct from traditional contracting where there is typically a direct binary relationship between the employer and the contractor. This is because workers are uniquely subject to forms of management and control embedded within the platform such as systems of rating and review and algorithms designed to control work quality standards (Cappelli & Keller, 2013; Veen *et al.*, 2020; Wood *et al.*, 2019). There is little empirical research that considers these control and management practices through an HR lens, nor if, as is typical in traditional firms, practices vary across platforms.

HRM in digital platform work

Spanning "the management of work and the management of people to do the work" (Boxall & Purcell, 2011: p.3), HRM on digital platforms is undertaken virtually through the platform website or app, regardless of whether the work itself is online or in-person. HRM in this context faces significant challenges. Platform workers are symbolically and materially distanced from the business and they are not contractually bound by an employment contract. This means the platform cannot directly control the frequency, amount, or standard of work produced. Platforms must however provide some assurances of quality to entice clients to use and reuse the platform, as well as attract sufficient workers to be competitively mobilised on demand (Jabagi *et al.*, 2019).

Discussions of HRM in relation to digital platform work have been primarily conceptual and focussed on the implications for the standard employer-employee relationship. Ellmer and Reichel (2018) for example, discuss how digital platform workers, as a labour source in traditional organisations, pose challenges for the implementation of HR practices such as compensation, performance management, recruitment, selection, training, and job design. In one of the few articles that extend HRM perspectives beyond traditional employment boundaries, Cascio and Boudreau (2017, p11) argue that HR processes can be conceptualised as a series of employment stages that occur outside "the boundary of a single employer and not necessarily through work experiences organized as jobs". Applying the talent lifecycle to nonstandard workers, they extend HR practices such as "attracting and sourcing" to activities that encourage worker engagement; "selecting" to the process of matching workers with available work; and "separating" as the end of a work assignment. Meijerink and Keegan (2019, p.220) describe digital platform work as an ecosystem where the platform, clients and workers create value through their "interdependence and multilaterality", and where HR practices govern the exchanges between actors in the ecosystem.

Aguinis and Lawal (2013) outline a research agenda for investigating how HR practices apply to work accessed *via* digital platforms. They call for a better understanding of recruitment and selection, highlighting how intermediary platforms potentially obfuscate assessments of person-organisation fit. Other scholars have similarly questioned if fit can be assessed in the rudimentary and seemingly hyper-efficient recruitment processes of digital platforms (Duggan *et al.*, 2020; Howcroft & Bergvall-Kåreborn, 2019). Building on an earlier paper about the relevance of HR practices to digital platform businesses (Kuhn, 2016), Kuhn and Maleki (2017) conceptualised how the constructs of employee satisfaction, commitment, organisational support, turnover and organisational citizenship behaviour might pertain to platform work, drawing attention to the need for a nuanced application of HR practices in this context. Duggan *et al.* (2020) relatedly explore how activities such as performance management and work assignment are incorporated into digital platform work through algorithmic management. In one of the few studies to empirically investigate the hiring of digital platform workers, Carr *et al.* (2017) demonstrated that clients use a series of informational cues taken from a worker's profile and reviews to form an assessment about the worker's person-job fit before offering them work. Although the Carr *et al.* (2017) study explored interactions on one platform only, it highlighted the complexities of selection in this context. Clients may ultimately select workers, but digital platforms may influence selection in subtle yet important ways.

As the number of digital platforms operating in a defined industry grows, the technology and business model that facilitates access to an on-demand workforce becomes less of a competitive advantage than the availability and quality of the platform labour force. Melián González's (2018) study of online reviews of workers posted on two platforms indicated that clients value professionalism, good service and high performance, suggesting that platforms may need to compete for high quality workers. Competition to recruit drivers already occurs between platforms such as Uber and Lyft (Lee *et al.*, 2015), where worker attrition is high (Cook *et al.*, 2018). Coyle (2017) further argues that the provision of high-quality services is essential for platforms to remain commercially viable, and that workers must therefore be incentivised to register with the platform. Attraction and selection of talented workers are thus crucial to the sustainability of platform businesses.

Attraction and selection in digital platform work

Schneider's (1987) widely used attraction–selection-attrition (ASA) framework posits that people are differentially attracted to organisations based on their analysis of the fit between their interests and personality, and organisational characteristics. Accordingly, recruitment processes attract and select people with similar attributes, and filter out individuals who are unlikely to fit, or these individuals subsequently leave the organisation (Acikgoz, 2019; Schneider, 1987; Schneider *et al.*, 1995). Organisations are thus reflective of the people who are recruited. Recruitment encompasses activities which identify, attract and influence individuals with the required capabilities to apply for job openings and accept a job offer (Breaugh, 2008). Assessments of fit by organisations and by individuals are made at three key stages; before joining (attraction), during early interactions (selection), and after commencing work, when poor fit may lead to attrition (Acikgoz, 2019).

Traditional methods of attracting job applicants include advertisements, use of employment agencies, and direct marketing to candidates (Acikgoz, 2019; Perez *et al.*, 2014). Recently e-recruitment, the use of web-based tools including social media, online job boards and corporate websites, have also been utilised by organisations to differentiate their employment offering to potential applicants (Alamro *et al.*, 2018). Websites and publicly available information now play a central role in communicating an organisation's employee value proposition (Barrow & Mosely, 2005), signalling job/organisational characteristics from which applicants assess fit (Dineen *et al.*, 2007; Dutta *et al.*, 2019). Prior research suggests that recruitment messages should contain credible and specific information on the career opportunities, salary and other benefits distinct to an organisation because an individual's preferences for certain job or employment conditions influence their perceptions of job/organisational attractiveness (Barrow & Mosely, 2005; Breaugh, 2008; Dineen *et al.*, 2007).

Decisions about relative compatibility and capability to do the job occur in the selection phase of the ASA framework (Acikgoz, 2019) usually against job-related selection criteria and pursuant to ethical and legal standards, including anti-discrimination legislation (Graves & Karren, 1996). Selection practices—shortlisting, interviews, abilities testing, and work sampling (Klotz *et al.*, 2013)—enable assessment of a candidate's person-organisation fit and person-job fit (Acikgoz, 2019; Rynes & Gerhart, 1990). Person-job fit refers to the match between the applicant's skills and qualifications and the job requirements, while person-organisation fit refers to the perceived match between the goals and values of the organisation and the applicant (Carless, 2005; Schneider *et al.*, 1995). Perceptions of fit influence employee retention, engagement, and performance (Alfes *et al.*, 2016; Stone *et al.*, 2019), and can induce candidate attrition during the recruitment process (Acikgoz, 2019). Candidates with low fit are rejected or self-select out during the recruitment process or soon thereafter (Acikgoz, 2019). The full cycle of attraction-selection-attrition thus occurs during the recruitment process producing a distinct applicant pool (Acikgoz, 2019).

Although usually applied to traditional organisations, the ASA framework, provides an ideal lens through which to examine the attraction and selection processes of digital platforms and explore the potential implications for assessments of person-job/person-organisation fit in this contemporary form of work. Since digital platforms match workers with jobs, or match clients who require work with available workers, the engagement and performance of workers is closely connected to client retention (Jabagi *et al.*, 2019). Hence, the ways in which attraction and selection processes are deployed by digital platforms - a context where workers have a high degree of agency in choosing the platforms on which they work, and when and how much they work - is crucial to economic success. For this reason, it is important to understand how digital platforms attract independent workers to register and engage in work, and how selection processes operate across a triangulated work relationship. Potential workers interact with digital platforms *via* their websites and are subject to the terms and conditions of platforms on which they register. Website content and terms and conditions are thus central to worker assessments of fit and provide insight into the processes of attraction and selection on digital platforms.

Methods

Sample

This study identifies and critically examines recruitment processes operationalised in the triangular labour-hire relationship central to digital platform work, through qualitative thematic analysis of the website content, and terms and conditions documents of eight digital platforms offering care services and nine digital platforms offering graphic design services in Australia. The sampling frame was developed following Drahokoupil and Fabo (2016, p.2) distinction between platforms that "facilitate the connection between demand in one location and remote suppliers that are possibly based abroad" and those that offer local labour, or more simply, "services provided digitally" and "services provided on-location" (Pesole *et al.*, 2018, p.4). With respect to the former, the work is virtual because it is completed and delivered online (e.g. graphic design work). In contrast, platform-mediated localised services involve a physical presence (e.g. care work). This sampling strategy (see Table 1) also allowed for comparisons between an industry in which platform work is relatively new (care work)[1] and one where it is more established (graphic design work). In both contexts, workers are required to possess skills that would usually require a vocational certificate/qualification to obtain employment in a traditional organisation. This stands in contrast to transport and food delivery platform work - a primary focus of research on digital platform work to date - which does not require formal qualifications. Care workers and graphic design workers who access work *via* platforms also share other commonalities including engaging with online processes that connect them with individuals or businesses who require

Table 1. Characteristics of sample digital platforms.

Platform	Summary of services offered	Platform operates (locations)	Commenced operations	Work is virtual/local
Care1	Aged and Disability Care	Australia	2015	Local
Care2	Aged and Disability Care, Childcare, Pet Care, Housekeeping	Global	2016	Local
Care3	Aged and Disability Care	Australia	2016	Local
Care4	Disability Care	Australia (4 States)	2014	Local
Care5	Aged and Disability Care, Home Nursing	Australia	2018	Local
Care6	Aged and Disability Care	Australia (2 States)	2016	Local
Care7	Aged and Disability Care	Australia	2014	Local
Care8	Aged and Disability Care, Childcare	Australia (2 States)	2016	Local
GD1	Graphic Design, Web and App Design, Illustrations	Global	2008	Virtual
GD2	Graphic Design, Web and App Development	Global	2008	Virtual
GD3	Graphic Design, Writing and Translation, Web and App Development, Illustrators, Social Media Marketing, Professional Services	Global	1999	Virtual
GD4	Graphic Design, Web and App Development, Social Media Marketing, Writing, Illustration, Programming,	Global	2009	Virtual
GD5	Graphic Design, Photography, Writing, Web Development, Social Media Marketing, Illustration, Animation	Australia	2015	Virtual
GD6	Graphic Design, Web and App Development, Writing, Professional Services	Global	2014	Virtual
GD7	Graphic Design, Social Media Marketing, Illustration, Web development, Data Entry, Writing, Professional Services	Global	2010	Virtual
GD8	Graphic Design, Social Media Marketing, Web Development, App Development	Global	2014	Virtual
GD9	Graphic Design, Web Development, Illustration, App Development	Global	2003	Virtual

work, and participation in advertising, bidding or matching activities, despite no guaranteed receipt of work.

Care platforms provide opportunities for work in either or both of the following ways: carers sift through jobs posted by care-seekers and respond *via* the platform; or carers advertise their services online and care-seekers view their profile and contact them directly. Clients can input their location and support needs and specify preferences for worker characteristics such as gender or spoken language to assist algorithmic matching. Matched workers manage bookings through the platform's app. Similarly, graphic design platforms allow designers to advertise skills and services to clients or, alternatively, to bid for posted work. Clients using graphic design platforms may also create a contest where designers submit completed designs and payment is awarded to the 'winner'. To access potential work opportunities, digital platforms uniformly require all users to agree to non-negotiable terms and conditions for use of the platform. These terms and conditions specify who can access the platform (and therefore work opportunities) and, to a lesser extent, define credentials, qualifications, experience, or skills that workers must possess.

Procedure

During November and December 2018, popular internet search engines Google, Yahoo and Bing, chosen to replicate the experience of platform users (Madden *et al.*, 2012; Weare & Lin, 2000), were used to identify digital platforms offering graphic design services or disability and aged care services in Australia. To enable a comparative analysis of HR strategies used by platform businesses in different industries within the same labour market and regulatory environment, we limited our search to platforms offering care or graphic design services in the Australian context by using the appended word 'Australia'. However, several platforms also provided other types of services and/or provided services outside Australia. To select graphic design platforms, search terms included 'graphic design work', 'find a graphic designer', 'graphic design jobs', 'website development' and 'logo designers'. To select care platforms, search terms included 'find a carer/support worker', 'care providers', 'disability care', 'home care', 'aged care'; 'support worker/carer jobs', and 'working in aged care/disability care'. Following Hurwitz *et al.* (2018), inclusion/exclusion criteria were developed and collector/review sites such as www.gigsmash.com were used to confirm the inclusion of prominent platforms.

Firstly, since our focus was on the recruitment of workers with skill sets specific to care or graphic design work, digital platforms that offered generic task services (that feasibly but not definitively included care or graphic design work) were excluded. Nine care platforms and thirteen graphic design platforms offering services in Australia were initially identified. Digital platforms were further distinguished from the websites of traditional organisations, job boards and online stores, by the existence of 'terms and conditions of use' that expressly denied that the business was an employer, agency or labour hire company, and the existence of digital worker-client matching and payment processes intermediated by the platform. One care platform and four graphic design platforms that did not display all these characteristics were further excluded. The final sample therefore comprised the entire population of digital platforms specialising in the provision of care and graphic design services that were operating in Australia at the time of the study.

A qualitative thematic analysis was undertaken of the terms and conditions documents governing the use of the platform and the content of each platform website. Website content included 'frequently asked questions', 'how it works' sections, and information for people seeking work. Both data sources, which were publicly available, were downloaded, saved offline and preserved for coding (Hurwitz *et al.*, 2018). Screenshots of relevant pages from the website enabled coding of embedded content (see Table 2 for a summary of website content). The researchers did not register or subscribe to the sample platforms so information available only to registered users was not included in the data.

Analysis

Applying thematic analysis, coding was undertaken in phases progressing from semantic description to interpretation (Braun & Clarke, 2006, p.13). For each platform and data source we first identified text directly relevant to the organisation and management of work on the platform. We excluded clauses in the terms and conditions relating to legal jurisdictions, third party services and copyright. With reference to the HR literature, two coders searched for text that indicated recruitment methods such as clauses in the terms and conditions that specified who could access the platform; outlined any required qualifications or vetting process; or stipulated how workers were selected by clients. Axial categories (Gioia *et al.*, 2013) were then developed and tested through a process of weekly meetings and iterative re-coding of data from the selected platforms across both industries, by two coders. A coding framework was agreed and applied across the sample, initially by one coder, then reviewed and independently used to re-code the data by a second coder (Gioia *et al.*, 2013). The material in Table 2 represents the "slices of data" (Glaser & Strauss, 2017, p.108) within each platform that were iteratively analysed and compared to achieve theoretical saturation within categories. The categorisation of data was peer-reviewed fortnightly by all authors and further reviewed by an independent HRM scholar (Gioia *et al.*, 2013). During these meetings, the utility of various platform practices (such as worker profiles) were debated to scrutinise and agree themes. A final phase of theory-driven analysis (Braun & Clarke, 2006) examined each identified theme in relation to ASA theory, refining and grouping the processes and mechanisms adopted by platforms. During this phase, comparisons were made across platforms within and between the two industries.

Table 2. Summary of data set.

Platform	Description of website pages reviewed*												Documents reviewed	
	Home/ Landing	About	How it Works	Why Join	FAQs / Help Centre	Workers – Find Work	Clients –Post a job, Find a worker	Worker Testimonials	Pricing	Safety	Create a profile	Other	Terms & Conditions	Other
Care1	x	x	x	x	x	x	x	x	x	x	x	Concierge	x	
Care2	x	x	x	x	x	x	x	x		x	x	Tips/Advice	x	
Care3	x	x	x	x	x	x	x	x			x	Tips/Tools	x	
Care4	x	x	x	x		x	x		x		x		x	
Care5	x	x	x	x	x	x	x	x	x	x	x	Services	x	
Care6	x		x	x	x	x		x	x	x	x		x	Worker Help
Care7	x	x	x	x	x	x	x	x	x	x	x	Services	x	Worker Guide
Care8	x	x	x		x	x	x	x	x		x	Carer Resources	x	User guides
GD1	x	x	x	x	x	x	x	x	x		x	Contests	x	
GD2	x	x	x	x	x	x	x	x	x		x	Jobs	x	'Rules' document
GD3	x	x	x	x	x	x	x	x	x	x	x	Jobs	x	
GD4	x	x	x	x	x	x	x	x		x	x		x	Worker Help
GD5	x	x	x	x	x	x	x		x		x		x	
GD6	x	x	x	x	x	x	x		x	x	x	Hiring guide	x	
GD7	x		x	x	x	x	x	x	x	x	x	Worker guide	x	
GD8	x	x	x	x	x	x	x	x	x		x	Contests	x	
GD9	x	x	x	x	x	x	x	x	x		x	Join Us Forum	x	

Note: Column headings describe sections of the website reviewed. Actual sections or web pages may have had a different title such as "become a carer" or "designers page" rather than "Worker – Find Work", however the content was similarly aimed specifically at platform workers.

Findings/results

The substantive findings are presented in three main sections: how platforms attract workers; the selection processes used by platforms; and the selection processes used by clients of the platform.

Attraction processes used by platforms

All care and graphic design platform websites contained substantial information directed at individuals seeking work. To attract workers, platforms promoted the benefits of platform work and publicised an abundance of work opportunities. Some benefits were, prima facie, common to both graphic design and care platforms, such as enticing workers to join a "community". However, illustrating distinctions between the two targeted industries, in graphic design, the community was "*creative*" and/or "*global*" (7 out of 9 platforms used one or both these terms), whereas in care work, community was referred to as "*local*", extending beyond workers to include clients:

> ""*... become a part of our global community of talented designers". (GD1web).*
>
> *"... flexible and rewarding work in your local community." (Care4web)*

Both care and graphic design platforms listed "*flexibility*", "*freedom*" and "*choice*" as reasons to register. Workers were invited to "*set your own rates*", "*choose your clients*", and select "*when you work, where you work, and for whom you work*" (see Table 3 for frequency of these terms). Care platforms emphasised control over work *hours*, whereas graphic design platforms referred to flexibility as *where* work could be undertaken.

Although workers engaged with the platforms as freelancers/contractors, they were often encouraged to register on the platform in order to '*build a career*'. Several care platforms cited additional benefits such as '*work close to home*' and the provision of, or discounts on '*carer insurance*'. Location, autonomy, flexible work arrangements, career opportunities, and discounted products, are offerings frequently used by traditional employers to attract top talent (Cappelli, 2015). Yet as freelancers, digital platform workers inherently have autonomy, flexibility and control over their work. These *benefits* may not therefore attract higher quality workers to the platform nor necessarily position one platform as more

Table 3. Statements made regarding choice and flexibility.

	Choose your clients/jobs	Set your own rates/prices	Choose when you work	Choose where you work
Graphic design	7	6	6	7
Care platforms	7	6	5	4

attractive than another, given the similarities of espoused benefits across platforms.

Distinct from conventional employment, platforms advertised an abundance of work opportunities to attract workers.

"Clients are now posting jobs in hundreds of skill categories," (GD6web)

Graphic design platforms promised access to global work opportunities and usually cited the number of job postings, projects completed, or logos of past clients, inferring that work was plentiful. For example, 7 graphic design platforms listed the number of "*designs*", "*completed projects*" or "*jobs*" as being in the hundreds of thousands or millions, and the remaining two presented long lists of reputable companies as potential clients. In contrast, only three of the care platforms in the sample provided numerical information on available work opportunities. Instead, all care platforms used the absence of costs as a selling point: for example, "*joining is free*" (Care1, Care8web). Yet a deeper investigation of the terms and conditions of care platforms identified that workers could indeed incur costs, including acquiring police checks and insurance, along with internet and vehicle expenses.

On both graphic design and care platforms, registering on the platform was described as '*easy*' (6 care, 4 graphic design platforms) and the many work opportunities available were described as enjoyable or '*rewarding*' (Care7). The apparently straightforward and efficient (*within 24 h;* Care7) processes involved in obtaining work through the platform was supported by worker testimonials on all care and graphic design platforms, except one.

Selection

According to ASA, organisations are more likely to select individuals who possess characteristics similar to existing members. In practice, this assessment is made using a linear series of selection processes. Carers and graphic design platform workers were subject to multiple layers of selection processes although these varied between industries.

Selection processes used by platforms

The terms and conditions of all care platforms specified that to register on the platform, workers must be "*over 18 years*", "*legally authorised to work in Australia*" and in possession of a National Police Check. Additionally, all care platforms required workers to undertake a "*working with children check*" and to supply proof of identification and referee details. For certain types of care, platforms also stipulated mandatory qualifications or accreditations such as first aid certificates. Care platforms further stipulated on their websites that workers were vetted against these standards, signifying the application (in principle at least) of minimum selection criteria.

However, contradicting these assurances that workers are screened, care platforms stated in their terms and conditions that they do not *"examine, determine or warrant the certification and/or licensing, competence, solvency or information of any Carer who uses or is listed on the platform"* (Care6). Arguably, such assertions may absolve care platforms from responsibility for, or endorsement of, worker credentials. Instead responsibility and risk shifted to the client who is explicitly

> *"responsible for verifying and satisfying yourself as to the accuracy of any information, content or qualifications provided or listed by a Care Provider, ... you engage Care Providers at your own risk." (Care5 terms)*

Unlike care platforms where police checks, referees and identification checks provided clients with an indicator of safety (if not quality) of service delivery, there were no such criteria in the terms and conditions of graphic design platforms. Minimum criteria reflected only the capacity for the individual to enter into a contractual agreement (i.e. aged 18 years or over). Prerequisites for credentials, qualifications, or experience that might indicate standards of design work, were noticeably absent. Rather, workers, were encouraged to list such details in their profiles. Although more than half (6) of the graphic design platforms in the sample indicated that they "*curated*" or "*verified*" their designers, in almost all cases this was confined to checking email addresses, bank details and other identifying information. Two graphic design platforms stated that they examined worker designs for quality but provided no information on how quality checks were undertaken.

In a traditional recruitment and selection process, job advertisements typically specify minimum or essential criteria, in addition to criteria for desirable or preferred skills and qualifications (Graves & Karren, 1996). Desirable criteria were visible in two different locations on the care platform websites: where care seekers/clients were guided on what to look for when selecting a carer; and where care workers were instructed on how to obtain work *via* the platform. For example, clients were advised to consider the qualifications held by workers, and care workers were advised to create a profile that was "*simple and to the point*" and would "*help clients get to know you better*" and "*stand out from the crowd*" (Care7 web).

Graphic design platforms also provided guidance to workers on how to make their profiles or bids for work appealing to clients. Through supporting information included in the FAQs pages, or in some cases on blogs written and managed by the platforms, workers were encouraged to make their profiles and/or bids more competitive and more attractive to potential clients in order to win more work. In this way, their profiles constituted a form of curriculum vitae and their bid operated as the job application in a competitive selection process. Both served to differentiate the worker from other platform workers – the applicant pool for the gig.

Client-driven selection processes

All terms and conditions explicitly stated that the platform was *not* an employer and, as noted earlier, contained clauses that placed the responsibility for verifying credentials and selecting a worker onto the client. The recommended selection processes that clients were encouraged to adopt varied considerably both between and within industries. Six of the eight care platforms recommended shortlisting, reference checking, interviews (telephone or face-to-face and sometimes both), verification of qualifications, and/or the development of a contract. Clients could shortlist workers from their profiles. One care platform further encouraged clients to:

> *"Conduct your own internet search on potential candidates and check any social network accounts associated with them." (Care2 web)*

Perhaps reflecting the in-person and intimate nature of the work, care platforms encouraged selection techniques similar to those applied in a traditional employment relationship, recommending face-to-face meetings between the client and worker. The extent to which clients or workers heed this advice is unknown, particularly as jobs may vary between brief or long-term care assignments.

In contrast, graphic design platforms rarely provided detailed guidelines on the processes (such as interviews) that clients should use to choose a worker, other than suggesting the use of filters to "*browse profiles*", "*compare proposals/bids/offers*" or "*check out the feedback*" from clients. Clients could review designer profiles and message workers *via* the platform to discuss an opportunity, or simply post a job and accept bids.

Given that graphic design platform workers complete the work online and can be located anywhere in the world, the potential applicant pool is considerably larger than for localised care work, increasing the likely competition for advertised jobs. Digital platforms are renowned for creating competition between workers through bidding processes. However, on graphic design platforms, competitive client-driven selection processes were intensified through contests. Five of the nine graphic design platforms in the sample allowed clients to initiate a contest where a crowd of designers would submit a completed design in response to a client-posted brief. The client could then review all the designs before awarding a 'winner' who would be paid for the work. This was expressed as a 'risk free' selection process for clients. Traditional selection processes for creative jobs (including freelance work) require workers to present work portfolios or samples. A contest however requires designers to fully complete the work with no guarantee of 'winning' or of being paid.

A final dimension of client-driven selection was algorithmic shortlisting. Both care and graphic design platforms provided search filters to assist clients to shortlist from the potential pool of available workers. Platform algorithms used inbuilt conditions to "match" workers against the client's search criteria and decide which worker profiles were presented. In this process the relevance of the worker's profile as a CV becomes critical because to be considered for a job the worker's profile must contain elements that matched client search terms. The position of a worker's profile on the web page was also determined by hidden processes that appeared to prioritise workers with high client ratings and good client reviews. On eight platforms, workers could pay for priority positioning to potentially receive more work opportunities, bringing the fairness of the matching process into question.

When recruiting and selecting a new employee, an organisation must comply with anti-discrimination and privacy laws. In Australia, it is illegal for an employer to discriminate against prospective employees or independent contractors on the basis of personal attributes such as race, age, gender or religion, unless the attribute is a genuine occupational requirement (FairWork Ombudsman, 2019). Any such information for clients undertaking selection was not provided by any platforms examined. While platform terms and conditions occasionally specified the need for clients to comply with 'laws', they did not specify which laws were being referred to or how clients should comply. Clients were '*solely responsible*' not only for selection and recruitment but also for '*compliance with all applicable laws*' (*Care1 terms*).

The matching process on care platforms in particular encouraged potentially discriminatory selection processes by suggesting that clients advertise for carers with similar values to their own, or select preferred workers based on 'interests', 'personality' or 'working styles', or even 'cultural background' or 'religion'. This was markedly different to graphic design platforms, where filters related to specific skills.

Discussion

This study examined the similarities and differences between attraction and selection practices used by digital platform businesses in two different types of digitally mediated work – online, virtual work, and in-person labour. Raising important questions about who is responsible for ensuring fair and equitable opportunities for work undertaken *via* digital platforms, the findings highlight that despite promoting to workers that they have the power to choose advertised work, selection is multi-layered and determines which workers receive preferential opportunities. Attraction-selection-attrition becomes attraction-selection-selection, with attrition less formalised and therefore less visible. Limited to an assessment of platform websites and terms and conditions, this study presents an important first step in understanding the mechanisms through which digital platforms create a pool of candidates available for on-demand work.

To be commercially viable, digital platform businesses need to build a critical mass of workers (Coyle, 2017). However, attracting workers is not only about acquiring unique talent as a source of competitive advantage. Nor is it simply a matter of meeting client demand with an adequate supply of willing and able workers. Rather, the major advantage for platforms in maintaining adequate numbers of workers is that access to a large labour pool encourages clients to post jobs, which in turn facilitates the attraction of additional registered workers who generate fee income for the platform. Building labour supply thus becomes the central source of profitability. Meijerink and Keegan (2019) argue that recruitment is aimed at maintaining the digital platform ecosystem through which value is constructed by balancing the supply and demand of labour. The findings here demonstrate that to achieve this goal, platforms offering very different types of work apply similar recruitment practices, but that there are also distinctions at the point where clients become responsible for selection. These processes are summarised in Figure 1 and discussed with reference to extant research on recruitment and the implications for digital platform businesses, workers, and clients.

In both virtual and in-person work, digital platforms present similar value propositions to attract workers, then pre-screen workers applying rudimentary, minimum criteria that permit a large pool of candidates to register on the platform. This increases the number of available workers that the platform can advertise to clients. It also fulfils the promise of "community" made to prospective workers, further legitimising their participation. Prior research into online communities has demonstrated that publicising a large community increases its perceived value and incentivises potential members to participate (Butler *et al.*, 2014). Consistent with the ASA framework, potential community members use available online information to assess their *fit* and self-select in or out of the online community (Butler *et al.*, 2014).

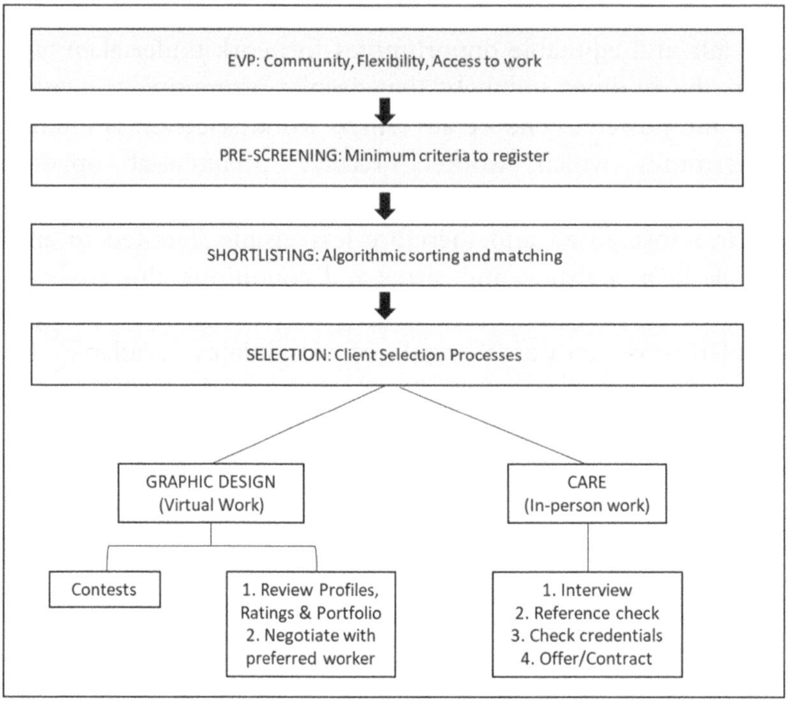

Figure 1. Digital platform attraction and selection processes.

Organisational attraction occurs when an individual, in light of available information, perceives that they share common values with an organisation (Perez *et al.*, 2014). Digital platform workers are allegedly attracted to the flexibility and autonomy of freelance work (Wood *et al.*, 2019) and these are the very values emphasised by all digital platforms examined for this study. Acknowledging that platforms may also employ additional methods of attraction and selection not evident on their websites or in their terms and conditions (for example via direct marketing), the results of this study showed little variance between the value proposition (Barrow & Mosely, 2005) offered across platforms. Platforms capitalised on the flexibility associated with self-employment, supplemented with the promise of ample work. For freelance workers (such as some graphic designers) accustomed to performing discrete tasks for multiple clients, additional work offered by digital platforms may be particularly attractive. However, platform workers frequently work across multiple platforms to supplement an existing income (Florisson & Mandl, 2018; McDonald *et al.*, 2019). This is especially the case in virtual work such as graphic design where 'multi-apping' (Veen *et al.*, 2020) and undertaking work across geographic boundaries is more common. Workers appear to be attracted by a perceived fit with digital platform work in general, rather than a perceived person-organisation fit with a specific platform.

After registering, workers are shortlisted *via* algorithms that control the prominence of the worker's profile and the job opportunities available to a given worker. Platforms thereby perform an algorithmic assessment of person-job fit, filtering out unsuitable candidates. Workers can influence this shortlisting by providing relevant information in their profile (a form of virtual CV), having good client ratings (akin to references) or, in some cases, by paying for priority positioning. Experimentally, Carr *et al.* (2017) demonstrated that clients on Fiverr use worker profiles to assess person-job fit. Our findings demonstrate however that jobs and profiles are first pre-filtered by the platform through processes that are not transparent to the worker. Despite the promise of being able to 'choose the jobs you want', the range of jobs (and applicants) presented to the worker (or client) and the opportunity to assess person-job fit, is restricted. The implications for the quality of work or the retention of platform workers requires further research, especially considering that in traditional employment relationships, ensuring fit during the hiring process improves worker satisfaction and citizenship behaviours (Stone *et al.*, 2019).

Using algorithms to shortlist and identify potential candidates is increasingly common (Alamro *et al.*, 2018). However, algorithmic selection, even in traditional employment, is not bias-free (Lambrecht & Tucker, 2019). In digital platform work, existing worker inequalities can be exacerbated by platform algorithms that preference workers according to listed skills and the platform's inbuilt review systems (see, Pelletier & Thomas, 2018; Wood *et al.*, 2019), while other studies suggest that digital platform work can improve opportunities for minority or disadvantaged workers (Burtch *et al.*, 2018; Chan & Wang, 2018). Our findings question this second view and instead support the findings of scholars such as Levy and Barocas (2017) and Graham *et al.* (2019) who suggest that platform businesses have at least a moral and ethical responsibility, if not a legal obligation, to consider the potential for bias that is built into platform algorithms. For example, selection processes in care work might be compared to dating sites where individuals are matched into a relationship based on their values, preferences, and algorithmically calculated suitability. Hence, rather than person-job fit, or person-organisation fit (Rynes & Gerhart, 1990), platform care work emphasises person-person fit. While there are some obvious benefits in ensuring carers and people seeking care are compatible, this approach to selection has the potential to undermine fairness and equity in selection decisions that would ordinarily be based on an individual's skills, qualifications and job experiences.

As illustrated in Figure 1, clients are responsible for the final stages of selection where the processes vary widely between online graphic design work and in-person care work. Work that is undertaken in-person, even if accessed online, necessarily involves a high degree of trust that seems reliant on labour-intensive selection processes such as job interviews. Virtual work however appears to have become increasingly commodified as a service divorced from the individual worker. In graphic design, where the qualifications and experience of designers did not need to be evidenced, contests offered a relatively 'risk free' selection process for clients. For the worker, participation in contests came with the substantial risk of undertaking work for no assigned value or financial return. More generally, high levels of global competition between workers registered on graphic design platforms places pressure on workers to distinguish themselves through positive client ratings, impressive worker profiles, and lower fees for service. Hence, the mechanisms of selection on digital platforms pose a threat to fair access to work, especially where pricing, or client reviews, over which workers may have little influence, affect shortlisting and client perceptions of 'fit' (Carr *et al.*, 2017). The ASA framework posits that recruitment processes shape the applicant pool and ultimately the homogeneity of an organisation's workforce (Schneider *et al.*, 1995). The different selection processes adopted by graphic design and care platforms reflect very distinct types of work and therefore different workforces, however the remarkable similarities between methods of attraction also imply values shared by all digital platform workers.

In both care and graphic design work, organisations can be clients of platform businesses. Using a third party to source contingent workers is nothing new; however, unlike agency-provided temporary workers, platforms shift responsibility for selection, and all associated costs and risks to the client, minimising some of the benefits organisations might obtain by using temporary labour (Burgess & Connell, 2006). Selection decisions are also synchronously reliant on the quality and function of platform algorithms (Ellmer & Reichel, 2018) and dependent on the comprehensiveness and trustworthiness of platform criteria for worker participation. Our findings further indicate that attraction is linked to the characteristics of platform work in general, raising questions about the likely return on investment in employer branding for organisations sourcing workers *via* digital platforms (Aguinis & Lawal, 2013). These are important considerations for HR in organisations that rely on platform workers as a supplementary source of employees.

Conclusion

Digital platforms offer a new mode of organising work that remains predicated on sufficient labour supply. Meijerink and Keegan (2019) argue that to realise their multilateral value, platforms must delimit access through methods akin to recruitment and selection. Building on this idea, this study revealed how recruitment practices vary according to the work context. Where work is virtual and the labour supply is global, there are few restrictive criteria placed on workers to access work opportunities, and selection processes require greater worker investment and a willingness to risk performing work that will never be paid. By contrast, where labour is local and 'in-person', workers are subject to more traditional methods of recruitment and selection including selection criteria and interviews. The opportunities presented to workers however are controlled by algorithmic selection processes that allow clients to select on work-related, as well as personal characteristics which may result in bias or discrimination and mitigate person-job fit.

Applying the ASA framework to consider how platforms attract and select workers and if these processes enable assessments of fit (by the platform, clients or workers), this study has contributed new knowledge on HR practices in this contemporary form of work. Specifically, this study has exposed the multi-layered and sometimes invisible processes of selection that raise doubts about equitable access to work on digital platforms. The study has demonstrated how platforms simultaneously abdicate responsibility for selection decisions to clients, while maintaining control over attraction of workers and key selection processes, such as algorithmic shortlisting or 'matching'. Digital platforms are thus reshaping established HR practices in ways that complicate employment relations (Duggan *et al.*, 2020). For example, many clients of digital platforms are also organisations who contract or 'employ' the platform worker, using processes inconsistent with those applied to traditional contractors or employees. Further, in Australia, it is illegal to discriminate in relation to work, potential work or in the supply of goods or services (FairWork Ombudsman, 2019), meaning that clients, if not platform businesses themselves, must ensure their processes of selection are equitable and free from discrimination. Although the transnational nature of virtual platform work complicates HRM practice, at the least, all client organisations should have a working knowledge of the underlying assumptions within the algorithms that distribute and match workers to work opportunities.

The model presented in this study, developed through an analysis of the websites and terms and conditions of digital platforms, provides a useful starting point for future research on attraction, selection and attrition in digital platform work. To test and expand the model proposed here, further research is recommended utilising alternate data sources, such as client or worker interviews, to explore the perspective of digital platform users. A future research agenda might also include investigation of targeted advertising and other attraction strategies adopted by digital platforms, or the specific methods, if any, that clients use to select workers. This study also establishes the basis for future research on retention and attrition on digital platforms, including why workers disengage from digital platform work and the potential impact of worker turnover on digital platform businesses.

Note

1. The recent emergence of care platforms in Australia has been facilitated by the introduction of cash-for-care schemes (such as the National Disability Insurance Scheme) that give individuals seeking care or their advocates the option to employ their own support workers, whereas graphic design digital platforms have been operating in Australia for many years (see Table 1).

Disclosure statement

No potential conflict of interest was reported by the author(s).

Funding

This study was funded by an Australian Research Council Grant DP180101191.

ORCID

Penny Williams http://orcid.org/0000-0002-2680-9129
Paula McDonald http://orcid.org/0000-0002-3549-4691

Data availability statement

The data that support the findings of this study are available from the corresponding author (PJW), upon reasonable request.

References

Acikgoz, Y. (2019). Employee recruitment and job search: Towards a multi-level integration. *Human Resource Management Review*, *29*(1), 1–13. https://doi.org/10.1016/j.hrmr.2018.02.009

Aguinis, H., & Lawal, S. O. (2013). eLancing: A review and research agenda for bridging the science–practice gap. *Human Resource Management Review*, *23*(1), 6–17. https://doi.org/10.1016/j.hrmr.2012.06.003

Alamro, S., Dogan, H., Cetinkaya, D., Jiang, N., & Phalp, K. (2018). Conceptualising and modelling E-recruitment process for enterprises through a problem oriented approach. *Information*, *9*(11), 269. https://doi.org/10.3390/info9110269

Alfes, K., Shantz, A., & Alahakone, R. (2016). Testing additive versus interactive effects of person-organization fit and organizational trust on engagement and performance. *Personnel Review*, *45*(6), 1323–1339. https://doi.org/10.1108/PR-02-2015-0029

Barrow, S., & Mosely, R. (2005). *The employer brand bringing the best of brand management to people at work* (2nd ed., rev. and updated.). Wiley.

Boxall, P., & Purcell, J. (2011). *Strategy and human resource management* (3rd edition.). Palgrave Macmillan.

Braun, V., & Clarke, V. (2006). Using thematic analysis in psychology. *Qualitative Research in Psychology*, *3*(2), 77–101. [Database] https://doi.org/10.1191/1478088706qp063oa

Breaugh, J. A. (2008). Employee recruitment: Current knowledge and important areas for future research. *Human Resource Management Review*, *18*(3), 103–118. https://doi.org/10.1016/j.hrmr.2008.07.003

Burgess, J., & Connell, J. (2006). Temporary work and human resources management: Issues, challenges and responses. *Personnel Review*, *35*(2), 129–140. https://doi.org/10.1108/00483480610645786

Burtch, G., Carnahan, S., & Greenwood, B. N. (2018). Can you gig it? An empirical examination of the gig economy and entrepreneurial activity. *Management Science*, *64*(12), 5497–5520. https://doi.org/10.1287/mnsc.2017.2916

Butler, B. S., Bateman, P. J., Gray, P. H., & Diamant, E. I, University of Maryland (2014). An attraction-selection-attrition theory of online community size and resilience. *MIS Quarterly*, *38*(3), 699–728. https://doi.org/10.25300/MISQ/2014/38.3.04

Cappelli, P. (2015). What it Really Takes to Attract Top Talent, *Harvard Business Review*, Retrieved from: https://hbr.org/2015/11/what-it-really-takes-to-attract-top-talent, March 2019.

Cappelli, P., & Keller, J. R. (2013). Classifying work in the new economy. *Academy of Management Review*, *38*(4), 575–596. https://doi.org/10.5465/amr.2011.0302

Carless, S. A. (2005). Person–job fit versus person–organization fit as predictors of organizational attraction and job acceptance intentions: A longitudinal study. *Journal of Occupational and Organizational Psychology*, *78*(3), 411–429. https://doi.org/10.1348/096317905X25995

Carr, C. T., Hall, R. D., Mason, A. J., & Varney, E. J. (2017). Cueing employability in the gig economy: Effects of task-relevant and task-irrelevant information on Fiverr. *Management Communication Quarterly*, *31*(3), 409–428. https://doi.org/10.1177/0893318916687397

Cascio, W., & Boudreau, J. (2017). Talent Management of Nonstandard Employees. In Collings, D., Mellahi, K., & Cascio, W. (Eds.), *The Oxford handbook of talent management*. Oxford University Press.

Chan, J., & Wang, J. (2018). Hiring preferences in online labor markets: Evidence of a female hiring bias. *Management Science*, *64*(7), 2973–2994. https://doi.org/10.1287/mnsc.2017.2756

Cook, C., Diamond, R., Hall, J., List, J. A., & Oyer, P. (2018). *The Gender Earnings Gap in the Gig Economy: Evidence from over a million rideshare drivers*. NBER Working Paper No. 24732, National Bureau of Economic Research. Retrieved from: http://www.nber.org/papers/w24732

Coyle, D. (2017). Precarious and productive work in the digital economy. *National Institute Economic Review*, *240*(1), R5–R14. https://doi.org/10.1177/002795011724000110

Degryse, C. (2016). Digitalisation of the economy and its impact on labour markets. *ETUI Research Paper-Working Paper.* Retrieved from: https://www.etui.org/publications/working-papers/digitalisation-of-the-economy-and-its-impact-on-labour-markets

Dineen, B. R., Ling, J., Ash, S. R., & DelVecchio, D. (2007). Aesthetic properties and message customization: Navigating the dark side of web recruitment. *Journal of Applied Psychology, 92*(2), 356–372. https://doi.org/10.1037/0021-9010.92.2.356

Drahokoupil, J., Fabo, B. (2016). The platform economy and the disruption of the employment relationship. *ETUI, The European Trade Union Institute.* Retrieved from: https://www.etui.org/publications/policy-briefs/european-economic-employment-and-social-policy/the-platform-economy-and-the-disruption-of-the-employment-relationship

Duggan, J., Sherman, U., Carbery, R., & McDonnell, A. (2020). Algorithmic management and app-work in the gig economy: A research agenda for employment relations and HRM. *Human Resource Management Journal, 30*(1), 114–132. https://doi.org/10.1111/1748-8583.12258

Dutta, D., Mishra, S. K., & Varma, A. (2019). Predictors of job pursuit intention across career stages: A multi-phase investigation. *The International Journal of Human Resource Management.* https://doi.org/10.1080/09585192.2019.1651376

Ellmer, M., & Reichel, A. (2018). *Crowdwork from an HRM perspective–integrating organizational performance and employee welfare.* Working Paper, HRM Group, University of Salzburg.

FairWork Ombudsman (2019). *Protections at work.* Retrieved from: https://www.fairwork.gov.au/employee-entitlements/protections-at-work/protection-from-discrimination-at-work

Florisson, R., Mandl, I. (2018). Platform work: Types and implication for work and employment–Literature review. *Eurofound.* Luxembourg: Publications Office of the European Union, (s 96). Retrieved from https://www.eurofound.europa.eu/data/platform-economy/records/platform-work-types-and-implications-for-work-and-employment-literature-review

Gioia, D. A., Corley, K. G., & Hamilton, A. L. (2013). Seeking qualitative rigor in inductive research: Notes on the Gioia methodology. *Organizational Research Methods, 16*(1), 15–31. https://doi.org/10.1177/1094428112452151

Glaser, B. G., & Strauss, A. L. (2017). Theoretical sampling. In Denzin, N.K., (Ed.), *Sociological methods* (pp. 105–114). Routledge.

Graham, M., Hjorth, I., & Lehdonvirta, V. (2017). Digital labour and development: Impacts of global digital labour platforms and the gig economy on worker livelihoods. *Transfer (Brussels, Belgium)), 23*(2), 135–162. https://doi.org/10.1177/1024258916687250

Graham, M., Woodcock, J., Heeks, R., Fredman, S., Du Toit, D., Belle, J. P. V., Mungai, P., Osiki, A. (2019). The fairwork foundation: Strategies for improving platform work. In *Proceedings of the Weizenbaum Conference 2019 "Challenges of Digital Inequality – Digital Education, Digital Work, Digital Life"* (pp. 1–8). Berlin https://doi.org/10.34669/wi.cp/2.13

Gramano, E. (2020). Digitalisation and work: Challenges from the platform-economy. *Contemporary Social Science, 15*(4), 476–413. Retrieved from: https://doi.org/10.1080/21582041.2019.1572919

Graves, L. M., & Karren, R. J. (1996). The employee selection interview: A fresh look at an old problem. *Human Resource Management, 35*(2), 163–180. https://doi.org/10.1002/(SICI)1099-050X(199622)35:2<163::AID-HRM2>3.0.CO;2-W

Howcroft, D., & Bergvall-Kåreborn, B. (2019). A typology of crowdwork platforms. *Work, Employment and Society*, *33*(1), 21–38. https://doi.org/10.1177/0950017018760136

Hurwitz, L. B., Alvarez, A. L., Lauricella, A. R., Rousse, T. H., Montague, H., & Wartella, E. (2018). Content analysis across new media platforms: Methodological considerations for capturing media-rich data. *New Media & Society*, *20*(2), 532–548.

Huws, U., Spencer, N. H., & Syrdal, D. S. (2018). Online, on call: The spread of digitally organised just-in-time working and its implications for standard employment models. *New Technology, Work and Employment*, *33*(2), 113–129. https://doi.org/10.1111/ntwe.12111

Jabagi, N., Croteau, A., Audebrand, L., & Marsan, J. (2019). Gig-workers' motivation: Thinking beyond carrots and sticks. *Journal of Managerial Psychology*, *34*(4), 192–213. https://doi.org/10.1108/JMP-06-2018-0255

Kässi, O., & Lehdonvirta, V. (2018). Online labour index: Measuring the online gig economy for policy and research. *Technological Forecasting and Social Change*, *137*, 241–248. https://doi.org/10.1016/j.techfore.2018.07.056

Katz, L. F., & Krueger, A. B. (2019). The rise and nature of alternative work arrangements in the United States, 1995–2015. *ILR Review*, *72*(2), 382–416. https://doi.org/10.1177/0019793918820008

Klotz, A. C., da Motta Veiga, S. P., Buckley, M. R., & Gavin, M. B. (2013). The role of trustworthiness in recruitment and selection: A review and guide for future research. *Journal of Organizational Behavior*, *34*(S1), S104–S119. https://doi.org/10.1002/job.1891

Kuhn, K. M. (2016). The rise of the "Gig Economy" and implications for understanding work and workers. *Industrial and Organizational Psychology*, *9*(1), 157–162. https://doi.org/10.1017/iop.2015.129

Kuhn, K. M., & Maleki, A. (2017). Micro-entrepreneurs, dependent contractors, and instaserfs: Understanding online labor platform workforces. *Academy of Management Perspectives*, *31*(3), 183–200. https://doi.org/10.5465/amp.2015.0111

Lambrecht, A., & Tucker, C. (2019). Algorithmic bias? An empirical study of apparent gender-based discrimination in the display of STEM career ads. *Management Science*, *65*(7), 2966–2981. https://doi.org/10.1287/mnsc.2018.3093

Lee, M. K., Kusbit, D., Metsky, E., & Dabbish, L. (2015). *Working with machines: The impact of algorithmic and data-driven management on human workers [Paper presentation]*. Proceedings of the 33rd Annual ACM Conference on Human Factors in Computing Systems, April). In (pp. 1603–1612). ACM.

Levy, K., & Barocas, S. (2017). Designing against discrimination in online markets. *Berkeley Tech. LJ*, *32*, 1183.

Madden, K., Nan, X., Briones, R., & Waks, L. (2012). Sorting through search results: A content analysis of HPV vaccine information online. *Vaccine*, *30*(25), 3741–3746. https://doi.org/10.1016/j.vaccine.2011.10.025

Mandl, I. (2019). *Platform work: Maximising the potential while safeguarding standards?* Eurofound. Publications Office of the European Union, Luxembourg. Retrieved from: https://www.eurofound.europa.eu/publications/policy-brief/2019/platform-work-maximising-the-potential-while-safeguarding-standards

McDonald, P., Williams, P., & Mayes, R. (2020). How professional photographers engage with and resist digital platform work. *New Media & Society*, https://doi.org/10.1177/1461444820917905

McDonald, P., Williams, P., Stewart, A., Oliver, D., Mayes, R. (2019). *Digital platform work in Australia. Preliminary findings from a national survey.* Melbourne (June). Retrieved from: https://research.qut.edu.au/work-industry-futures-research-program/wp-content/uploads/sites/35/2019/06/Report-of-Survey-Findings_18-June-2019_PUBLISHED.pdf

Meijerink, J., & Keegan, A. (2019). Conceptualizing human resource management in the gig economy. *Journal of Managerial Psychology*, *34*(4), 214–232. https://doi.org/10.1108/JMP-07-2018-0277

Melián González, S. (2018). What do consumers appreciate about on-demand economy workers? *Psychosociological Issues in Human Resource Management*, *6*(2), 29–43.

Pelletier, A., & Thomas, C. (2018). Information in online labour markets. *Oxford Review of Economic Policy*, *34*(3), 376–392. https://doi.org/10.1093/oxrep/gry005

Perez, E. M., Walton, A. L., Cooper, D. M., & Pacheco, M. R. (2014). Unpacking organizational attraction: A process model. *International Journal of Business and Social Science*, *5*(10), 108–120.

Pesole, A., Brancati, M. C. U., Fernández-Macías, E., Biagi, F., & Vazquez, I. G. (2018). *Platform workers in Europe: Evidence from the COLLEEM survey.* (No. JRC112157)., Publications Office of the European Union. https://doi.org/10.2760/ 742789

Riso, S. (2019). *Mapping the contours of the platform economy*, Automation, digitisation and platforms: implications for work and employment, European Foundation for the Improvement of Living and Working Conditions (Eurofound), Dublin. Retrieved from: https://www.eurofound.europa.eu/sites/default/files/wpef19060.pdf.

Rynes, S., & Gerhart, B. (1990). Interviewer assessments of applicant "fit": An exploratory investigation. *Personnel Psychology*, *43*(1), 13–35. https://doi.org/10.1111/j.1744-6570.1990.tb02004.x

Schneider, B. (1987). The People Make the Place. *Personnel Psychology*, *40*(3), 437–453. https://doi.org/10.1111/j.1744-6570.1987.tb00609.x

Schneider, B., Goldstiein, H. W., & Smith, D. B. (1995). The ASA framework: An update. *Personnel Psychology*, *48*(4), 747–773. https://doi.org/10.1111/j.1744-6570.1995.tb01780.x

Stone, R., Leuty, M., Rayburn, R., & Wu, B. (2019). Person–environment fit at work: Relationships with workplace behaviours. *Australian Journal of Career Development*, *28*(3), 234–244. https://doi.org/10.1177/1038416219870205

Taylor, J., & Joshi, K. D. (2019). Joining the crowd: The career anchors of information technology workers participating in crowdsourcing. *Information Systems Journal*, *29*(3), 641–673. https://doi.org/10.1111/isj.12225

Ticona, J., & Mateescu, A. (2018). Trusted strangers: Carework platforms' cultural entrepreneurship in the on-demand economy. *New Media & Society*, *20*(11), 4384–4404.

Veen, A., Barratt, T., & Goods, C. (2020). Platform-capital's 'App-etite' for control: A labour process analysis of food-delivery work in Australia. *Work, Employment and Society*, *34*(3), 388-406. https://doi.org/10.1177/0950017019836911.

Weare, C., & Lin, W. Y. (2000). Content analysis of the World Wide Web: Opportunities and challenges. *Social Science Computer Review*, *18*(3), 272–292. https://doi.org/10.1177/089443930001800304

Wood, A. J., Graham, M., Lehdonvirta, V., & Hjorth, I. (2019). Good gig, bad gig: Autonomy and algorithmic control in the global gig economy. *Work, Employment & Society : a Journal of the British Sociological Association*, *33*(1), 56–75. https://doi.org/10.1177/0950017018785616

Index

Page numbers in **bold** refer to tables and those in *italic* refer to figures.